THE AMERICAN REVOLUTION
A General History, 1763–1790

The Dorsey Series in American History

REVISED EDITION

The American Revolution
A General History, 1763-1790

E. JAMES FERGUSON
Professor of History
Queens College
The City University of New York

1979

 THE DORSEY PRESS   Homewood, Illinois   60430
Irwin-Dorsey Limited   Georgetown, Ontario   L7G 4B3

ISBN 0-256-02195-3
Library of Congress Catalog Card No. 78–70958

Printed in the United States of America

1 2 3 4 5 6 7 8 9 0 ML 6 5 4 3 2 1 0 9

Preface

This revision alters the original edition of *The American Revolution* in significant ways. It enlarges the scope of the book to include subjects not previously covered, it incorporates the results of recent historical research, and it reflects the shifts of emphasis induced by that research. There are several additional chapters and a new conclusion.

I have done a good deal more with English antecedents, not only by way of explaining disputes between colonies and mother country, but in order to show the affinity and contrast between the American Revolution and those that occurred in England in the previous century. A comparison of these revolutions and their consequences exposes the critical differences in institutional growth that took place in the "metropolis" and in the "provinces," differences that were conducive to the alienation of the colonies. In analyzing social structure in America, I have taken advantage of statistical tabulations only recently available, and to the topics covered I have added sections on Indian society and the status of women, as well as an improved version of black history and race relations.

The analysis of the Revolutionary movement is greatly expanded, more sensitive to social class tensions and sectional controversies, and more emphatic in treating the "popular movement," the "disaffected," and the loyalists. The implications raised by discussion of these subjects are reviewed in later discussion of the social results of the Revolution, to which material is added on religion and the progress of anti-slavery after the war. The shifts in emphasis require some expansion of the sections on British and American military policy as well as the domestic issues that divided Americans as civilians. Finally, in spelling out the role of the Nationalists, the adoption of the Constitution, and the enactment of the Hamiltonian funding program, I have tried to link these movements with corresponding developments in 18th-century Britain.

The revisions are in many respects the outward sign of inner changes, because since the first edition was written my general interpretations have acquired a new look, both in substance and in emphasis. One insight I have gained is into the continuity between British history in the 18th century and the subsequent history of the United States, at least up to 1800, when Thomas Jefferson pronounced that the final phase of the revolution of 1776 had taken place. Perhaps the proper date for the end of the continuum is 1815. At any rate, general works on early American history seem to ignore these continuities, which constitute the background of public controversies in the early national period. Another insight, crystallized for me by the work of many young scholars, is that the Revolution was not only the first modern revolution; it was also the first *popular* revolution of modern times that succeeded. In ways I hope this book will clarify, the existence of the popular movement—and the necessity the American elite was under of accommodating it—present a set of factors that gives an imperative meaning to much of what happened in the country's domestic affairs: the conflicts over public policy, and the fear and hostility with which the upper classes reacted to popular initiatives. It explains, finally, why the upper classes sought refuge and political stability in the establishment of a national government and in the sphere of economic policy were willing to abandon the traditional, agrarian-oriented modes of public finance in favor of a funding system modeled upon the more advanced capitalist institutions of Great Britain. A people's revolution had occurred in America.

January 1979   E. JAMES FERGUSON

Contents

ix

Chapter V
The Empire Divided   119

The Setting. Sources of British Colonial Policy, 1760–1765. The Grenville
Acts. The Stamp Act and Popular Resistance. Natural Rights. The Theo-
retical Defense of American Rights. America's "Friends" and the Repeal of
the Stamp Act. The Townshend Acts. British Troops and the Boston Massacre. Tea Party and the Intolerable Acts. The First Continental Congress.
War and the Overturn of Government. The Failure of British Policy. Independence Declared.

Chapter VI
War and Diplomacy   165

The War on Land: Strategy of Survival. The War at Sea: Privateers and
Ships of the Line. Sources of Internal Disunity: Blacks and Loyalists. The
Disaffected and the Strategy of Popular Leadership. Problems of Man-
power, Organization, and Money. Campaigns in 1776 and 1777. France
Enters the War. The War in the Doldrums, 1778–1780. Victory at York-
town. Foreign Entanglements and the Peace Treaty.

Chapter VII
Not without Effort: Stresses and Strains in Wartime Society   199

Conventional and Partisan Warfare. Raising the Continental Army. Merchants in Government and the Deane-Lee Affair. The War Economy. Committee Rule. Mass Expropriation. The Unity of Patriots.

Chapter VIII
Social, Economic, and Political Change   225

Interpretations. The Loyalists. The Distribution of Land. Expansion of
Small Farmer Society. Political Ideas and the State Constitutions. Govern-
ment by the People. The Articles of Confederation. Business Enterprise.
Religion: Definitions of Freedom. Blacks and Slavery. The Nationalist
Movement, 1781–1783. The Newburgh Conspiracy.

Chapter IX
The Confederation   265

The Postwar Economy. Federal Regulation of Trade. Western Lands and
the Ordinances. The West in International Relations. Loyalists and Planter
Debts. The Failure of Constitutional Revision. The Revival of Social Radicalism. Origins of the Movement for the Constitution.

Chapter X
The Formation of the National Government, 1786–1790   289

Forces behind the Constitution. The Framing of the Constitution. The Constitution as a Political Act. The Constitution as a Social Document. Ratification. The Inauguration of the Government. The Funding Program. Assumption of State Debts. Epilogue.

CHAPTER I

American Colonies 1763

Colonies within the Empire: A Liberal Inheritance

The American Revolution was the first successful colonial revolt of modern times. It created the first independent nation to emerge from the colonial empires carved out by European powers in the Western Hemisphere. The commitment of the new republic to the advanced and humane social values of the time provided a model for contemporary reformers and profoundly influenced the direction of social change in the Western world. The principles of the American Revolution, although in many ways transmuted by their adaptation to an industrial age, still provide a basic standard by which Americans judge their society.

Foundations of Nationality

After the first settlements, nearly a century elapsed before the British colonies in North America began to acquire the attributes of a nation. In 1690 they were a mere fringe of coastal settlements, penetrating, except in a few river valleys, scarcely more than 50 miles into the forest. The population was less than 250,000, strung along the Atlantic coast, the main clusters being in New England and Chesapeake Bay. The principal towns were hardly more than villages; the largest, Boston, in 60 years had gained only 7,000 inhabitants. Philadelpha had just been founded, and Baltimore did not exist. Except for a few settlements such as those of the Dutch in New York and of the Swedes in Pennsylvania, the people were almost entirely of English stock, bred in a common national tradition.

During the three quarters of a century before the American Revolution, the populaton increased to nearly 2.5 million. Settlement pushed inland to the Appalachian barrier and began to spill over into the great midcontinental valley. Philadelphia, the leading city, contained nearly 30,000 people and in the opulence of its urban life rivaled important European centers. America had become a melting pot of nationalities. Except in New England, where the stock remained 95 percent English, the white population was a mixture of national cultures and religons. In the south, the vast infusion of enslaved blacks out of Africa had transformed the demographic structure.

The rapid growth of the white population during the 18th century was accelerated by heavy immigration. Thousands of Germans came from the Rhineland after 1710, driven by hardship and war in their own country, but also by the promise of land and religious freedom in America. Most of them settled in Pennsylvania, where there was both good land and religious toleration. An estimated 70,000 had arrived by 1756, and before long the province was one-third German. Frequently adherents of radical Protestant sects, the "Pennsylvania Dutch" tended to remain unassimilated, forming communities which preserved native language and customs. Coming after the Quakers who had founded the colony, they settled in the interior. Following the Germans were the Scotch Irish, whose migration, from Ulster in northern Ireland, began about the same time. Like the Germans, they were impelled to migrate by economic hardship, religious discrimination, and the hope of bettering their condition. Pushing west, they struck the fertile valleys of the Appalachians. Then, mingling with Germans, they turned southward into the western sections of Maryland, Virginia, and the Carolinas. The southern backcountry filled up and soon contained the majority of the south's white population.

The influx of people was a powerful stimulus to the economic growth of the colonies, enlarging their labor forces and expanding their resources in agriculture, commerce, and manufacturing. It also widened gulfs between Britain and America. After the initial obstacles to assimilation had been overcome, intermarriage brought a steady fusion of peoples which weakened identification with Old World culture and particular national traditions. Heretofore almost entirely English, the colonial population became a conglomerate. The immigrants, moreover, were often refugees from persecution, and many of them were foes of England. Their presence contributed heavily to the emergence of a distinct American nation. Mere physical separation and the different conditions of life in America further depleted the stock of common experience shared with the people of England. As people moved deep into the interior they were cut off from easy or habitual communication with the outside world. The east was remote, and England scarcely imaginable.

Political Traditions

The colonies inherited from the English past a libertarian political tradition which, by the 18th century, the mother country itself had grown away from. The England that the colonies rebelled against in 1776 had in the previous century gone through two major revolutions, beheaded one king, and driven out another. It was then in the forefront of the movement against royal power. Elsewhere in Europe social and economic changes were elevating kings to the status of absolute monarchs. Autocratic rulers could pretty well say, like the king of France, "the state, it is I." Representative bodies of the Middle Ages, such as the Estates General of France and the Spanish Cortes, had fallen into disuse or been reduced to a shadow of the king's will. Only in England had the national representative body, Parliament, preserved its integrity. One reason was that the Tudor kings who built up a strong monarch in the 16th century were domesticated to English traditions and content to rule through, not against nor independently of, Parliament. Representative government and the "rights of Englishmen" therefore survived as existent realities. These rights were challenged early in the 17th century, however, when the Stuarts, a Scottish dynasty, fell heir to the English throne with the accession of James I. James professed to rule not only by divine right but in defiance of Parliament. A prolonged struggle ensued, culminating in the outbreak of civil war in 1642, the victory of the parliamentary forces over the king, the execution of Charles I, and the establishment of a republic, the "Commonwealth," which lasted from 1649 until the Restoration in 1660, when Charles II came back from exile to take the throne.

It was perhaps too early in modern history for a large nation to succeed as a republic, but the proximate reason for the failure of the Commonwealth was its being embroiled in religious controversy. This controversy stemmed from the Reformation, which had occurred in England in 1527, when Henry VIII detached the state church from Catholicism. The resulting Church of England could not, however, contain the spiritual fires kindled by the Reformation. Toward the end of the 16th century an intensely pietistic movement spread to all ranks of society, to Parliament, to the universities, and to the Anglican Church itself. The Puritans, as they were called, desired a church more typically Protestant, austere, less wordly, and more in line with Protestant doctrine. They wanted it divorced from royal control, self-governing, and some Puritans even believed that it should consist of independent congregations. The Puritan crusade against the state church controlled by king and bishops merged with the political struggle of Parliament against royal authority.

In its political aspects the struggle was over the rights of Englishmen: the customary and legal rights and privileges which had been acquired by citizens of varying wealth and rank in English society as it was then constituted. The emphasis was on legal and constitutional safeguards against arbitrary acts of government, security of property, Parliamentary control of taxation, and procedural guarantees under law to protect the individual against improper arrest and punishment. In an age when, in other countries of Europe, the symbols of growing royal absolutism were the priest, the dragoon, and the hangman, such rights were of no mean importance, and they were England's pride. They were essentially conservative in effect, however, in that they confirmed and tended to perpetuate the existing order of the society and its class privileges. In its religious aspects, on the other hand, the struggle against royal authority had radical implications. The outstanding characteristic of Puritanism, a tidal wave of religious emotion, was its transcendence of vested interests, its justification of the existing order only in terms of God's will. Puritanism was inherently radical because it subjected every aspect of public and private life to uncompromising moral judgment.

What one might expect of religious radicalism unfolded in the course of the civil war when, after Charles I was defeated, the Puritans fell out among themselves. A war broke out between Parliament and the army, led by its chief general, Oliver Cromwell. His "Roundheads" constituted a redoubtable fighting force, "Saints" who sang hymns on the eve of battle and fought with passion and discipline. A stronghold of radical Puritanism, the army became a breeding ground for ideas potentially subversive of English institutions and class relationships. Over their camp-fires the Saints pursued the implications of Christian doctrine to such lengths as to advocate human equality, universal manhood suffrage, democratic control of the army, a revision of the taxing system to relieve the poor, religious toleration for all Protestants, and the redistribution of landed property. The Puritan army soon defeated the parliamentary forces and possessed supreme power in the nation. After the execution of the king, England became in form a republic, but no elected Parliament would conform to the views of the army, whereupon Cromwell was forced to dissolve Parliament and rule England as a military dictator, his orders executed throughout the country by military generals. Although Cromwell managed to suppress the most extreme Puritan elements in the army, government by the godly at this time implanted in most Englishmen an ineradicable distaste for any sort of official ideology. Moreover, the gentry and nobility received an unforgettable lesson as to the consequences of letting political power slip into the hands of common men. Loathing Puritanism now, the landed gentry and nobility combined with Parliament to restore the monarchy in 1660.

The Restoration lasted only 30 years. Charles II, as he said, had no desire to resume his travels, and hence ruled with sufficient restraint to live out his days on the throne. Hs successor, James II, was less cognizant of the practical limits of kingly power in England. He coupled efforts at personal rule with a foolish attempt to reestablish Catholicism, and thereby alienated all those who would otherwise have been disposed to uphold the monarchy. When the Dutch leader, William of Orange, responded to invitations of a number of great English noblemen and landed on the coast with an army in 1688, nobody would fight for James, and he fled.

The Glorious Revolution of 1689 settled the question of ultimate sovereignty in England. Thereafter, for a century, the kings had great powers both actual and in principle; they conducted the government and chose ministers to do their bidding. The people looked up to them as the embodiment of the nation, placed on the throne by God, and entitled to every man's obedience. They ruled, nevertheless, by the consent of Parliament, not in their own right, and under the limitations of the English constitution and the common law. Although free to select their ministers, they could not in practice govern without Parliament or in defiance of it; hence they had to choose ministers who could gain Parliament's support. Thus the foundations of Britain's modern cabinet system were being laid in the 18th century.

Religious toleration also won a victory in the Revolution of 1689. The Toleration Act still required all citizens to pay taxes for the support of the established Anglican church, but Dissenters (non-Anglican Protestants, such as the former Puritans), although barred from public office and excluded from Oxford and Cambridge Universities, were allowed to worship in their own churches and establish their own institutions of learning. The Toleration Act did not extend to Catholics; in the course of time, however, the restrictions upon them were lifted, as were those still in effect against Dissenters. Relgious freedom gradually took its place among the rights of Englishmen.

The Glorious Revolution brought in a century of intense social conservatism. Nothing in the Revolution settlement reduced inequality in the distribution of wealth, widened the suffrage in voting for members of Parliament, nor altered relations between social classes. Class distinctions, in fact, became more rigid than before and the government less representative of the common people. The landed gentry that ruled the countryside and dominated Parliament remained in a state of shocked reaction against the democratic upsurge of the Puritan Revolution, clutched its privileges and clung to the certitudes represented by royal authority and the established church. Any suggestion of reform was shunned as "enthusiasm." Mediocrity became a cardinal virtue as all advancement in government, church, or military services hinged on patronage and was limited to the upper classes. In the words of an English historian, "England in 1760 exhibits all the qualities identified with the 'old regime' of pre-industrial Europe. Government is dominated by a hereditary aristocracy which uses it as a vehicle to maintain the social order; institutions of church and education also are harnessed to support the status quo and at the same time serve the family interests of the ruling class." It was this England, not the England of the preceding century, against which the Amercans revolted.

It was appropriate that the political regime established by the Revolution of 1689 was sustained by monolithic corruption. Many Englishmen at first considered the regime to be illegitimate, and there were plots to bring back the Stuarts, hence the stability of the government was for some time in danger. Political unity was eventually restored, however, under the leadership of Robert Walpole who became the chief minister of the king in 1721 and held his position for the next 20 years. It was Walpole's belief, candidly admitted and openly acted on, that it was better to buy off enemies than to fight them. The British political system gave him ample resources. Not only did the government have numerous offices to bestow, but the mounting public debt (discussed below) and the staggering taxes levied to support it caused a huge flow of money in and out of the Treasury, providing endless jobs, favors, and profits to dispense for political purposes. Outside the administration, the House of Commons was pervasively corrupted by the "rotten borough system." Most members of the Commons sat as delegates of boroughs, some of which were incorporated and therefore controlled by a handful of voters whose choice could be manipulated. In any case, many boroughs had lost or were losing most of their populations as people for economic reasons migrated to other parts of the country. The sparsely populated boroughs were in the political pockets of the local gentry or nobility, and borough seats in the Commons were openly bought and sold. Although rotten boroughs and patronage at the disposal of the ministry were never quite enough to corrupt a majority of the Commons, under normal circumstances they provided a marginal advantage which enabled the ministry to reconcile conflicts of interest and carry out policies. Actually, corruption was the cement that attached Parliament to the new monarchy and that conciliated those who disputed the succession to the throne. Although never considered in formal discussion of the English constitution, corruption was a vital element in the system of government.

Colonial Self-Rule and the Structure of Government

The American colonies were founded in the century of England's civil war and its climactic struggle against kings; and events in the colonies reflected the incidents of that struggle. During the English civil war of 1642–48, Massachusetts declared its independence, and in 1649 an English army was necessary to compel royalist Virginia and Catholic Maryland to submit to the Puritan government of Cromwell. Later, when James II was ousted by the Glorious Revolution, concurrent uprisings in several colonies drove out proprietary and royal governors and proclaimed allegiance to William and Mary. As political turmoil in England subsided during the 18th century, however, the colonies were no longer disturbed by waves of strife spreading out from the homeland. Rapidly increasing in population and wealth, the colonies became more diversified and less subject to the parochial and partisan impulses of their 17th century beginnings.

During the 18th century, up to the beginning of the controversies that led to the American Revolution, the empire in North America existed with the consent of the colonists. This was partly because they had acquired a large measure of control over their own affairs. Since representative government was an English institution, they had been allowed from the beginning to have elected assemblies. But the colonies were founded at different times and in varying circumstances, and their governments were not always, in fact, very representative of colonial interests nor of the common people. In structure, the governments were roughly similar, patterned after the British government, with a governor, an upper legislative house called the council, and a lower legislative house, the assembly. These bodies corresponded to king, House of Lords, and House of Commons. The governors had general powers to enforce laws, commanded the armed forces, appointed judges and local officials, and had an absolute veto over legislation. The council, in most instances appointed by king or proprietor, was a small, select group of perhaps a dozen men who sat with the governor as an executive council and also shared, with the assembly, in the enactment of laws. The more numerous assembly was the only branch of provincial government which was popularly elected. Variations on this pattern as of 1760 were: the election of all branches of government in Rhode Island and Connecticut; the election of the council by the assembly in Massachusetts; and in Pennsylvania, the existence of a single-house legislature, without a council.

In the early years of colonization, English kings and their advisers had expected that colonial governments would be subservient to royal and proprietary governors. The English view was always that colonial governments had the legal status of English municipalities, which were in charge of local matters but had no powers independent of the crown. Originally, it was also the official view that within the colonies authority should rest with appointed governors and councils, and that the elected assemblies should function mainly to give advice and assistance.

During the course of a century of development, a twofold evolution occurred. First, effective power passed from the governors, who represented the interests and purposes of king or proprietor, to the councils, and finally to the elected assemblies. By virtue of incessant struggle and the fact that they represented the body of the inhabitants rather than an outside influence, the elected assemblies won a dominant position over both governors and councils. Second, colonial governments achieved a remarkable degree of independence of royal control. From the beginning colonial legislatures acted like little parliaments, asserting legislative rights established by the English constitution. The councils first carried on the struggle; then the lower houses, rising to dominance, claimed the right to regulate their membership and control their adjournment, the immunity of their members from arrest, and, above all, their exclusive power over taxation. As the 18th century wore on, the assemblies managed to exclude governors and councils from any share in raising public revenue. Power over taxation was an effective weapon, for, except in Georgia, Britain never provided funds either to pay the governors' salaries or to support their administrations. By withholding money and bargaining for concessions, the assemblies steadily invaded the governors' prerogatives. On the eve of the disputes that led to the Revolution, the assemblies in most colonies had won not only exclusive control over taxation, but the right to determine how public money was spent. They managed Indian relations, directed the use of the militia, appointed militia officers, and controlled the local courts, whose judges they nominated and protected against removal. They had all but won the battle against royal authority.

The assemblies were elected on the basis of a broad suffrage. In the first years of settlement, it appears that in most colonies nearly all free, white males could vote, but, as the provinces grew, property qualifications similar to those in England were introduced. In America, as in England, it was the common belief that voting should be restricted to persons who, by virtue of their ownership of property, had a "stake in society" and who would therefore be more responsible than those without property. But in contrast to England, where only a small minority met the qualifications, the wide ownership of land in America allowed large numbers to vote, perhaps 60 percent to 75 percent of adult males in New England and 40 percent to 50 percent in the south. Women, bound white servants who had an unfree status, and slaves were excluded from suffrage, but the idea that any of these groups should participate in government was wholly alien to the thought of the times.

Local government was based upon the county and modeled after the English shire, with a corresponding set of appointed civil and military officers. South of New England the principal officers were the justices of the peace, who were appointed for life by the governor upon recommendation of the legislature. In previous centuries, the Tudor monarchs of England had reduced the influence of the nobility by building up the powers of the justices, who were drawn from the non-noble gentry. In America, the justices were therefore powerful figures. They decided minor civil and criminal cases and met periodically with other county justices to preside over more important cases. They were also the chief local administrative officers, in charge of such matters as poor relief, road construction, and the enforcement of laws laid down by the provincial legislature. In the southern and middle colonies, the justices ruled the countryside.

In New England, town government was more important than county government. It was modeled upon the organization of the Congregational church and in form was democratic. The town meeting elected delegates to the legislature and chose selectmen to administer all local affairs. How democratic the town meetings were, however, is an open question. Although everybody could speak, voting on many matters was restricted to those who met property qualifications, and there is much to suggest that proper-tied men and church leaders dominated the proceedings. But democratic or not, local government, whether in the towns of New England or the counties of the middle and southern colonies, was basically antipathetic to British rule. It attached the people to local authority, and not to crown or Parliament. This was an unassailable source of patriot strength when Britain's rule was challenged.

Neither a wide suffrage nor vigorous local governments made politics democratic. In fact, the people as well as their leaders were steeped in a tradition of elite stewardship. Politics was nearly everywhere a gentleman's game. There were no organized parties; the upper class led and the people followed. Monopoly of public office by the elite was seldom challenged, and elections, although sometimes fiercely contested by gentlemen, turned on the personality and reputation of the candidates rather than on pledges to implement the views of the electorate. Popular influence over government was further reduced by the fact that governors and councils, which still exercised power, were appointed from England and beyond the direct reach of the voters.

From this description of colonial politics, one might surmise that they were not much different from those of Georgian England. Indeed, there is a distinctly similar flavor if one talks about some parts of the colonies, say Tidewater Virginia. Nevertheless, compared with governments elsewhere, even in England, those in the American colonies were singularly responsive to the people. The suffrage, for one thing, was much broader; the wide distribution of property qualified more people to vote, hence the freeholders whose favor the upper class candidates courted were a much larger proportion of the population than in England. Also, corruption of the English sort was not much of a factor. There were abuses in the electoral system and political practices. Western counties frequently did not have the number of delegates to the legislatures that their population entitled them to. Personal influence, for those who had it, typically secured whatever benefits governments had to offer, notably in New York, where wealthy and influential men received enormous land grants. Nevertheless, public virtue was more typical of America than public corruption. There were no rotten boroughs, and colonial governments usually did not generate enough patronage for much bribery. They performed few functions, spent little money, and collected only minor taxes. In mid-18th century, the peacetime expense of running the government of a populous colony such as Pennsylvania was no more than the income of many English noblemen.

Moreover, the American colonies were spared the complacency and reaction that settled down on Britain in the 18th century. Americans were the intellectual heirs, not of 18th century England, but of the 17th century Commonwealth. In consequence of the original settlement and of later migration, the great majority of Americans were what in Britain were called Dissenters, successors to the Puritans. It is true that social ideas and conventions in the colonies generally tended to follow patterns set in England, and that as America grew populous and wealthier in the 18th century it acquired an upper class fond of reciting some of the conservative platitudes of Georgian England. Nevertheless, the legacy of the English civil war and Commonwealth was still vigorously alive. The political writings read by Americans were those of England's revolutionary age or the descendant literature of that age written by 18th century popularizers. The closest political communicants of Americans in England were Dissenters, always in that country the most persistent critics of government and exponents of libertarian ideas.

British Political Control and "Salutary Neglect"

Despite the progressive enlargement of its empire, Britain failed to develop a rational system of colonial administration. The colonies were originally founded, not as projects undertaken by the king or government, but as private enterprises conducted by business corporations or proprietors, and the king at first exercised only a distant supervision over them. As the empire in North America grew, both king and Parliament showed a disposition to control colonial affairs, but in the first half of the 17th century their efforts were frustrated by political upheavals at home. After the Restoration in 1660, the Stuart kings tried to reorganize colonial governments upon the model of the French empire. James II was overthrown in the revolution of 1689, however, and the new structure collapsed.

British rule, as it impinged upon the colonists in the 18th century, was the outgrowth of the era of political stability in Britain that followed the revolution of 1689. It was a series of contrivances rather than a coherent system. The balance of power in Britain between the king and Parliament was itself undefined, and colonial administration reflected this duality. Royal government started with the king acting through his Privy Council, which was in turn influenced by the Board of Trade, the principal agency concerned with colonial affairs. The Board, although it advised as to policy and appointments to colonial offices, had no powers of its own. Any action had to be taken by the Privy Council, which also consulted the customs, the admiralty, and other departments of the British government as occasion suggested. This decentralized and to some extent irresponsible administration, conducted by agencies that handled Britain's internal affairs, was further handicapped and diverted from a steady pursuit of goals by its involvement in the corruption and intrigue that characterized British politics in this era.

The Privy Council could and frequently did disallow acts of colonial legislatures; but the main instrument of royal authority in the colonies was the governor, who was appointed by the king and responsible to him. In proprietary colonies the chain of authority passed through the proprietor and his appointed governor. Whether royal or proprietary, however, colonial governors were ineffective. With few exceptions they were strangers in the land, having secured their office through patronage in England. Many were mere placemen with no other motive than to make their fortune. In any event, although they had an absolute veto over legislation, they were usually overmastered in a conflict between their instructions and the will of the colonists as voiced by the legislature. Without powerful family connections or enough patronage at their disposal to corrupt the legislatures, they were unable to build up a purely personal following and had to operate by cultivating one or another faction in colonial politics. To make matters worse, they were always exposed to rear assaults in the home country, where political rivals studied how to exploit any failures or embarrassments they might incur. A governor too resolute in following his instructions risked dismissal and personal failure.

Parliament frequently took a hand in colonial affairs during the 18th century, not only in passing economic legislation but in enacting into law the substance of royal instructions to colonial governors. Nevertheless, the joint authority of crown and Parliament was a source of weakness rather than of strength, for neither would concede predominant authority to the other. The checks and balances built into the English government prevented the development of a unitary and effective colonial administration. Some efforts along this line were indeed made from time to time. When opportunity arose, the king revoked original charters granted to corporations and proprietors, instituting direct royal government; as a result, by the time of the American Revolution, only two proprietary colonies remained: those of the Penns in Pennsylvania and Delaware and of the Baltimores in Maryland. Only two corporate, or "charter," colonies survived: Connecticut and Rhode Island, which were all but removed from direct royal control. Occasionally, the Board of Trade also proposed to consolidate separate colonies into larger units which could be more effectively ruled from Britain. Such a plan was sponsored by Britain at the Albany Congress of 1754, which recommended a central government seated in America. The idea was unanimously rejected by the colonies, and the Revolution cut off any further efforts of this kind.

If for no other reason than its inefficiency, therefore, British rule of the colonies was benign, allowing them to widen the scope of self-government and to advance their own interests. This state of affairs was tolerable to British leaders because the colonies' increasing consumption of imported manufactures and their production of reexportable staples like tobacco were visible economic assets to the mother country. As long as Britain's interest in the colonies was primarily commercial, their economic growth justified "salutary neglect" in political matters. Another deterrent to rigorous administration was the presence of France and Spain in North America. The colonies were, in this respect, the beneficiaries of Old World conflicts, which were carried on not only upon the battlefields of Europe but as struggles for empire in North America. Britain was not in a position to alienate colonists whose assistance she needed in war. Similarly, the colonists relied upon British protection against the French in Canada. As a result of mutual dependence, disputes between colonies and mother country, although frequent and often exasperating, were conducted in a low key.

British Economic Regulation: Colonial Gains and Losses

That colonies should serve the economic interest of the mother country was a universally accepted principle in the 18th century, one which was never disputed by Americans. It was easier for them to acquiesce in it because British economic regulation, as it evolved, was not rank exploitation and seldom conflicted directly with established colonial interests. British mercantilism envisaged a reciprocal development of the empire, in which the mother country would be the source of manufactures and the colonies producers of raw materials. Within this framework the needs of the mother country had priority, yet it was recognized that, if they were to buy manufactures, the colonies had to be given opportunities to prosper. Their enterprises, however, had to be compatible rather than competitive with those of Britain.

The Navigation Acts, adopted by Parliament during the 1660s, had three main objectives. The first was to confer a monopoly of colonial trade upon English nationals, including the colonists. All ships in colonial trade had to be English built and owned, commanded by an Englishman, and manned by a crew three-fourths English. A second objective was to channel colonial exports to northern Europe through England, with consequent benefits to English merchants and the royal customs revenues.

Certain commodities produced in America, most importantly sugar and tobacco, which were commonly reexported to Europe, were designated as "enumerated articles." These could be shipped only to the British Isles or other British colonies. By the time of the Revolution, nearly all goods exported by the colonies had been enumerated. Finally, under the Staple Act, nearly all products originating in Europe and destined for the colonies had to be landed in Britain. Apart from channeling trade through Britain, the act enabled the government, if it wished, to price European goods out of colonial markets by levying high duties on them.

To trade regulation Parliament added restrictions upon colonial manufactures which threatened to compete with those of Britain. The colonies were forbidden to export wool or wool products and beaver hats. Although they were encouraged to produce raw iron, they could not legally after 1750 construct mills for manufacturing finished iron products. Whenever the colonies tried to stimulate home manufacturers by imposing high duties on British imports, the acts were disallowed by the Privy Council.

Parliament, on the other hand, tried to promote colonial development in ways compatible with British interests. Bounties were given for tar, pitch, and turpentine, formerly imported from Scandinavia and necessary for the British fleet. The Chesapeake colonies, which produced reexportable tobacco, were encouraged to continue doing so by the prohibition of tobacco raising in England. Bounties on South Carolina's rice, marketable in Mediterranean countries, and her indigo, which was useful in British textile manufactures, were the mainstay of the colony's prosperity. Beyond these inducements, Parliament allowed varying rebates of duties laid on colonial goods reexported to Europe and in some cases granted bounties on British goods shipped to the colonies, thus reducing their price in America.

The total effect of British economic regulation is hard to estimate. Obviously, the prohibition of direct trade with Europe and the duties laid upon colonial exports imposed burdens upon American commerce and drew money out of the colonies. The system was designed to keep America in a subordinate economic relation to Britain. Yet the disadvantages were in part offset, not only by bounties and other encouragements, but by the restriction of colonial trade to English vessels. This regulation was the basis of a thriving ship construction industry in the northern colonies, which built a third of the British merchant fleet. The colonists also shared in the monopoly of colonial trade conferred upon British nationals; they owned an estimated third of the ships in the trade of the southern colonies, half of those in the trade of the middle colonies, and three fourths of those in New England's trade. To these tangible benefits were added various privileges which colonists enjoyed as members of the empire. At no cost to themselves, they received the protection of the expensive British fleet, which enabled them to trade during war and reduced their maritime insurance rates. They drew upon credits extended by British merchants, and they had free access to the goods and markets of a country that by the middle of the 18th century was the world's leading industrial nation. It has been argued, too, that parliamentary restrictions had little practical effect, that the colonial manufactures prohibited were as yet nascent and were unable in fact to compete with those of Britain, that the trade with Europe channeled through Britain would have followed the same route even if not restricted, and that, in any event, the really damaging regulations were evaded by massive smuggling, which Britain's lax enforcement of the customs laws did little to check. British controls as they operated up to 1760 were not a major issue in the public debate that preceded the Revolution, but they were no doubt an ulterior factor in the situation. Given their strong economic growth, it is questionable how long the colonies would have tolerated subordination to Britain in the imperial system.

CHAPTER II

The Metropolis and
the Provinces

Britain's Emergence as a Military
and Industrial Power

When the colonies were first planted, Britain was not among the wealthiest, most populous, or most powerful states of western Europe. By the middle of the 18th century, however, it was the leading military power and economically the most advanced nation of Europe. An important element in its progress was success in war. Spain had once been the dominant military power in Europe, and as spearhead of the Counter-Reformation posed a serious threat to the security of Protestant Britain. The defeat of the Spanish Armada in 1688 and a subsequent war which Britain won tempered the Spanish menace, and Spain later declined as a major power. Emerging then as Britain's chief rival was France, which was larger than Britain in territory, population, and wealth. Britain became wholly committed to opposing French expansion when William of Orange assumed the English throne in 1689; as head of the Dutch republic, William had been the leader of Protestant resistance to Catholic France. He immediately declared war, and in nearly half of the next 60 years, the two countries were fighting. There were four declared wars with some fighting in between: the War of William III (1688–97), the War of the Austrian Succession (1702–13), the War of the

Spanish Succession (1739–48), and the Seven Years War (1756–63). These wars, which had other names in the American colonies, were part of a longer series, sometimes called the second Hundred Years War, that eventually included the War of the American Revolution (1776–83), and the wars of the French Revolution, which, with a brief intermission of two years, lasted from 1793 to 1815.

In all the wars preceding the American Revolution, Britain had the benefit of at least one major ally on the continent, such as Holland, Austria, or Prussia, and the allies stood the shock of massive physical conflict and slaughter. Britain sent out expeditionary forces, which were often hired mercenaries, and supported its European partners with heavy financial subsidies. Britain itself was protected from invasion by the English Channel and a powerful navy; hence it tended to seek encounters in distant parts of the world where smaller forces and naval supremacy could be effective. The wars against France and its European partner, Spain, developed into a struggle for overseas empire, in which Britain gained the advantage, eventually dislodging Spain from Gibraltar and France from India and North America, besides enlarging its island possessions in the Caribbean. The British empire spread over the globe.

The wars left a mark on British society. In terms of men and armaments they were conducted on an ever-increasing scale, and though fought in part with mercenaries, usually Germans from the Rhineland hired under contract with their rulers, each war left Britain with a larger standing army. In the previous century Britain's army had usually disbanded between wars. The British people were by tradition hostile to keeping an army in peacetime, regarding it as the king's force and an instrument of despotism. Armies of the time consisted of the dregs of the population, and soldiers stationed in Britain were quartered in private houses. Dr. Samuel Johnson coupled them with criminals and horrible stinks as equally unwelcome in a household. Such troops were in peacetime used mainly to put down rioting and to suppress smuggling, both of which activities were popular with the people. All classes of the population hated the troops.

There had been at one time an alternative to professional soldiers in the militia, which had existed since the Middle Ages: "English society with a weapon in its hand." Every man from 16 to 60 years old had to serve in the militia; in peacetime that meant practicing drill during the summer. The militia in each county was headed by a Lord Lieutenant and officered by the landed gentry who, under one regulation, were ranked according to the amount of their taxable property. The militia fairly represented the people and was presumably a force in reserve against foreign invasion or royal oppression. Many people in Britain continued to believe that it was superior in valor and military effectiveness to any body of men who fought only for pay. There were few occasions to test its mettle, however, and although a tradition of military amateurism persisted, warfare became so distant and so evidently professionalized by the 18th century that interest in the militia waned. It continued to exist on paper, but no longer assembled regularly after 1714. Thus the people's army decayed. Britain did not adopt national conscription, which was being introduced in European countries; instead, it depended on a professional army.

The cost of continuous war brought far-reaching changes in British economic life. Midway through King William's War, it became evident that the government could not pay its debts. In this crisis, the king's advisors made a fascinating discovery which was to play a key role in Britain's rise to greatness, namely, that there is no limit to the money a government can borrow if it can just pay the interest on its debts. This discovery was the basis for the creation in 1694 of Britain's *funded debt,* which for a century was the marvel and the envy of Europe. Thenceforth, whenever the government borrowed, it promised only to pay interest but never the principal of the debt contracted. Since the British people dutifully paid taxes and the government regularly discharged the interest, British national bonds always sold at par value and foreign capitalists as well as the country's own capitalists eagerly bought them up. The debt was administered by the newly created Bank of England and other great corporations, which were responsible for discharging the interest and were in turn reimbursed out of the income from regular taxes levied by the government. Britain's "public credit," its astonishing ability to borrow money, was crucial to victory in the wars of the 18th century. The cost, however, was high. At the end of the Seven Years War (the French and Indian War in America), the national debt was £130 million, an astronomical figure for those times, and the interest paid on it consumed a large proportion of the government's annual revenues. The taxes levied to support the debt were a heavy burden, especially on the landed gentry. A larger percentage of national income was absorbed by taxation in Britain than in France, where the Old Regime was eventually ruined as a result of the government's financial insolvency.

High taxes were not the only drawback of the funding system; it was believed by many people to be the chief source of the corruption that pervaded every aspect of politics and public life. The enormous sums handled by the government and by large corporations afforded an inexhaustible source of patronage. Some critics said that patronage on so massive a scale had placed such power in the hands of the monarch as to undermine the constitutional restraints established by the Revolution of 1689. In any case, it was believed that war profiteering, banking operations, stockjobbing, and speculation had undermined the moral standards of the country, elevated swindlers above honest men, impaired the work ethic, penalized the productive part of the nation, and overturned the traditional relations between social classes.

Complaints about loss of morality and traditional values were no doubt a predictable reaction to fundamental social and economic changes that were dismantling the existing order without a political revolution. New methods of agriculture had increased the supply of food and raw materials for industry; the agricultural revolution threw laborers off the land into the industrial cities and by mid-century had made farming in many parts of the country a large-scale, capitalist enterprise. The industrial revolution was under way, stimulated by investment capital derived from war profits and financial speculation as well as by the mass production and standardization involved in continuously equipping and arming large military forces. Factory production, power machinery, and division of labor were propelling Britain into the industrialism of the 19th century.

A Pre-Industrial Economy

Throughout the 18th century, the American economy was in a pre-industrial stage, its industries largely extractive. Perhaps 80 percent of the people were directly dependent upon agriculture; this, outside the slave plantation areas, was basically subsistence farming, supplemented in varying degree by the production of cash crops. Slave plantations were also largely self-subsistent, but they differed markedly from small farms in the amount of capital and resources applied to the money crop. Production for the market, whether on a small farm or on a plantation, went into export commodities like tobacco, rice, wheat, and wood products. Since America's population was overwhelmingly rural, there was not much of a domestic market for the products of its farms and forests.

Most manufactured articles were made in the home, or in small shops or mills that tended to local needs in every village and town. With few exceptions, manufacturers were organized on a handicraft basis, in which the master of a shop was assisted by apprentices learning their trade and by hired journeymen who had received their license to practice. The factory system, with its extensive use of machinery and division of labor, had not been introduced. Probably because transportation was difficult, particularly in winter, the putting-out or domestic system, which had converted the cottages of rural England into sweatshops, was not much in evidence. There were two or three industries, such as iron manufactures and flour and lumber milling, which sometimes were large-scale and produced for distant markets; otherwise, manufactures were small and local; the goods that they turned out were generally inferior to imports from Britain, which dominated the American market for high-quality manufactures until long after the Revolution. Except for ship construction, in which Americans excelled, colonial towns were not manufacturing centers; they were distribution points for exports and imports.

Commerce, although vigorously pursued, was on a modest scale. Ships owned by Americans were generally smaller and carried cargoes of less value than those of English merchants trading to America. As their trade grew from small beginnings, the colonists tended to move into lines of enterprise that could be carried on with little capital: they marketed low-value colonial products, such as foodstuffs and lumber, in the West Indies, for example, and returned West Indies goods to the colonies. For the most part they left to British merchants the direct trade with Britain, particularly the marketing of southern staples and the importation into the colonies of high-cost manufactures.

As a new and undeveloped country America lacked capital, for which it relied upon British merchants. A chain of credit crossed the Atlantic and extended to the remotest edge of the inland frontier. American merchants in the coastal towns got goods on consignment from British merchants and passed them along to rural storekeepers; these in turn sold the goods on credit to farmers. The harvesting of the farmer's crop started a reverse flow of commodity payments that eventually allowed the wholesale merchant in the coastal town to send a cargo to England in cancellation of his debts. Since British credit was directed toward financing the consumption of British goods rather than investing in the colonial economy, it had only a partial effect in promoting American economic growth. However, it allowed merchants to employ a larger trading capital, overseas as well as at home, and it provided southern planters with the slaves to work more land.

In terms of the institutional growth, the colonies were in many ways a backward area. A general commitment to agriculture and extractive industries, dependence upon imported manufactures, and a shortage of domestic capital are in modern times the earmarks of an underdeveloped economy. Moreover, there were no banks in America to provide credit. No business corporations had yet been formed; trade and other enterprises were still on such a small scale that local partnerships sufficed to raise the necessary capital. The country lacked a transportation network which would tie it together in an economic unit: roads were few and usually primitive, bridges unbuilt, and many back-country areas virtually cut off from access to markets and sources of supply. Since land transportation was expensive, commerce moved by water, and, although there was a certain amount of coastal trade, the colonies traded mainly with the outside world rather than with one another. Up to the time of the American Revolution, economic development in the colonies had not proceeded far enough to suggest, either to the government or to the people, that it was feasible to promote economic growth by any considerable investment in internal improvements.

Yet the colonies were pre-industrial only in the sense that Britain had been a century earlier; that is, they were on the threshold of an economic expansion that would lead to the industrial revolution. Few of the handicaps that beset modern underdeveloped nations afflicted the colonies. Although population increased rapidly, it exerted little pressure on resources. Before the Revolution, when westward expansion was blocked by the Appalachian mountains, the supply of land relative to population declined, yet in the country at large there was enough land to maintain the habitual standard of living. Ideas and attitudes inherited from the past were an advantage rather than an obstacle. The common American was middle class in viewpoint, acquisitive, and nearly devoid of allegiance to feudal or non capitalist values that might have interfered with his commitment to economic progress. The merchant and planter elite had a modern orientation, and was accustomed to investing its wealth in productive enterprise. In both their circumstances and their attitudes, Americans were "the first-born children of extended commerce."

The ability of the colonies to live above mere subsistence levels depended upon their earning money in foreign markets, either by producing a desirable commodity or by getting into the international carrying trade. Their efforts to do either were shaped by their relations with Britain and its economic regulations. The southern colonies had no problem; their development conformed with mercantilist theory: they specialized in valuable staple crops and provided noncompetitive markets for British manufacturers and for British slave traders. Moreover, British merchants handled the bulk of the south's carrying trade. Ironically, however, the south's accommodation to the empire was its undoing. By the time of the Revolution, the Chesapeake planters were hopelessly in debt and tobacco planting was a declining industry. The rice planters of South Carolina, sustained by British bounties, were better off, but they too were in debt.

New England and the middle colonies had difficulty in finding lines of enterprise that were compatible with the imperial design. Except for timber products and ships, the things that they produced lacked markets in Britain, which excluded New England fish and levied nearly prohibitive duties on the wheat of the middle colonies. The difficulties of the northern colonies in adapting to the imperial scheme proved, however, to be their salvation. A vast empire of slave plantations stretching southward into the tropics was a potential field of exploitation. The southern colonies, the tip of this slave empire, did not at the time offer much promise; they were self-sufficient in the timber and foodstuffs which the north produced, and the manufactured goods which the south needed were supplied by Britain until the north became industrialized in the 19th century. Farther south, however, lay the sugar islands of the West Indies, utterly specialized in growing their single crop, crowded with slaves, rich, and dependent upon outside sources for the very goods that the northern colonies had in abundance. The West Indies could be supplied from North America with foodstuffs, barrel staves, and lumber 20 percent cheaper than from any other area. Accordingly, the northern and middle colonies traded, not only with the British West Indies, but with the French, Dutch, and Spanish islands, whose ports were opened to them. On return voyages they took away the sugar, molasses, cotton, dyestuffs, and tropical woods of the islands, sometimes carrying them to Britain, but more often to colonial ports from which they were transported overseas by British merchants. By cultivating their natural advantages in the West Indies, the northern colonies gained a share in the lucrative commerce between these islands and Europe. Their economy was expanding rapidly in the years before the Revolution.

Currency Finance: The Paper Money System

The problems of the colonies with foreign trade came to a focus in the difficulties which they had with money and with international payments. As the first explorers had learned to their dismay, the North American coast held no deposits of precious metals. The only way that the colonists could get hard money was by selling abroad, but, since in trading with Britain they normally bought more than they sold, the money that they earned from other sources, such as the West Indies, tended to flow to Britain in payments for goods and the discharge of debts. Hence there was a perennial shortage of hard money in the colonies. This did not greatly matter in the early, primitive days, but as the domestic economy grew there was not enough hard money to handle commercial transactions and pay taxes. The inhabitants felt the need of a circulating medium which, unlike gold and silver, would stay in the country and not "take unto itself wings and fly away."

A solution adopted by every colony except Virginia was to emit paper money through a land bank. The legislature printed "bills of credit" and lent them to farmers and other persons at low rates of interest. The loans were secured by mortgages on the borrowers' property and were repayable in installments over a period of years. As borrowers spent the money, it passed into general circulation. As borrowers repaid their loans and the money in circulation declined, the legislature nearly always started another land bank to sustain the flow of loans and keep sufficient money in circulation. For a nation of farmers, land banks provided agricultural credit as well as the means of discharging debts and improving farm property. The injection of money into the economy had inflationary effects, tending to raise prices and ease the burden of debt. Although not everyone agreed, paper money was generally regarded as the cure for economic depression. Moreover, the interest paid in by borrowers was an important source of revenue to the government; it enabled Pennsylvania and some of the other middle colonies to exist for many years without levying direct taxes.

There was another way that colonies issued paper money: directly, in the conduct of public finance. The method originated as a means of financing wars. Faced by an emergency that required large, immediate expenditures, the colonies could not borrow from their citizens or greatly increase the rate of taxation. There were no banks or other financial institutions, and the country's wealth was in land, slaves, and commodities, not in liquid capital which could be drafted to public use. In these circumstances, all colonial governments resorted to paper money. The legislature simply printed bills of credit, which were paid out to meet governmental expenses, and at the same time levied taxes which, paid in paper bills, eventually drew the bills out of circulation. The money issued by this process (as well as bills issued through the land banks) was not redeemable in gold or silver. It was usually legal tender, that is, by law declared acceptable in public and private transactions. Its value depended, however, not on convertibility into precious metals, but on the unreflecting acceptance of the bills by the people and the confidence of the people in their government—their knowledge that the need to pay taxes would sustain a demand for the money and thus preserve its value.

The risks inherent in the system were fully understood. If emissions were too large, they were likely to cause price inflation and a depreciation of the currency. This happened in New England and the Carolinas, but most of the other colonies handled their paper money successfully. Not only did paper money have generally beneficial effects upon the economy, but it enabled the colonies to finance the wars in which they engaged. During the French and Indian War, in which the colonies laid out what were for them enormous sums, no serious depreciation occurred. The colonies were greatly assisted by a British subsidy which they received as compensation for their war expenditures. Nevertheless, in terms of the demands made upon it, the paper money system stood the test of war.

Since the amount of money in circulation affected price levels, any emission involved a conflict of interest between debtors and creditors. Debtors favored a large amount, which could be expected to raise price levels and therefore reduce the real value of their debts. Creditors, who had an opposite interest, desired small emissions. In Massachusetts and South Carolina, bitter disputes arose over this issue; but elsewhere, although paper money legislation, like taxes, always created a division of opinion, there was little objection to paper money itself, even among propertied men and creditors. In most colonies it was considered indispensable.

Paper money emissions were a constant source of friction in colonial relations with the British government. Although the Board of Trade generally acknowledged that the colonies had to issue paper money to cope with their problems, it tried through instructions to governors to keep down the amounts and to ensure that sufficient taxes were levied to withdraw the money from circulation. Its greatest concern was to protect British merchants against having to accept payment of debts in depreciated currency; hence it resolutely opposed laws making paper money legal tender. Colonial governors were instructed not to approve paper money acts which did not have a clause suspending their operation until they could be reviewed by the Privy Council. The Board's efforts were not very successful; during the frequent wars of the period, governors approved nearly any kind of paper money legislation, since only in this way could the colonies furnish aid to Britain.

Although wars still hindered the enforcement of policy, British control tightened after 1740, when Parliament, as well as the Board of Trade, showed a tendency to heed the complaints of a few British merchants more than the desires of the colonists. In 1751 Parliament passed an act, applying to New England, which prohibited land banks and declared that paper money could no longer be made legal tender. The other colonies were, for a time, left untouched. However, Britain seemed irresponsible in its adopting regulations which in the view of the colonists crippled their efforts to deal with monetary problems, and, at the same time, did nothing to help solve them.

War and Social Change in the Colonies

The last and biggest war in which Americans engaged as British colonies was the French and Indian War (called the Seven Years War in Europe), which began in 1754, two years before it broke out in Europe, and lasted until 1763. Britain and France were the main protagonists in North America. By this time the westward expansion of the colonies had reached the Appalachian barrier in many areas and was beginning to break into the Ohio Valley. Alarmed by the threat to their possessions, the French reinforced posts in the Ohio country which linked Canada with French settlements along the Mississippi River. The war decided which nation was to possess Canada and the trans-Appalachian west. Early encounters were disastrous for the British, but the turning point came in 1757 with the appointment of William Pitt to head the British ministry. His strategy was imperial rather than European. While conducting a holding operation in Europe, he applied British resources to the war overseas. In North America the groundwork for victory was laid by strengthening the British fleet until it could cut off France's reinforcement of its troops. Quebec fell to the British in 1759, and within the next two years every remaining French fort in North America was taken. In Europe, India, and the West Indies, Britain and its allies were victorious. Exhausted, France made peace in 1763, surrendering all possessions in North America.

Although not ordinarily inclined to make sacrifices for the empire unless their own interests were affected, the colonies were involved in this war as never before. Not only was it conducted on a larger scale than previous wars, but for the first time a major expeditionary force of British regular troops was sent to the colonies. British troop strength in North America rose from about 3,000 before the war to over 30,000 men, and this army was maintained in the colonies for several years. Although most supplies were shipped from Britain and Ireland, the military forces purchased many things locally, American merchants shared in war contracts, and the soldiers spent their pay in America. The British government spent a great deal of money, and so did American governments. After the war, Britain kept stronger garrisons in North America and the Caribbean, and these required regular outlays of money.

Such large injections of cash heated up the colonial economy. Individual merchants made profits, but in the middle and New England colonies—which were most directly affected by British expenditures—profits spread out broadly among farmers, master craftsmen, and other people who could sell their products or services to the armies. Historians trace a general change in colonial society beginning about 1750, attributable at least in part to war. General prosperity resulted in mounting colonial imports of British luxuries, in housing shortages and in sharply rising property values in the towns, and higher standards of consumption among the middle and upper classes. Behind the wave of war prosperity came a steep and disruptive economic recession which lasted for several years after the fighting stopped.

In spite of the postwar depression, the war left behind it a larger and more productive American economy—relative to population, more products of the land and of the forest were produced for sale. The carrying trade had expanded—relative to population, the colonies employed more ships, more goods, and more capital in voyages to the Caribbean and Canada, in the coastal trade, and in commerce with southern Europe, Britain, and Ireland. There is evidence, particularly for Philadelphia, that American merchants were getting rich enough to invest in the larger ships and more expensive cargoes required to compete with British merchants in the trade between Britain and the West Indies. American competition was becoming so bothersome to British merchants, in fact, that proposals were made in Parliament to restrict or prohibit colonial ships from engaging in the trans-Atlantic trade. Although British merchants still had a virtual monopoly of the lucrative commerce of the southern colonies, there is evidence that American merchants were ready to challenge British supremacy in other segments of imperial commerce.

Rise of a Native Elite

A product of social change was the rise of an upper class grounded in the colonies rather than in the mother country. This process started long before the changes that occurred after 1750 but were enhanced by them. Although few noblemen ever came to America, the immigrants included people of every other class. In the 17th century, wealthy merchants and landowners of good family in England at first formed the upper crust of colonial society. By the turn of the century, however, social rank was reshuffled as new men made their fortunes in America and rose to prominence. Such men, who were the leaders of colonial society, had a basic allegiance to their own provinces and, insofar as American culture diverged from that of England, a sense of their identity as colonists rather than as Englishmen. The emergence of a native elite was a potent element in the development of American nationalism.

The Metropolis and the Provinces

By mid-18th century, America's population was nearly a third that of England, wealth was accumulating, society was becoming more sophisticated, and plenty of Americans were alarmed by the thought that the colonies were becoming like the mother country. Nevertheless, there was a marked contrast between public institutions in the two countries and, to some extent, in the quality of life, which persuaded many Americans as well as Englishmen that Britain was an aging and decadent nation whereas America was youthful and virtuous. A similar attitude was expressed by the idea that the colonists had inherited the best and

most wholesome in British traditions, while the mother country
had fallen on evil ways. Americans were inclined to such views
because what they read about Britain was usually critical of its
society and government. The criticism was by no means without
substance or foundation in fact. It could be said rightly that
Britain was moving toward bigger government and bureaucracy,
that politics and administration were lubricated at every point
by corruption, that Parliament with its rotten boroughs was less
responsive than ever to popular will, that the militia, the people's
army, had been displaced by professional soldiers who did only
the government's bidding. It could be said with equal justice,
of course, that Britain had gotten the better of its national rivals
in war and had expanded its empire over the globe—every Brit-
isher's self image was enhanced by the nation's military victories.
It could be said, too, that in an age of absolutism, Britain had a
limited, constitutional monarchy, that civil and religious rights
were existent realities, that the government was stable and its
public credit almost unassailable, and that the British nation
had overwhelmed all rivals in trade, manufactures, and financial
power.

Americans were unsympathetic toward many of these accom-
plishments, tending to think instead, of the evils entailed. They
cited the staggering burden of the national debt and heavy taxes
which bore heavily on the landowners who paid most of them.
Admittedly, the funding system promoted financial and industrial growth, and the government's financial strength gave it
enormous power to wage war or to achieve any other national
objective which cost money. Yet the system could be said to
reward those already rich, including the idle rich who performed no services, to raise speculators and cheaters over honest
men; and in the countryside the taxes it required were wiping
out the lesser gentry. Britain's yeoman farmers, once considered
the backbone of the nation, were already extinct, and the wholesale enclosure of common fields was further transforming England's rural population into an agricultural proletariat which
labored at low wages or was pushed destitute into the industrial
and mining centers. The countryside of Britain was already a

land of large estates worked by hired labor, and in both the country and city, class distinctions had intensified. London, although the seat of government and the cultural center of the nation, was widely regarded as the most sinful and vice-ridden city in Europe. King George himself shared the sense that Britain was decadent: years later, when the colonists had won their independence and he saw the definitive treaty of peace, he said: "This completes the downfall of the lustre of this Empire; but when religion and public spirit are quite absorbed by vice and dissipation, what has now occurred is but the natural consequence."

In America, by contrast, if one disregarded the institution of slavery, public and private life could be viewed as resting upon higher foundations of virtue and humanity than in Britain. Colonial governments were small, cheap, broadly based, and far more responsive than in Britain to popular will. Public debts were small or nonexistent, and taxes were but a slight burden upon any form of productive enterprise. Without standing armies and relying upon their militia, the colonists were exempted from almost any element of militarism. Governments were relatively free of corruption, if only because they lacked patronage to dispense; in any case, official corruption was certainly not institutionalized—whenever it occurred, it made the people who witnessed it highly indignant and was likely to become a public issue. The financing of government did not enrich individuals nor benefit some classes at the expense of others. Although economic opportunity for the common man was declining and the urban poor were a growing problem, the colonists still enjoyed the blessing of a relatively bountiful supply of land which, in comparison with Britain or other European countries, was widely distributed among the population. The typical American was a yeoman farmer, and he was not a disappearing class.

In comparing their own social arrangements favorably with those of Britain, Americans thought in terms of Commonwealth principles, and also in terms of agrarian attitudes that had been appropriate to 17th-century England and now had some relevance to 18th-century America. Like the "country party" in

Britain, which was the vehicle of the landed gentry typically in opposition to the "court party" leagued with administration and the ministry in power, Americans viewed with deep misgivings the trends in Britain, perceptible in America, that were transforming a relatively simple, personal, parochial, stable, and agrarian-oriented society into one that was unboundedly competitive, wildly unstable, impersonal, and commercialized in values. In embracing this point of view, Americans were broadly inconsistent, for they themselves were always acquisitive and thoroughly addicted to speculative enterprises. It should be said that by no means all of them had an anticapitalist attitude. Merchants and members of the social elite, especially if travelled and well educated, were likely to be more worldly, and willing or eager to embrace what they considered progress. Nonetheless, most Americans, at least until they had an opportunity to share in it, interpreted the economic revolution of their time exhibited in Britain as a sacrifice of much that was fine and moral in human relations to what was false and immoral. They had a "country party" cast of mind.

CHAPTER III

Social Conditions,
Social Classes, and
Race Relations

The Sociology of Agriculture

The typical American was a farmer who owned his own land. In the backcountry or in districts remote from transportation, a man could buy a large tract for little money and often on credit. Going into the forest with his family, the frontier farmer built a crude shelter and began to cut down the trees, usually at first merely girdling the larger ones so they would die and let in enough sun to grow corn between the stumps. His efforts the first year or two were devoted to survival, raising enough food for subsistence, As soon as possible, however, he grew a cash crop, usually corn or wheat, which he could take to market As the years passed, he constructed a simple house of two or three rooms and a loft, built a barn, planted an orchard, and cleared more land at the rate of perhaps two acres a year. A farm of 30 cultivated acres and a cleared pasture was the work af half a lifetime, but at the end a farmer was assured of a rude but ample subsistence. Meanwhile, he had greatly increased the value of his property. "They maintain themselves the first year, like the Indians," wrote an English traveller, "with their guns, and nets; and afterwards by the same means with the assistance of their lands; the labour of their farms they perform themselves, even to being their own carpenters and smiths: by this means, people who may be said to have no fortunes, are enabled to live, and in a few years maintain themselves and families comfortably." With little or no capital, with only his own labor and that of his family, the American farmer could in time become a property owner and achieve a level of existence respected by the society in which he lived. America, it was said, was "one of the best places in the world for a poor man."

That was high praise in a world in which most of the people in every country were poor. Certainly, as all foreign visitors noted, the American farmer was vastly better off than the mass of England's impoverished agricultural workers, who toiled their lives through with no hope of gaining their own land. Yet, though an American farmer could improve his condition, his progress was difficult beyond a certain point. Without capital, and in a society where labor was relatively scarce and expensive, he proceeded only by exhausting the soil. The material plenty which formed the essential ingredient of American "democracy" sprang from the waste of natural resources.

Typically, a farmer planted a single cash crop on the same land until the soil's fertility was lost. He was indifferent to the use of fertilizer, refusing, as one agricultural reformer urged, "to toss about dung with an air of majesty." Fertilizer was, in any case, expensive or unobtainable, since domestic animals were seldom kept except for family use because they were expensive to buy and required much labor to maintain. To save labor and expense, the farmer allowed the livestock he did have to forage for food and thus lost their manure. For the same reasons, he made little or no use of soil-restorative crops which were then being employed in England. As long as land remained abundant, it was always cheaper to clear another acre than expend the capital and labor necessary to preserve the fertility of an acre already cultivated.

Such methods were, in fact, a successful adaptation to economic circumstances. American farms provided a decent living, and their products competed successfully in foreign markets with those of other countries. Yet agriculture, as practiced, moved in a circle of diminished returns. As the farmer cultivated more fields, the first fields wore out; he could not, therefore, greatly expand production. Even if he was prosperous enough to buy additional land, he could not farm it himself; the crude technology of the times did not permit large-scale methods, and hired labor was too expensive. He might lease extra land to another farmer, but his return was likely to be low, for leaseholds were not popular and tenants ordinarily paid little rent. Thus, if farming was a man's only occupation, he might gain a competence, but he could seldom rise to affluence.

There was one way he could make money —by selling out and moving to a new frontier. Increasing population and the universal demand for land in older areas, as well as in the backcountry as population moved westward, steadily increased land value. This was true even of worn-out lands, particularly if they had been improved by the construction of houses and barns. Thus, if a farmer was prepared to renew the arduous labor of his youth, he could escalate his economic chances by selling his property and migrating to a region where land was still cheap. Hence, American farmers were typically but half farmers; they were also land speculators. In settling a new area, they characteristically bought several times as much land as they could ever use, putting as much money as they could into the purchase. This was one reason, according to critics, why they had so little to spare for keeping up their farms once they had them. In any case, buying and selling land was an American avocation. It was a unique feature of American society, which set it apart from others, that the wide distribution of land enabled the common people to profit from the increase in land values that accompanied population growth.

Behind the newly cropped lands of the expanding backcountry, whose virgin soils yielded good crops, was a widening belt of declining land in the east. The country's total agricultural production was thus limited and, in "old" farming communities of the east, economic opportunity for the farmer decreased. A man's father or grandfather might have owned hundreds of acres, but through the generations the size of landholdings shrank as estates were divided among heirs. At some point there was no land left, even poor land, for the next generation. In many parts of the east, landless sons were in oversupply. Sometimes they lived in their father's house, working as hired men for other farmers or as occasional laborers at harvest. In most villages there were a few nonfarming occupations they might get into, such as blacksmithing, milling, weaving, brickmaking, keeping a store, and sometimes operating an iron mine. Near the cities it was not uncommon for people to occupy small plots of land, often having no horse or plow of their own and needing to hire the plowing done to raise corn for themselves and stalks to feed their cow. Their wives might raise vegetables to sell in town, while they worked for other farmers or engaged in occupations like driving wagons. They lived in tiny houses and, as an observer commented, sometimes had "nothing in the house but water to drink." But, as landless men frequently did, they might move about to try their luck in different places, working as laborers, perhaps leasing a farm, and, if they managed to acquire land, remaining as permanent residents. If not, they moved on. Home, tradition, and habitual circumstances seemed to have little hold on them. "They do and will remove as their avidity and restlessness incite them," remarked the English governor of Virginia. "They acquire no attachment to Place; But wandering about Seems engrafted in their Nature; and it is a Weakness incident to it that they should for ever imagine the Lands further off, are Still better than those upon which they are already Settled." Whatever the habits of Americans, however, wanderlust was inspired by dire necessity in some of the older sections of the country. In the late 18th century, Connecticut and other densely settled parts of New England had more people than agriculture alone could support.

Conditions naturally varied a great deal among individual farmers and in different areas of the country. The straitened economy of agricultural New England was masked by the industry and civil habits of the people. One Englishman wrote:

The face of the country [near Boston] has in general a cultivated, inclosed, and cheerful prospect; the farm houses are well and substantially built, and stand thick; gentlemen's houses appear everywhere, and have an air of a wealthy and contented people.

These freeholders of small tracts of land, which comprise the greatest part of the province have, almost to a point, the necessaries of life and nothing more . . . Their farms yield food—much of clothing—most of the articles of building—with a surplus sufficient to buy such foreign luxuries as are necessary to make life pass comfortably, but [also] more of necessaries—a greater capability of hospitality, and decent living than is to be found among the few remains of their brethren [small farmers] in England.

The same observer remarked that poor and indigent people were seldom seen.

Life in rural Pennsylvania had fewer amenities. Speaking of the Germans of Lancaster County, who owned some of the best land in America and were among the country's wealthiest farmers, a Frenchman observed: "I have found them having for dinner potatoes, bacon, and buckwheat cakes; tin goblets, a dirty little napkin instead of a table cloth . . . for downstairs rooms, a kitchen and a large room with the farmer's bed and cradle, and where the family stays all the time; apples and pears drying on the stove, a bad little mirror, a walnut bureau—a table—sometimes a clock; on the second floor, tiny little rooms where the family sleeps on pallets, with curtains, without furniture." These affluent Pennsylvania Dutch farmers had little regard for external appearances. "No care is taken to keep the entrance to the house free of stones and mud—not one tree—not one flower. In the vegetable garden, weeds intermingled with cabbages and a few turnips and plants. In brief, with the exception of the barn and a larger cultivated area, you do not distinguish between the rich Pennsylvania farmer and the poor farmer of other states." The French traveller once spent the night at an inn with 14 German farmers: "each one was driving a big 4-horse wagon, with 12 barrels of flour, to Philadelphia. I found them in a room next to the kitchen, all lying on the floor in a circle, their feet to the fire, each one on one or two bags of oats which they have with them to feed the horses on the way; they were all covered with a poor blanket, no cap, and all dressed . . ." The innkeeper made no charge for the space, counting on the liquor they would buy.

If manners in interior Pennsylvania were occasionally boorish, many communities in the remote South Carolina backcountry existed in what one Anglican minister described as a state of nature.

> In many places they have nought but a Gourd to drink out of. Not a Plate, Knive or Spoon, a Glass, Cup, or anything. It is well if they can get some Body Linen, and some have not even that. They are so burthen'd with Young Children, that the Women can not attend both House and Field. And many live by Hunting, and killing of Deer. There's not a Cabbin but has 10 or 12 Young Children in it. When the Boys are 18 and Girls 14 they marry, so that in many Cabbins you will see 10 or 15 Children and Grand Children of one Size—and the mother looking as Young as the Daughter.
>
> It would be . . . a Great Novelty to a Londoner to see one of these Congregations. The Men with only a thin Shirt and pair of Breeches or Trousers on—barelegged and barefooted. The Women bareheaded, barelegged, and barefoot with only a thin Shift and under Petticoat. Yet I cannot break them of this, for the heat of the Weather admits not of any but thin Cloathing. . . . The Young Women have a most uncommon Practise, which I cannot break them of. They draw their Shift as tight as possible to the Body, and pin it close, to shew the roundness of their breasts, and slender Waists (for they are generally finely shaped) and draw their Petticoat close to their Hips to shew the fineness of their Limbs, so that they might as well be in Puri Naturalibus. Indeed Nakedness is not censurable or indecent here, and they expose themselves often quite Naked, without Ceremony, Rubbing themselves and their Hair with Bears Oil and tying it up behind in a Bunch like the Indians, being hardly one degree removed from them. . . .

The minister estimated that 94 percent of the young women he married were already pregnant and that nine tenths of the back settlers had venereal disease. Left unprotected by the eastern-dominated provincial government, they lived under siege by organized bands of outlaws, who ransacked their homes, stole their livestock, and carried off their young women. In 1768 the entire Carolina backcountry was in disorder and the frontiersmen were on the point of rebellion.

Sociology of the Cities

The cities were the repositories of higher culture. With their concentration of wealth and education, the opportunities they provided for frequent exchange of ideas and information, and the commercial and intellectual ties that they had with Europe, the principal cities of America had, in some degree, come to resemble European cities. The metropolis of North America was Philadelphia, which with its nearly 30,000 inhabitants rivaled Bristol as the second city, after London, of the British Empire. New York in 1775 had nearly 25,000 inhabitants, Boston 16,000, Charleston 12,000, and Newport 11,000. Foreign visitors were impressed by the sumptuous houses, dress, and manners of their wealthy inhabitants and by the relative sophistication of the common people. Except for Boston, these cities had recently grown rapidly in population, by an estimated 33 percent between 1760 and 1775.

They were bustling, noisy places, their narrow streets congested with pedestrians, horsemen, carts, trucks, and freight wagons. Speeding was a problem; stray children often died under hooves and wheels. The air was frequently polluted by the stench of garbage and sewers, and the ordure of men and beasts. As the result of a universal housing shortage coupled with a sharp increase in real estate values, space was at a premium. The middle of town was a compact mass of wood and brick buildings, two or three stories high, built close upon the street and often sharing common walls. Residences were interspersed with shops, warehouses, taverns, stables, and an occasional church or assembly hall. The costly residences of big merchants, as well as their counting houses, mingled with the dwellings of shopkeepers and artisans, who carried on business in front rooms adjacent to the street, sharing living quarters upstairs with their apprentices. Laborers lived in rented rooms or in cottages along back alleys. High rents, however, had forced many people of low income into working-class districts at the outskirts of the city, where they often had little farms or vegetable gardens. Also seeking the suburbs were the gentry, in quest of pure air and genteel surroundings; their fashionable estates dotted the near countryside.

A relatively few individuals of outstanding wealth and position dominated urban society; in different towns, the upper 10 percent of taxpayers held from 65 percent to 85 percent of taxable property, without counting the wealth which they possessed in other forms. At the top of the pyramid in northern cities were the wholesale merchants who dealt in exports and imports. They usually came from affluent families, inheriting their professions as well as wealth and social position. Closely associated with them were lawyers, some of whom, unlike the common run of lawyers in America, had received distinguished and expensive legal education in London. Coupled with these two groups in pursuing honorific, if not always as profitable, professions were physicians and ministers, particularly of the Anglican church. These groups, joined with a sprinkling of "gentlemen" with independent incomes, constituted the native elite. Since the cities were the hub of British administration and commerce, their upper class also included a number of American and British officials, as well as merchants, whose careers were linked to British patronage and influence; they formed the most elegant and stylish element of the gentry. The various segments of the urban upper class were bound to one another, and in some colonies to the landholding gentry, by intermarriage, mutual patronage, and common business interests. They were universally recognized as "the better sort."

The increasing wealth of the urban upper class generated a taste for luxury and a tendency to imitate the life style of the English gentry. Rich men vied with one another in building sumptuous town houses, elegantly paneled and furnished. Some of their country mansions bore favorable comparison with those in England, and reproductions of the better known ones were printed and sold as wall displays. Wives and daughters adorned themselves in English fashions and spent much time visiting back and forth in their country estates. Lavish balls and dinner parties became a subject of public notoriety, arousing the indignation of the lower classes. Ironically commenting on the details of an extravagant dinner party reported in a Boston newspaper, one critic wrote: "In a few years we shall all become Turtle Eaters."

Citizens of the "middling sort" watched such goings on with less envy than might be expected because, if they did not ordinarily eat turtles, they often ate meat. The top brackets of this segment of the urban population consisted of skilled artisans and shopkeepers who operated their own businesses; below them in descending rank were artisans trained and in varying degree established in the practice of their crafts. Artisans performed the multitude of tasks generated by the city's economy and the personal needs of its inhabitants. Many skills were required in the construction and outfitting of ships, the manufacture of barrels and boxes in which to export commodities, the making of cloth and leather for clothes, the building of houses and other structures, besides such technical occupations as tailoring, cabinetmaking, metalworking, shoemaking, and distilling.

In an age before factory production, a large percentage of the highly skilled artisans were self-employed, producing and selling their own goods, taking orders from customers, or contracting for jobs. They spent most of their waking hours at their trades, working from sunrise to sunset, although at a leisurely pace, taking an hour off for breakfast, a break in the afternoon, an hour for dinner, and time off in between for conversation with friends or a quick round at the tavern. Their wives went out for the daily shopping required when small shops sold but one line of articles and there was no refrigeration: to the baker's for bread and to hire the use of his oven for roasting meat and baking pies, to the butcher and the greengrocer, and two or three times a week to the city market for general supplies. A successful artisan and his family lived under conditions that by contemporary standards were no more than merely comfortable. Typically, he inhabited a small, narrow house, less than 20 feet wide and 25 feet deep, a story and a half high. His workshop was located in a downstairs front room, and if he was fortunate there was space enough in the back yard for a garden, a chicken house, or perhaps a cowshed. If he did not own his own house, which was usually the case, he paid high rent. An artisan could not expect to have carpets on the floor, upholstered furniture, or a fine glass mirror. He ordinarily wore homespun or leather garments. But if industrious, he could support a family without his wife or children working out, and the steady demand for skilled labor gave him a reasonable degree of economic security. Many craftsmen and shopkeepers accumulated enough property to get on the tax rolls and to vote in city elections. An exceptional few graduated into the upper class.

The road was always open for men to become artisans. Training usually started with an apprenticeship in the early teens, during which a boy was bound out to a master, lived with the master's family, learned the trade, and was under the master's discipline. At the completion of his training, the youth might then work for wages as a "journeyman," but since it did not require much capital to set up his own shop and, in any case, he could easily get credit if he had a good reputation, there was no great obstacle to his becoming a master himself. By the middle of the 18th century, in fact, the apprenticeship system itself was beginning to break down. Artisans were in such demand that men without formal training and often with inferior skills managed to set up shop and to compete with established craftsmen. Compared with Europe, where the right to enter into occupations was closely restricted by law and by the monopolies of craft guilds, America was an open society. Newcomers as well as natives could practice any craft or enter into any line of business that they chose.

At the lower end of the urban social scale were the "inferior sort." Seamen constituted the largest component of this segment of the population, along with journeymen and apprentices, carters, porters, boatmen, male and female servants, day laborers, and blacks, both slave and free. Not all these working people were permanently fixed in a laboring status, and even if they were, they received high wages by European standards. "By day laborers," wrote one Englishman, "which are not common in the colonies, one shilling will do as much in England as half a crown in New England." Nevertheless, as we shall see, laborers possessed little property, and they were victimized by unemployment and economic changes.

Social Problems

The poor were singularly respectful and law-abiding compared with similar elements of European cities—in fact the level of conventional morality was higher in all ranks of American society—but the floating and unstable population that existed in colonial cities of any size was the principal source of crime and other social problems of the day. The profanity, rowdy behavior, and insolence of the lower classes toward their superiors was a subject of frequent complaint. More consequential was their addiction to alcohol, which among the poor constituted a social rather than a merely individual problem. Drunkenness was endemic at every level of American society. Taverns, segregated according to the social rank of their clientele, were the main social centers and places of public recreation, where men gathered for entertainment, gossip, and the exchange of information, a practice deplored by some moralizers like John Adams, who claimed, "Here the time, the money, the health, and the modesty of most that are young and of many old, are wasted; here diseases, vicious habits, bastards, and legislators, are frequently begotten." But Americans were also habituated to taking liquor at meals and on social occasions. Hence the average consumption of hard liquor sold commercially, to say nothing of the brandy and beer made at home, was in the neighborhood of 16 gallons a year for each family, in a country where families consisted mostly of children. But whereas the pint received by the agricultural laborer at the end of the day, along with his two shillings, usually created no problem, the congregation of drinkers at city taverns frequently led to brawls. And although the inebriety of the better and middling sort sometimes led to personal tragedy, chronic drunkenness of day laborers reduced their families to want and dependence upon the community.

The cities engendered other vices. Prostitutes operated out of bawdy houses and lingered in dock areas. Thefts and petty robberies were increasing in the late colonial period. Since police forces were negligible, consisting of a few constables employed in daylight hours and privately hired watchmen at night, authorities were unable to cope with frequent or general disorder. It appears that troop movements during the late colonial wars, economic change, population increase, and the influx of foreigners were disrupting the parochial order of the past and creating new conditions in urban communities. It was said at the time that general morality was declining.

Although a humanitarian attitude toward the poor and the legal offender scarcely graced the thought of colonial America, cities and rural communities did afford public relief to destitute and disabled people. Many seamen and other laborers were unemployed during the winter; their jobs were seasonal. The sick and the crippled had to be taken care of. There were many impoverished widows, particularly in New England, where men often died at sea. Poverty was regarded as the fault, or at least the private misfortune, of individuals, not as the failure of the society. Town officials in New England had no qualms about "warning out" newcomers likely to become public charges. Yet the measures of public relief afforded by American communities were for the time humane. All the principal cities had poorhouses and in some cases workhouses, but, because this form of relief was humiliating to the recipient, they spent considerable sums for outdoor relief, giving partial or complete assistance to poor families. An unsought result was an annual winter influx of would-be relief recipients from the neighboring countryside. The problem of orphans and pauper children was disposed of by binding them out as apprentices at age eight or ten. The mentally ill, if they had no means of support, were handled in much the same way as paupers. Those who could work were bound out or consigned to relatives who received public assistance. In the years before the Revolution, the rising costs of public relief constituted one of the main expenses of city governments.

Although colonial America was a law-abiding society, there was a small criminal element. In sexual behavior, the latitude actually countenanced in the 18th century was greater than in any subsequent period until the 20th century, but severe penalties were prescribed by law, particularly for sexual acts regarded as unnatural, and the laws were sometimes enforced, even though the age was more concerned with the protection of property than with morality. Professional crime was largely confined to persons who made a career of counterfeiting the currency, an offense punishable by death in some colonies. However, the death penalty was sparingly invoked for this or any other offense. The colonies had inherited from England a barbarous criminal code, unchanged from the Middle Ages and so unrepresentative of more modern attitudes that it was scarcely enforceable in England; it was further tempered in the colonies. Even so, colonial attitudes were not softened, as yet, by any humanitarian impulses or by the idea of reforming the criminal. Punishment was retaliatory and based on the idea of deterrence. Long prison sentences were unusual, in part because the maintenance of prisoners was an expense to the community. Offenders not punished by fines received summary physical punishment, such as whipping, disfigurement, or being put in the stock, penalties to which the poor were more exposed than the rich. However, those who were imprisoned received no quarter. Colonial jails were stinking dungeons, in which prisoners of both sexes and of all kinds were indiscriminately thrown together, often in a single room, with scarcely any light, heat, sleeping facilities, or sanitary provisions. Food was passed in through a hole in the wall. Of Boston's stone prison, one upper-class inmate, confined briefly for printing a pamphlet, wrote in 1754: "If there is any such thing as a hell upon earth, I think this place is the nearest resemblance I can conceive of." Prisoners were often allowed a short walk in the yard during the day, but the main alleviation of their lot seems to have been the ease of escape. A high percentage of those held for any length of time managed to escape, sometimes with the connivance of authorities who wanted to relieve the community of their upkeep.

The only ethical problem of law enforcement that received much attention concerned debtors, who usually comprised the majority of those in jail at any one time. Not paying debts was regarded as immoral, and imprisonment was considered necessary to persuade people to meet their obligations. Beyond that, the purpose was to protect the creditor, the debtor being imprisoned in order to force him to deliver up any concealed assets. The irony was that in jail he had no means of earning money and, if truly insolvent, was in theory confined forever, a result beneficial neither to his creditors nor to the community. The laws operated mainly against the poor, who were often imprisoned for nonpayment of petty sums. The laws also affected a small number of bankrupt merchants and businessmen who, even if they gained their release, were not absolved of their debts and were therefore prevented from raising the capital to start in business again.

The debtor and bankruptcy laws persisted until long after the colonial period, largely because the sense of the community was that insolvent debtors should be penalized and that a deterrent was necessary. In practice, however, the rigidity of the laws was everywhere relaxed. Debtors were often confined, not to jail, but to the community, provided they did not try to leave. After serving a short term, they were released upon petition or upon taking a "pauper's oath" that they were truly destitute. Although debtor laws constantly menaced the poor, their severity was mitigated.

Social Structure and Mobility in the North

The northern elite was predominantly urban in its composition. Except for a minority of large landholders, notably the great proprietors of the Hudson River Valley, it consisted of merchants and others connected with trade and a professional class of lawyers, physicians, and ministers. While not all members of elite families managed to hold their positions, the unsuccessful branches of prominent families subsiding into the lower ranks of society, those who did steadily fortified their wealth and status by intermarriage. Although most of the upper class had been born into it, it was constantly recruited from below by absorption of the talented and newly rich. Its members occupied most political offices, were predominant in government, and had a virtual monopoly of high civil and military positions. They were distinguished from the general run of people not only by honorific occupations, but by leisure, the expensive clothes they wore, the pews they occupied in church, the taverns they frequented, usually by superior education and manners, and by the deference accorded to them by ordinary men. Scarcely a nobility, for there was no order of nobility in America and few noblemen ever came to the country, the colonial elite nevertheless resembled the contemporary aristocracy of Europe as a visible upper class of wealth, talents, and officeholding.

Wealth was fundamental to social position, and among the upper classes a few large fortunes overshadowed the others. This was true of all parts of the country. A recent study by Alice Hansen Jones, *American Colonial Wealth*, provides a sophisticated sampling of wealthholding in 1774 and allows us to state the amounts in terms of 1975 price levels. While this procedure cannot convey a sense of the vast difference in the significance of equivalent amounts of money then and now, it does give a better impression than bare figures. In New England, according to Jones's study, the top 1 percent of free adult wealthholders had an average net worth of $92,600 in 1975 dollars. The average in the middle colonies was $128,000. The top 1 percent held 14.4 percent and 13.3 percent respectively of all wealth in these colonies. This population bracket represented a miniscule number of individuals, say 300 of Philadelphia's 30,000 population or 120 of Boston's 12,000. Including these largest fortunes, the top 10 percent of wealthholders in New England had an average net worth of only $27,000 and in the middle colonies $40,200. Nevertheless, the top 10 percent held nearly 42 percent of total wealth in both colonies. Within the elite itself there were striking differences according to occupation and geographical location. New England's upper classes were by comparison not very well off. Its ministers, lawyers, and physicians were well rewarded, compared with the middle colonies: professional men in New England had an average net worth of $13,700 compared with $10,300 for the middle colonies, but New England's merchants ($19,400) and its "esquires, gentlemen, and officials" ($14,700) were distinctly less affluent than merchants ($44,000) and esquires ($50,300) in the middle colonies.

Although wealth was concentrated at the top, there was a broad middle class, neither very rich nor poor, which held substantial amounts of property. Below the top 10 percent in New England, the next 50 percent had an average net worth ranging from $12,900 in 1975 dollars down to $3,000. This group held over 58 percent of total wealth in New England. In the middle colonies the same 50 percent had an average net worth of from $17,400 to $5,000, and it held just over 51 percent of total wealth. Possession of property did not necessarily denote affluence nor, at the lower levels, even comfort; to a common farmer his acres provided only the chance to earn a living by hard work and to an artisan an opportunity to practice his craft. Nevertheless, in an age when property determined status, possession of it elevated the average American to a social rank above that of the mass of people in Britain.

Unskilled laborers, whether rural or urban, earned hardly enough to live on and could scarcely support a family. Even so, wages were higher than in England, and there was more chance to move upward into skilled crafts or leave town and take up farming. Nevertheless, the fact remains that a substantial segment of the colonial population, about 40 percent in New England, had little or no property, and in all sections of the country the lowest 10 percent was in debt. Estimates for New England show the lowest 40 percent with an average net worth ranging from $1,300 in 1975 dollars to an indebtedness of $2,350. The share of total wealth possessed by this group was a minus figure, debts exceeding possessions. In the middle colonies, the lowest 40 percent was a little better off, with an average net worth running up to $3,500 and down to an average indebtedness of $450. Collectively, this group had just under 7 percent of the wealth.

A pre-industrial society places natural limits upon social mobility. Before the Industrial Revolution multiplied the range of economic pursuits, when most people in America lived mainly by subsistence farming, social mobility upward tended to be glacial in its progress. Farming, as we have seen, was not ordinarily a path upward. In the cities, opportunities were greater and more diverse, but even here the volume of commercial business was so limited that acquisition was likely to be by slow degrees, except as wars or other exceptional conditions allowed for windfall profits. Thomas Hancock, one of the greatest colonial merchants before the Revolution, had a busy day if he handled three transactions. Artisans were prevented from becoming large manufacturers by a handicraft technology that did not permit large-scale production and also by the limited markets of a society in which most goods were made in the home. There were few careers open in the church, none in the military forces, and, in an undiversified society, not many in the professions. Social classes therefore tended to remain stable, and if men rose to higher rank they usually mounted slowly on the acquired positions of their forefathers.

There were, however, enough examples of people improving their original station in life to make the ideal of America as a land of opportunity credible. Although the greatest merchants, with few exceptions, came from elite families, there were always substantial merchants who had risen from less affluent circumstances, some who came from artisan beginnings, and a few who were completely selfmade men. Unrestricted freedom of enterprise placed no barriers in the way of laborers becoming artisans and, if fortunate, setting up their own business. In agriculture, the frontier, with its continual reconstitution of a social order, always provided avenues upward, usually by land speculation, trade, or moneylending.

The major fact about American society, however, was not mobility upward, which tended to decrease in the years before the Revolution. It was rather the abundance of resources and continuing economic expansion that enabled the common man to make a decent living. "You see no where in America," wrote one observer, "the disgusting and melancholy contrast, so common in Europe, of vice, and filth, and rags, and wretchedness in the immediate neighborhood of the most wanton extravagance." There was extravagance, surely, but much less wretchedness, in spite of economic trends that by mid-century had begun to adversely affect the poor and laboring classes.

Decline of Economic Opportunity

Since most Americans were farmers, the availability of land was the principal measure of economic opportunity for the common man. In the first century of settlement land was abundant, offered cheap or free by proprietors and provincial governments in order to attract settlers. An ordinary man could easily acquire land, with nothing more than the sweat of his brow could make a substantial, if crude, livelihood, and could have land left to will his sons. In the cities and towns common laborers received far higher wages than in England, and there were more openings for skilled craftsmen. Many immigrants, in fact, were young men who had learned their trade and came to the colonies in search of better opportunities than those awaiting them in their home country. Only a small capital was needed to set up a shop or a store, to own a fishing boat, or even to engage in commerce.

By the middle of the 18th century, however, the supply of good land was diminishing. A population of farmers needed much land in proportion to its numbers. Expansion westward was limited by the Appalachian barrier and slowed by French and Indian depredations on the frontier. In older settled areas of the east, land values rose as people bid for the available supply. The successive partition of farms through inheritance reduced the size of farms to the point where they did not provide a full living for the owner. Young men without inheritance found the situation difficult as they faced the prospect of being agricultural laborers, moving to the frontier, or trying to find employment in the few nonfarm jobs that agricultural communities offered. A "wandering poor" had become part of the rural landscape.

In old sections of the Chesapeake colonies small farmers lost out before the end of the 17th century. Overproduction of tobacco and the resulting decline in prices reduced profits and placed a premium upon large-scale production, which the increased availability of slaves by then made possible. Planters with the means to buy slaves and reserves of fresh land survived the economic changes and grew wealthy. A planter elite indigenous to America came into being. For others opportunity was blocked. Tenantry was more often a permanent condition than a step in progress toward individual ownership. The Tidewater became a land of large plantations with a relatively sparse population of small farmers. Immigrants into Virginia and Maryland during the 18th century went into the backcountry and took up subsistence farming.

Cities, too, grew "old" in terms of economic opportunity. They did not afford a wide variety of potentially expansive business enterprises. The greatest opportunities lay in occupations connected with commerce and shipping. The scale of such enterprises expanded as the economy grew, yet they were conducted by a smaller segment of the population. In early times, when seagoing ventures typically needed little capital and employed tiny ships, many people took shares in them. By the time of the Revolution, although trade had expanded greatly, shares in it were confined to a relatively small part of the population. Entry into professions such as law and medicine was more difficult as they became more institutionalized and required more education. Urban society became increasingly stratified as wealth centered in fewer hands and the relative number of poor increased. Jonathan Boucher, a minister, wrote in 1773: "Both employers and the employed, much to their mutual shame and inconvenience, no longer live together with anything like attachment and cordiality on either side; and the laboring classes, instead of regarding the rich as their guardians, patrons, and benefactors, now look on them as so many overgrown collossuses, whom it is no demerit in them to wrong." In both cities and countryside, the colonies grew to a "precocious maturity" as the population surged upward toward the limits of what their simple economy could support without fundamental change.

Sociology of Sex: The Status of Women

The status of women was governed by their biological functions in reproduction and by long-standing traditions brought over from Europe. Training in sex roles started for women, as for men, in infancy as girls were coached in behavior appropriate to wifehood and motherhood, and in the skills pertinent to keeping the house and caring for a family. It appears that the average age of marriage, lower than in Europe, was between 22 and 23 for women and between 26 and 27 for men; however, a third of the women married before age 20. Nearly everyone of sound mind and body got married sooner or later. Couples were usually about the same age, the man slightly older. Bachelorhood was frowned on, a fact which may have helped to induce all but 12 percent of men to marry compared with the 16 percent of women who were spinsters. The percentage of unmarried women was higher than in earlier days of colonization when women were less plentiful and therefore more eagerly sought. Nevertheless, as a result of early marriages and a larger percentage of people getting married, the natural increase of population was above that of Europe. The Americans multiply, said an English wit, with the fecundity of their own rattlesnakes. One result, at least, was a young population; in 1790, 49 percent of the American people were under 16 years old. Once married, a woman could expect to be pregnant about a third of the time, bear a child every 24 to 30 months, and raise six to seven children. Childbirth was a leading cause of female mortality, the evidence suggesting that it was involved in perhaps one sixth of female deaths. Even so, husbands more often than not died before their wives.

The pain and danger of childbirth, which women alone suffered, was interpreted as divine punishment inflicted upon the "daughters of Eve" for their vicarious role in bringing evil into the world; on the other hand, it was thought that nature had endowed women with spiritual qualities befitting their specialized role as wives and mothers. They were considered softer, gentler, and more perceptive of and sensitive to emotion, than men. They were commonly praised as "modest" and "agreeable" and reproached as "bold" or "shrewish." They were expected to be skilled in housewifely arts, and to be neat and frugal. They were not, however, expected to be very brainy, particularly with respect to anything that required logic or abstract reasoning. Higher education was deemed inappropriate to the quality and capacity of their minds, indeed as a blemish upon their femininity. Upper-class girls were likely to receive some training in music, polite literature, and the decorative arts, and to be expected to cope with a sophisticated company; nevertheless the education of women remained generally at an elementary level because they were considered to be the intellectual inferiors of men.

Men, in common opinion, were innately endowed with superior strength of body and mind, precisely the attributes suitable to their being providers, protectors, and advancers of the family fortunes in a harsh and competitive world. These qualities were thought to complement those of the female, the idea being that the gentle nature of the female would blend with the virility of the male to produce a single, fully realized person. To this end, under English common law which prevailed in the colonies, women by the act of marriage were merged with their husband and virtually lost their legal identity. Their personal property passed to their husbands, along with any land not reserved to them by premarital contracts. They had little freedom in matters involving property, and the husband had complete charge of the children. He, of course, had legal responsibility for supporting the family and paying its debts.

Marriages were indissoluble under canon law. In England marital disputes were judged by ecclesiastical courts, and although marriages were sometimes annulled or couples allowed to live apart, divorce with the right to marry again was never permitted. People who were very wealthy could at enormous cost get a divorce by act of the House of Lords, but in practice only husbands, never wives. In the colonies, where marriage was regarded as a civil contract, it appears that divorce was more often permitted and extended to all classes. The commonest method of divorce, of course, was simply running away; men did this more often than women, and the lower classes more often than the upper classes. But legal divorce with freedom to remarry could be secured by either wife or husband only by act of the governor and council or of the colonial legislature. Husbands more frequently obtained divorces than wives, usually on grounds of adultery. The prevalence of a double standard of sexual morality is exhibited, however, by the fact that until the time of the Revolution, records in Massachusetts show that wives never sued for divorce solely on grounds of adultery, nor, indeed, on grounds of cruelty alone. Women themselves did not regard these offenses as sufficient to procure them a divorce.

Legally, wives were less under their husbands' domination in America than in England. When couples in America married, both of whom owned property, the rights of both parties were usually protected by contracts made before and sometimes after marriage. In America, moreover, a husband had to get his wife's consent before he could sell or transfer land. Upon a husband's death, the widow was guaranteed a third of his personal property and real estate; most colonies, if there were no children, allowed her a half share.

Sexual bias was generally evident in the legal relationships of marriage, the division of occupations that gave productive functions mainly to men, and in the widely accepted idea that women were intellectually inferior. There was nothing new in all this; such bias was universal in western culture. More notable was the fact that in some ways American women had more privileges as well as legal rights than European women. If one can believe what contemporary European visitors said, American girls were less restricted before marriage than single women in Europe. They were allowed to move about freely, to behave naturally, and to express themselves with candor in social situations; they went out with men on dates unchaperoned. Indicative of the latitude permitted in courting was the custom of bundling, practiced mainly in New England, where unmarried couples often occupied the same bed separated by a board, an adaptation to isolated farmsteads, cold nights, and lack of rooms in small farmhouses. It also facilitated courtship. Freedom of association between the sexes led to frequent premarital pregnancies, which usually aroused little comment and were regarded as a normal incident of the progression toward sex pairing and marriage. Such a degree of permissiveness was indicative of a closely knit society and high levels of common morality. Although standards of sexual conduct varied among different social classes, foreign observers were often struck by the basic *innocence* betokened by sexual conventions in America.

Women in colonial times had more status in some ways than women had later. In an age in which social class and family connection figured heavily in the general estimation of an individual, a woman might have a position in society independent of her husband and his place in the social scale. More important, women in pre-industrial society shared with men in productive labor. Most Americans lived on farms, and although men and boys planted the seed and harvested the crops, women and girls also had tasks which were essential to the farm economy. They cultivated the kitchen garden, fed the livestock, tended chickens and collected eggs, milked cows, and whipped out the cream and butter. They spun and wove cloth, and made most of the family clothes and house furnishings. They nursed the sick, cooked the food, and at harvest time prepared the huge meals consumed by hired crews. On a southern plantation, the planter's wife was the busy manager of a labor force of slaves and supervised a whole range of essential enterprises. The frontier woman, in her isolation, was driven to perform tasks that under other circumstances would have violated eastern conceptions of femininity. Traveling in the North Carolina backcountry, the aristocratic planter William Byrd observed a "very civil woman" with "nothing of ruggedness or immodesty in her carriage, yet she will carry a gun in the woods and kill deer, turkey, etc., and shoot down wild cattle, catch and tye hogs, knock down beeves with an axe and perform the most manful exercise as well as most men in these parts." Whether in the backcountry or in the east, however, American women, except in a few German immigrant families, never worked in the fields. That labor was reserved for men.

The fact that in a pre-industrial economy work was so largely done in the household or shop and on a small scale gave an important role to women, allowing them to participate as helpers to men or even as principals in an enterprise. Women in colonial times not only ran farms, they acted as tavern operators, blacksmiths, gunsmiths, silversmiths, shipwrights, tanners, barbers, butchers, printers and newspaper publishers, teachers, nurses, midwives, surgeons, and physicians. Until mid-century they virtually monopolized the practice of midwifery, one woman alone being said to have brought 3,000 infants into the world. Until the Industrial Revolution, when production moved from the household and shop, and men went out to labor as the family breadwinner, women had important and remunerative tasks to perform.

Indians and Whites

Colonists as well as the British had to deal on a continuing basis with Indians, the original inhabitants of North America. Modern conceptions of Indian prehistory and the nature of Indian society are constantly revised as new information comes to light; however, it is virtually certain that the Indians came out of Asia, possibly as early as 40,000 B.C., when expanding glaciers had soaked up enough sea water to uncover a land bridge from Siberia to Alaska. Except for the Eskimos and the Aleuts, who came later, these people were not of the same stock as present inhabitants of China, Manchuria, and Japan, but were related to the ancestors of other peoples now living in southeast and west central Asia. They kept coming at intervals in small hunting bands, moving eastward of the Rocky Mountains, where glaciation was less extensive, then southward, pursuing herds of animals, and eventually reaching the tip of South America. Except for a brief interval, the land bridge was permanently submerged about 20,000 B.C., after which the New World Indians developed in virtual isolation except for landfalls of the occasional survivors of long sea voyages from Europe, Africa, or Asia. About 8,000 B.C., as the last Ice Age ended, the climate grew arid, deserts expanded west of the Rocky Mountains, and 50 or more species of the great beasts of the Pleistocene era, such as the mammoths, the mastodons, and the big-horned bisons, became extinct, victims of climatic change and possibly slaughter by man. The Indians then turned to collecting wild plants to supplement hunting, and reduced some of these to cultivation, showing themselves to be remarkable horticulturists. On the basis of intensive cultivation of maize, beans, and squash, plus tomatoes, chile peppers, and dozens of other plants, a populous and sophisticated civilization arose in Mexico, beginning about 3,000 B.C. and reaching its first major expression in the Olmec culture, about 1,000 B.C. to 300 B.C. Indian cultures waxed and waned thereafter; at the time of the Spanish conquest, the population of Mexico is variously estimated at between 11 million and 30 million.

Within the area of what is now the United States, there were possibly 1 million Indians before the whites arrived. They were backward, at least by Mexican standards, having scarcely reached neolithic levels of cultural development. They were extremely diversified, speaking as many as 1,000 to 2,000 languages, each mutually unintelligible and as different from each other as English is from German. The eastern woodlands eventually colonized by the English were thinly populated by Indians; hence, the tribes enjoyed a relatively abundant life. There were two major groups of tribes in that area, the Algonquin and the Iroquoian speakers. The Algonquins tended to be more nomadic, less oriented toward agriculture, and far fewer in number. It was the Iroquoian speakers with whom the English had the closest relations. The Iroquois were not nomadic. Typically, they lived in villages of bark and wooden houses, often surrounded by palisades for defense. Outside the villages were cultivated fields, where they practiced slash-and-burn agriculture, using methods later copied by English settlers. They girdled and burned trees to let in sunlight, planted corn and other vegetables between the stumps, cultivated with wooden shovels, and, when soil fertility declined, cleared new land and from time to time moved the whole village to a fresh site. Something less than 50 percent of their food requirements was met by agriculture, the remainder by hunting and fishing, which also supplied skins and furs for clothing, blankets, and tents. Some tribes manufactured baskets and stone tools, trading them for other things, or they specialized in trapping animals. After the whites arrived, the Indians took up making wampum, which became a general medium of exchange among Indians. Some tribes engaged in commerce itself as a business, going on long-distance trading expeditions.

Iroquois nations or tribes consisted of clusters of villages, and the villages consisted of clans, the most important unit of personal relationship. Clans were groups of families thought to be descended from a single, ancient ancestor. They were scattered in different villages and distinguished by a totemic symbol such as the turkey, the wolf, the turtle, and others. Since lineage and blood relations were usually traced through the maternal line, the ancestral head of most clans was a woman, and the closest blood relative of an Indian child was the mother and members of her immediate family, such as her brother or sister. Although a husband resided with his wife, he did not belong to her clan. Within the villages, members of a clan with their affiliates lived together, several families and as many as 50 individuals sometimes sharing a large, extended dwelling. Clan relationships determined whom one was permitted to marry, and they gave an individual the security of having numerous blood relatives, even in distant villages, with whom he was united by ties of mutual obligation. Since women were the heads of families, owned the agricultural lands and disposed of their products, usually took part in the election of chiefs, and were protected by clan ties, they had considerable status, a position relatively superior, in fact, to that of most women in white society of the time. Before marriage they were often allowed much sexual freedom, marriages were arranged but not forced, and unhappy marriages were dissolved. Polygamy was practiced, but wives who objected to it could get divorced; in any case, family harmony was often fostered by the marriage of sisters or mothers and daughters to the same man. Although Indian women cultivated the fields while men hunted—a division of labor adapted to the bearing and rearing of children—white observers sometimes commented that squaws' work was neither ignoble nor as hard as that of most white women.

Indians had only an attenuated sense of property rights—not surprisingly, for societies that depend upon hunting and gathering for subsistence must learn to share as one of the conditions of survival. In any case, Indians shared so freely that some early anthropologists thought they were communistic. Their generosity, although proverbial, was, of course, confined to a narrow range, for they had few personal goods beyond clothing, tools, and weapons, and they did not have many ways of either accumulating or preserving wealth. Land was vital to their existence, but there was land to spare in the eastern woodlands. A tribe or nation usually laid claim to a loosely defined territory; within it, hunting areas were shared by members of the tribe and agricultural lands belonged to the people who tilled the soil for as long as they did so, after which the land reverted to the tribe. Among Indians, the emphasis was on the rights of users, not of nominal owners.

No written language or written number system developed in North America. Indian culture was communicated over the generations by word of mouth. Although religious beliefs varied greatly, Indian religion was characterized by a generalized animism and a profound sense of the supernatural. It was thought that a spirit existed in all living things and in many inanimate objects as well. Animals had souls, and a hunter propitiated the spirit of the animal he killed for food. Indians generally believed in life after death, and many tribes conceived of a bipolar universe in which a good spirit—remote, abstract, and impersonal—contended with a bad spirit which was always at hand

and busy in the affairs of man. Religious observance often took the form of soliciting the aid of spirits by dances and sacrifices. Sometimes individuals went on a "vision quest," withdrawing themselves from human association in order to experience deprivation and ordeals, in the course of which dreams and visions might indicate they had won the support of a powerful spirit. People so favored could become shamans, and, whether men or women, gain importance in the tribe.

Iroquoian institutions of government were scarcely understood by whites. Chiefs were elected at both the village and tribal levels, and occasionally tribes were loosely united in confederacies. A few tribal chiefs, particularly in the southeast, had a degree of personal authority suggestive of an Inca or Aztec ruler. More typically, however, a chief's leadership rested upon consent, and his pronouncements were obeyed only to the extent that his followers agreed with them. Government among Indians was a means of meeting emergencies by collective action if a consensus existed. Lacking such a consensus, authority was not effective, and commands from above were ignored by the individual, the village, and the tribe. Nevertheless, order rather than anarchy generally prevailed in Indian society. Tradition was deeply ingrained, tending to bind individuals to accepted norms of conduct. Moreover, in the course of an average year, Indians ordinarily met only people with whom they had relationships, either through simple family ties or through clan affiliations. Kinship affiliations united them in customary, traditional behavior.

Order and harmony stopped at the limits of the tribe, however, for war was institutionalized in Indian life and affected nearly every aspect of it. Although sometimes waged over territory, war was ritualistic: it served to confer prestige, determine the ranking of men, and create solidarity in the social group. It was usually associated with retributive justice: a wrong had to be revenged upon the perpetrator or his kin. Blood feuds were therefore frequent and persistent. Indian warfare, moreover, was cruel and characterized by torture, partly because it was regarded as a contest in manly courage. Cruelty was mitigated by the custom of enslaving captives, both men and women, and of adopting them, whereupon they were protected by membership in a family.

Almost unfailingly, Indian societies degenerated upon contact with whites, mainly as a result of the spread of contagious disease. Acute epidemic diseases such as smallpox, mumps, and measles, apparently need large populations to keep them going, otherwise they die out. Such diseases could not have afflicted early man; they must have existed only since neolithic times when larger human populations arose subsisting by agriculture and men began to share modified forms of viruses and parasites with domesticated animals. Certainly the ancient hunters who crossed over from Asia bore no such diseases, not only because they were small bands but because virulent organisms, if adapted to warmer climates, would have been cut off by the "cold screen." Hence, American Indians acquired no immunity to white diseases, and when exposed to them died in great numbers, often hundreds of miles beyond the frontiers of settlement. In eastern North America, diseases spread by fishermen and explorers decimated the Indians of coastal New England before settlers came, leaving extensive cleared lands without cultivators. It is thought that the tribes comprising the Huron and Iroquois confederacies lost half their populations in the 1630s and 1640s, and that devastation was equally great among the southern Indians.

Trade with whites was also ultimately destructive to Indian institutions. Indians instantly recognized the superiority of European firearms, knives, hatchets, and other implements of war, as well as metal traps, fishing hooks, and pots and pans. The squaws enjoyed European mirrors and jewelry, and both sexes admired European clothing, furniture, and wool blankets. The only way Indians could get these valuable goods was through the fur trade. In consequence, beaver trapping was promoted to a systematically pursued business, "the ladder by which the Indian could climb to a higher standard of living." It also became a primary element in physical survival, because tribes that could get firearms could dominate or destroy those armed only with stone hatchets and bows and arrows. An enormous dislocation and shifting of tribes occurred in the eastern woodlands as tribes fought to control the fur trade, either by taking possession of the areas where pelts were gathered or by interposing themselves as middlemen between more distant tribes and European traders. Tribal wars were on a larger scale and fought with an intensity seldom known before the whites came.

Eventually, the beaver supply ran out, and unless tribes could act as middlemen for distant tribes, as the Iroquois did, or adapt more wholly to agriculture as the Civilized Tribes in the south did, they sank into poverty. Apart from the continuing need for European weapons, a return to the old ways was difficult because native crafts tended to decline and were even forgotten; if hunting grounds were near European settlements, the game had been destroyed or driven away. The devastation of Indian communities often ended in massive addiction to alcohol, for which the Indians were culturally unprepared. Alcoholism was widely prevalent among the tribes and a major cause of death.

Unlike Mexican Indians, the males of eastern woodland tribes considered labor in the fields to be women's work, hence they were very unwilling field slaves. Besides that, it was hard to make slaves of them: slave raids on Indian settlements risked retaliation, and the proximity of tribes to white settlements facilitated escape. Probably the most important factor, however, was that the northeastern Indians recognized no individuals as superiors; their society was wholly unstratified, and they were unaccustomed to servility. Indians from the southeast were somewhat more susceptible to enslavement because they were familiar with social ranking, and some were, in fact, held as slaves in the southern colonies or sold to the West Indies. They were not highly valued, and, in general, North American Indians were not enslaved on a large scale. Therefore, in contrast with the Spanish colonies, where Indians were subjugated and on that basis brought into prolonged association with whites, little racial intermingling with Europeans took place. Furthermore, North American Indians did not migrate into white society. Their folkways had such a strong hold on them that they almost never voluntarily left their own people to join the whites, who in any case rejected them as inferior. The only cultural transfers occurred when whites "reverted to savagery" and moved in with Indians. This happened often enough to arouse comment, particularly in cases in which white women and children taken captive refused to return to their own kind. "By what power does it come to pass," wrote Crèvecoeur, "that children who have been adopted when young among these people, can never be prevailed on to readopt European manners? . . . There must be in their social bond something singularly captivating . . . for thousands of Europeans are Indians, and we have no examples of even one of those Aborigines having from choice become European."

Since Indians did not make good slaves, the main interest of the English after the fur trade declined was to get rid of them and seize their lands. All the major European powers in North America, including Spain, France, and Britain, acknowledged that Indians had some kind of right to their land. The British founded their claim to territory in North America upon discovery and conquest, but they recognized Indian rights based on usufruct, that is, actual occupation and cultivation of the land— rights which had to be extinguished by treaty before British nationals could properly take possession. Whatever pious declarations of principle accompanied the process, however, the results were always the same: if the British or other European nations wanted Indian land, they took it. In the case of the British, the process followed a well-established pattern: white encroachment on tribal land and Indian attacks upon whites, followed by war and a treaty which forced the Indians to surrender their lands.

Indian warriors had always taken part in the struggles between France and Britain for dominion in North America. Although fully aware that some tribes carried on war by merciless slaughter without regard for age, sex, or the condition of the victims, both European powers nevertheless solicited Indian support, offering inducements for military aid and threatening retaliation if it was refused. Frequently, tribes had little real interest in contests between the whites, but were forced into them by fear of white reprisal or by the need for military aid if rival tribes allied themselves with one of the European powers. In the latest outcropping of this sequence of events, the French and Indian War of 1754–63, the Iroquois Confederacy in western New York supported Britain, but France secured the backing of tribes in other areas, which furnished 800 of the 900 men that ambushed and destroyed Braddock's expedition in 1755. By 1758, however, the French were losing and their Indian allies were deserting. Even for the tribes which stood by the British, however, the war proved to be a disaster. When France surrendered its territory in North America to Britain, the tribes lost the opportunity to play off whites against one another, and the Indians were then hard pressed to resist colonial encroachments upon their lands.

Slavery and Race Relations

The discovery of the New World created an enormous demand for labor, and in response to it the European powers revived the ancient institution of slavery. Slavery had died out in northern Europe during the Middle Ages, but still existed in some Mediterranean countries at the time of the discoveries, and it was generally prevalent in Africa and the Middle East. The Europeans revived slavery on a massive scale; the result was the forced migration of 10 million people out of Africa over the course of some 450 years, a transfer of population of world historical proportions. Over the entire span of the slave trade, the death rate in passage across the Atlantic averaged about 5 percent although through the 18th century it was probably closer to 15 percent, and within a year or two after arrival in the New World, perhaps 30 percent to 40 percent of those who survived the ocean voyage died. Of approximately 9.5 million blacks reaching the Western Hemisphere, only a small proportion landed in British North America, not more than 400,000 and possibly less than half that number, of which nine out of ten were transported by British traders.

What chiefly distinguished modern from ancient or African slavery was its racial character. Only blacks and American Indians were enslaved, the Indians unsuccessfully, hence black

Africans became the prototypal slaves. One scholar has suggested that without its racial content, modern slavery would probably have disappeared like medieval serfdom, without lasting social consequences. Under the circumstances that prevailed in the Western Hemisphere, however, blacks made the best slaves. For one thing, they could resist disease. Human populations become adapted to diseases they are commonly exposed to. American Indians, as we have seen, had been isolated and therefore lacked resistance to Old World diseases; the Caribbean Indians enslaved by the Spanish died quickly of disease and hard labor. Europeans themselves were notably susceptible to tropical diseases, especially malaria and yellow fever, both of which originated in Africa but were soon endemic in the New World. Among Europeans who manned slave depots on the coast of Africa, the death rate of new arrivals was 50 percent the first year, and European crews of slaving vessels often suffered more deaths than the blacks they transported. Black Africans, however, had a degree of inherited or acquired immunity to tropical diseases, and although more prone than whites to pulmonary disorders and the effects of a cold climate, they were not destroyed as were the Indians by white diseases. They were also more useful than Indians because they were skilled in the cultivation of the very sort of tropical and semitropical crops the Europeans wanted them to raise. They were easier to manage than either white servants or Indians because they had no allies, no sources of rescue, and no outside support. Their skin color identified them; it was easy for their masters to enforce plantation discipline and capture runaways. Drawn from diverse African cultures and speaking many different languages, new arrivals often remained long isolated among their fellow slaves, and it was hard for slaves of varying tribal origins to organize concerted resistance.

Africa provided a nearly inexhaustible supply. Before the whites came, sub-Saharan Africa was studded with Bronze Age kingdoms, some possessed of considerable wealth and sophisticated culture. Typically they had developed elements of an exchange economy with their commerce oriented toward the east, focusing on the export of gold, ivory, and slaves to the Islamic countries of the Middle East. Slavery existed nearly everywhere, although it was not the mainstay of the economy nor the basis of a ruling class, and it was only to a limited degree hereditary; the descendants of slaves purchased or captured in war usually gained their freedom within a generation or two and were absorbed into the population. Once the Europeans arrived, their purchases and the prior existence of slavery transformed sub-Saharan Africa into a grand slave market. The Africans were not necessarily victimized by Europeans; the slave trade was highly profitable and eagerly sought by both parties. The initial effect was to disrupt the balance of power among African kingdoms in favor of those along the Atlantic coast. The slave trade loomed ever larger in the economies of most countries, enriching classes of the population connected with it and altering the social structure. By the end of the 18th century, however, the effects were similar to the disaster that befell the Indians in North America. Firearms derived from the slave trade had become crucial to the survival of African kingdoms in wars among themselves. To get firearms, they had to put their entire resources into the slave trade, which was enhanced beyond all former proportions. African kingdoms made war to capture slaves to get weapons to make war—a vicious and destructive cycle. The slave trade had a brutalizing and disintegrative effect upon African societies.

Ultimately, the slave trade created racial problems of incalculable gravity for the European nations who engaged in it. More immediately, it was a source of wealth, and the European powers vied with one another to control its western segment. The Portuguese were first in the field, then the Dutch, and all the European powers tried to gain a footing, but by the end of the 17th century the British had drawn ahead. Earlier, the British had been obliged to buy slaves for their Caribbean colonies from the Dutch at high prices; but with the formation of the Royal African Company in 1672 the British broke into the Guinea trade and, later, as a prize of war, gained the right to supply Spain's colonies with slaves. Britain soon became the world's greatest slaver, and the trade itself the largest branch of world commerce, employing more capital than any other commodity. Entire cities such as Bristol and Liverpool rose on the basis of it, as well as Bordeaux, Cherbourg, and Nantes in France. Some scholars have said that the profits of the slave trade financed the initial phases of the industrial revolution. This claim is no doubt excessive, but the trade was undeniably a source of major capital accumulation; slave labor was instrumental to a huge commerce in sugar, tobacco, and other tropical products; and by the 19th century, slave plantations in the Western Hemisphere were important markets for British and, eventually, American industry.

Slavery was relatively slow to take hold in the American colonies. Until the 1690s, Virginia and Maryland relied upon white indentured servants brought over from England. When these servants had completed their terms, they took up land and became tobacco farmers. The shortage and relatively high expense of white labor retarded the growth of large plantations, and Tidewater Virginia remained a land in which small farmers predominated. The situation took an adverse turn, however, as reliance upon white labor eventually raised the specter of class conflict. After a half century, tobacco prices declined as a result of overproduction. The small farmers no longer prospered as before, and ex-indentured servants often could not be independent farmers themselves, especially because good land with access to navigable waters had become relatively scarce and expensive. The growing class of poor and landless men posed a threat to the wealthier planters. Bacon's Rebellion, which broke out in 1676 and for a while overturned the colony's government, stemmed from social unrest and class tension, clearly showing what could be expected from continuing to people the colony with white servants.

The alternative was black slaves, more tractable than white servants, without rights, and easier to apprehend when they ran away. Once purchased, they were laborers for life and, besides, they augmented the master's capital by reproducing themselves. If widely enough distributed, slave ownership promised to allay conflicts of interest among whites. It helped, besides, that slavery was quite acceptable to the English settlers. Bound—that is, unfree—white labor, was usual among them, and blacks were already enslaved in the British West Indies. Blacks, in fact, had come into Virginia in 1619, and since British law did not recognize slavery, it appears that their status was for some time equivocal. In theory they were considered to be indentured servants, but in practice they were treated like slaves, held in lifelong bondage and their status imposed upon their children, who belonged to their masters. Fact soon overtook theory: within a half century, Virginia had enacted a slave system into law.

Until the end of the 17th century, there were not many slaves in the tobacco colonies. Virginia in 1680 had only 3,000 out of a total population of 43,500. That was because slaves were expensive. However, British involvement in the slave trade soon made them cheaper and more available. By 1710 Virginia had 23,000 slaves and by mid-18th century over 100,000, at that time about 44 percent of the total population. In all the American colonies, there were approximately 460,000 blacks, slave and free, in 1770, of which 409,000 resided south of Pennsylvania, where they made up 40 percent of the population.

Slavery in the American south differed from that in Latin America or even the British Caribbean mainly in the degree of racial exclusiveness associated with it. There were historical reasons for this. Unlike the Spanish and Portuguese, who in the centuries before the discoveries had known Moslem blacks as conquerors, their culture as superior, and, at least among the Portuguese, their women as models of beauty, the insular English had had little exposure to blacks. Hence, Americans regarded them from the beginning as a lower species. In the Latin colonies whites were relatively few in number, often men without women, and consequently they interbred freely with blacks. Moreover, white wives had little status, and the society placed no restraint upon male sexual promiscuity, which steadily "bleached" the colored races, producing a mixed population. In the American colonies, racial prejudice was undiluted by the scarcity of white women, who by the time slaves arrived in large numbers were in ample supply. Miscegenation was regarded as immoral and subject to legal penalties, and, although frequent, was not on a sufficient scale to mix the population and ameliorate racial distinctions. White identity was kept exclusive and intact, as illustrated by the fact that any degree of black ancestry, however slight, classified a man as black, whereas, in the Latin colonies, any degree of white ancestry classified a man as nonblack or mulatto.

Nor, in the American colonies, did social conditions lessen race distinctions. In the Latin colonies, where blacks and mulattoes constituted the great majority, the normal functions of government, business, and military defense could not be executed without their participation. Racial consciousness was intense and a carefully scaled social hierarchy existed, based upon visible physical characteristics. Nevertheless, the society provided a range of places and occupations, with corresponding degrees of status, which blacks could aspire to and occupy. In the American south, on the other hand, a fully elaborated white society existed before any considerable number of blacks arrived. Except on the rice coast of South Carolina, whites always formed the majority of the population and needed blacks only for labor.

No outside force intervened to protect slaves against absolute subjection to their masters. In the Latin colonies, the crown and the Catholic church attempted to regulate slavery. Under law, slaves were not merely chattels; they had rights as human beings. The crown prescribed the conditions under which they could be held in bondage. The church fostered their conversion to Christianity, admitted them to the sacraments, including that of marriage, and encouraged their manumission. Slaves had the right to purchase their freedom, and by cultivating a piece of ground customarily alloted to them and by working on the numerous Catholic holidays, they could acquire the money to do so. In the southern colonies slaves had no such rescue. Their status was governed by colonial laws under which they were classified as property, except when they committed crimes; then they were punished as human beings. There were no customary ways for them to purchase their freedom. Before the American Revolution the established Anglican church sponsored their conversion to Christianity but made little headway against the opposition or indifference of masters. Only a minority of blacks, whether free or slave, were baptized or taught religion. Although the churches in America opposed slavery in principle they made no considerable effort, except for the Quakers, to promote manumission. Hence, there was never a large class of free blacks.

Slaves were probably better fed and treated in the American south than in the Latin and British Caribbean colonies, where many planters deliberately worked them to death, the mortality of the entire slave population ran as high as 4 or 5 percent a year, and constant importations were necessary merely to sustain the labor force. In North America, on the other hand, once the initial imbalance in sex ratios was corrected by generations born in America, the slave population grew rapidly by natural increase. There was less chance, however, for a slave to become free in America, and, whether black or mulatto, he was condemned after freedom to a degraded status.

The slave system was sustained by legal codes, which were similar in all the southern colonies. The codes were designed to control slaves, guard against insurrection, and enforce racial barriers. Slaves were forbidden to leave the plantation without written permission, to congregate in large numbers, or to carry clubs or other weapons. Any white person was authorized to apprehend any black who could not give a satisfactory account of himself and demonstrate that he was not a runaway. In areas of heavy slave concentrations, whites served on patrols, particularly on Saturday night and Sunday, in order to protect the community. Killing a slave was not a felony, and slaves had no right to defend themselves against attack. They could not hold property, nor could they marry. Manumission was made as difficult as possible, because free blacks were hard to control and their existence interfered with the arrangements of a system that coupled slavery with race. Miscegenation, when it came to public attention, was punished by whipping and fines levied upon the white person; mulattoes were punished for consorting with either whites or blacks. The status of children was adjudged to follow that of their mother and, since miscegenation nearly always involved white males and black or mulatto females, white exclusiveness was preserved: the product of racial admixture was classified as black and, in most cases, as slave.

Slavery rested on force, but its racial component tended to obscure the fact, and the English preferred to think that enslavement of blacks denoted the superiority of the white race. Since blacks presented a mean appearance, performed servile tasks, and bore other marks of debased status, it was easy to regard them as a lower species and to dismiss their African culture as mere barbarism from which they were fortunate to be rescued. Neither master nor slave, however, rested easily in this assumption. The claim of racial superiority invited a comparison of the human beings involved and generated constant tension. White attitudes were laced with myths and fancies directly or inversely expressive of varying shades of guilt, aggression, and insecurity. Blacks acted out their hostility by playing stupid, sabotaging work and damaging property, using insolent language, and speaking in dialects unintelligible to whites. Running away was an act of defiance; slaves tried to join the Indians, to reach Florida, to get out to sea in a ship, or simply "go underground," staying out of sight and existing by theft or with the aid of sympathizers. The slaves who had a craft, who were born in America, and who knew the English language well had the best chance of getting away and not being caught.

The whites never believed that slaves were reconciled to their condition. Rumors constantly circulated that slaves poisoned their masters and committed arson. Outright slave rebellion, however, was feared as the ultimate horror by whites who understood that "freedom Wears a Cap which Can Without a Tongue, call together all Those who Long to Shake off the Fetters of Slavery." Plots and actual rebellions occurred often enough to keep the fear alive.

Maryland uncovered slave conspiracies in 1738 and 1739, and in the latter year South Carolina experienced a rebellion in which 50 slaves were killed, some in pitched battle, along with 25 whites. In New York an outbreak occurred in 1712, but in 1741 a more famous revolt exploded in which 4 whites were hanged, 13 blacks burned, 18 hanged, and 70 shipped out of the colony. Nevertheless, considering their numbers, American slaves were relatively docile. Of all slaves in the Western Hemisphere, those in America were least affected by the arrival of undisciplined blacks from Africa. They were the most domiciled to American conditions and the furthest removed from the influence of native culture and tribal affiliations, which might have furnished a rallying point for organized revolt. Besides, they had no place to go. They could not long defend themselves against the white majority, nor did the alternative exist, as in some parts of South America, of fleeing into the wilderness and founding communities. The Indian tribes which ringed the settlements were sometimes hostile or made a business of returning escaped slaves, and, unlike the tropics, the North American wilderness hardly afforded a living to those not habituated to it.

Slaves were apparently better off in the early years of settlement and on the frontier than later. On small plantations, and this was always true, they worked beside their masters and in early times beside indentured servants. Frontier conditions put a premium on initiative and the ability to solve problems, not only in the course of ordinary duties but in such tasks as herding livestock and handling pack animals, wagons, and canoes. As a result of their African experience, slaves were not infrequently more versed in forest lore than whites, and they were trained in agriculture. Rice cultivation, which was fundamental to South Carolina's economy, may have owed a great deal to techniques introduced by slaves from Africa, where rice had been grown for many centuries. With craft skills in high demand, masters eagerly purchased and highly valued the slaves who possessed them. Under such "egalitarian" conditions, blacks appear to have interbred more casually with whites and Indians; many of them learned to read and write, and they were sometimes given guns and sent out to fight Indians. As the frontier receded and plantations became larger, the number of slaves on plantations increased, the tasks of most slaves became routine, and the necessity of maintaining discipline among a greater number restricted their freedom and the scope of their activities.

The northern colonies were involved with slavery and the slave system. All of them had slaves, the fewest in New England, the most in New York, but with substantial numbers in Pennsylvania and New Jersey. Yankee merchants participated in the slave trade, although it was regarded as a risky enterprise and none of the colonies except Rhode Island made a regular business of it. But slavery never became integrated with any of the economic functions of northern society. The reasons were probably circumstantial rather than moral. The north lacked a staple crop whose profits, given the agricultural methods in use, could be vastly increased by large-scale production. The initial investment required to buy a prime field hand before the Revolution was in the neighborhood of $150, which was nearly the cost of hiring a farm laborer for three years. The return from the labor of a slave employed in the diversified tasks of small farming was not sufficient to justify the investment. In the cities slaves and free blacks worked as laborers, the latter at wages uniformly lower than those received by whites, but the availability of white artisans and their resistance to black competition prevented blacks from moving into skilled trades. Northern slaves were for the most part laborers or house servants.

In the south, by contrast, the economy rested squarely on slave labor, a fact illustrated by the universal habit of calculating the output of a plantation, not according to the number of acres, but by the number of slaves. There was, however, a sharp sectional division of slave ownership. In most parts of the back-country, where the majority of whites lived and farmed in much the same way as in the north, slaves were few. Slaves were concentrated in other areas of the Chesapeake colonies, along the Tidewater and in the more accessible sections of the Piedmont and interior valleys. Farther south, slaves were exceedingly numerous on the coast of South Carolina, where they sometimes outnumbered whites by 20 to 1. In 1790, the first year for which reliable figures are available, only 7.6 percent of the whites in such a state as Virginia held slaves, and most of the slaves, some 72 percent, worked on substantial or large plantations. They planted, tended, and harvested the cash crop, raised nearly all of the plantation's food, and in off-seasons worked at lumbering and other forest industries, while they cleared more land. They performed all the skilled tasks, such as blacksmithing, carpentering, coopering, and baking. In the fields they worked long hours, 15 or 16 hours a day during harvest, spurred on by drivers who set the pace and whipped them at the end of the day for not keeping up. They had only Sundays off, and during the year but three or four other holidays and Christmas. House servants and skilled craftsmen constituted a slave elite, whose lot was tempered by less arduous labor and close personal relationships with the master and his family.

Plantation slaves were often hired out by their masters, frequently on an annual basis, but the practice was also common in towns and cities, where the rental of slaves augmented many a master's income. Slave artisans became so numerous in Charleston during the 1760s that the protests of white artisans finally led to legislative restrictions.

Before the 1760s, only feeble, isolated voices rose against slavery. Most southerners accepted it without attempting to rationalize it, or they justified it in terms of biblical authority or as benefiting the blacks by lifting them out of African savagery. More perceptive southerners denounced it, although they did not know what to do about it, because it degraded labor and populated the country with an alien race which could not be assimilated to white society. "I am sensible," wrote William Byrd of Virginia in 1736, "of the many bad consequences of multiplying these Ethiopians amongst us. They blow up the pride, and ruin the Industry of our White People, who seeing a Rank of poor Creatures below them, detest work for fear it should make them look like Slaves." An even greater evil was the danger of submerging the white population in a sea of blacks. There were already 10,000 blacks in the colony capable of bearing arms, Byrd said, and the number was increasing every day. "In case there should arise a Man of desperate courage amongst us, exasperated by a desperate fortune, he might . . . kindle a Servile War. Such a man might be dreadfully mischeivous before any opposition could be formed against him, and tinge our Rivers as wide as they are with blood."

If southerners regarded slavery as an evil, however, they generally saw it as an inheritance from the past which had to be lived with. The southern economy, they thought, depended upon slave labor, too much money was invested to think of abolishing the institution, and the slaves, even if liberated, would still remain as blacks who could not live side by side with whites except in bondage. In the late colonial period, southern colonies sometimes attempted to restrict slave importation. Their laws for this purpose were invariably disallowed by the Privy Council, which was concerned with promoting the British slave trade rather than curtailing it. However, such laws did not necessarily denote moral opposition to slavery; they were designed to stop the flow of money out of the country in slave purchases.

What antislavery feeling existed in the colonies derived mainly from religious belief. All the churches in America were in some measure sensitive to the contradiction between slavery and Christian doctrine, yet slavery was so strongly entrenched and racial feeling everywhere so pronounced that the churches generally found it more expedient to save black souls for heaven than to promote black equality on earth. As a result, increasing numbers of blacks were converted to Christianity, but slavery as an institution was left untouched. The Anglican church, which was established in the southern colonies and had Britain's backing, was so much a creature of the planters themselves that it was powerless to interfere. The only vigorous criticism of slavery came from Quakers, who were in part moved by repugnance toward the idea of increasing the number of blacks in the population.

Nonetheless, what one scholar has described as "an international antislavery opinion" began to appear by the 1760s, and it presaged in the fullness of time the end of modern slavery. In some areas slavery was weakened by declining profitability. The older British sugar islands in the Caribbean, once jewels of the empire, had lost their fertility, and their proprietors no longer had the same commanding influence in Parliament. Similarly, British interest in the slave trade, although still important to individuals, was no longer of the utmost concern to the government because the trade supplied slave labor for new French and Spanish possessions that were competitive with Britain's exhausted islands. In North America, the oldest plantation colonies, Virginia and Maryland, were finding tobacco culture less profitable and their slaves sometimes an encumbrance; after 1750 many Chesapeake planters turned to diversified agriculture. The northern colonies specializing in trade and manufactures had little interest in slavery. It was still a vigorous institution on the rice coast of South Carolina and Georgia; nevertheless, in the colonies at large it had lost some of its economic power and its ability to withstand challenges on religious and intellectual grounds.

One challenge came from the Enlightenment, with its emphasis upon natural goodness, the determining influence of the environment on the individual, and the perfectibility of man; slavery was contrary to reason and nature. Another challenge came from the pietistic religious revivals of the age, Methodism in Britain and the Great Awakening in America, which rejected worldly hierarchy and emphasized the equality of man before God. Still another challenge came from republican ideals nourished by the American resistance to Britain. Americans found it embarrassing to reply to Samuel Johnson's sarcastic comment: "How is it that we hear the loudest *yelps* for liberty among the drivers of negroes." Throughout the northern colonies there was a growing consensus that "Every Argument which can be urged in Favor of our own Liberties will certainly operate with equal Force in Favor of that of the Negroes: nor can we with Propriety contend for the one while we withhold the other."

Polemics against slavery increased in number during the 1760s and 1770s, and stirred up more public discussion. In 1771 the Massachusetts assembly voted to end slave importations but the governor would not sign the bill. In 1772, the year that slavery was abolished in Britain by judicial decree, the Virginia legislature enacted a prohibitive duty on importation of slaves, calling it "a Trade of great inhumanity." In 1774 the Philadelphia Society of Friends forbade Quakers to buy or sell slaves and ordered them to get ready to emancipate the ones they had. In adopting the Declaration of Independence in 1776, Congress, for the sake of colonial unity, was obliged to delete Jefferson's charge that by perpetuating the slave trade, George III had waged "cruel war against human nature itself, violating its most sacred rights of life and liberty." By the time of the American Revolution, slavery, although entrenched in many parts of the world, was becoming an anachronism, an offense to the moral sense of mankind.

Planter Elite

The planter elite was the nearest thing to a European aristocracy that America produced. The dominant families of the Chesapeake colonies owed their position to tobacco fortunes increased by the acquisition of large tracts of land. As in the north, entry into the elite was based on wealth, and successful men were absorbed from below, often by marriage. There was mobility downward, too, and some great names sank into obscurity, except for hallowed memory. Nevertheless, the Chesapeake elite was a more exclusive set than the northern upper class, more self-conscious, more elevated above the common rank and set apart by pretensions to superiority. Visitors from the north and foreigners alike were often struck by the haughtiness and pride of great planters, who, surrounded from infancy by slaves and dependents, were bred to be the masters and disposers of lesser men. "Every master of slaves," observed George Mason of Virginia, himself a slaveholder, "is born a petty tyrant." Almost by hereditary right, they occupied the seats of political authority, from the vestry boards and county courts that handled local government to the provincial assemblies and councils that managed the affairs of the colony. This ascendancy was fully concurred in by the common people, who looked up to them for leadership and the display of a life style that reflected the ideals of the community.

The southern elite was considerably wealthier than its counterparts in New England and the middle colonies. The study by Jones already cited gives the top 1 percent of southern wealthholders average net assets of $537,000 in 1975 dollars, and this group alone held an extraordinary 22.5 percent of total wealth. Including these great planters, the top 10 percent averaged $140,000 in net worth and owned 55.8 percent of the wealth. Below this group, the next 50 percent in the scale represented a substantial middle class which was relatively affluent in its upper brackets, with net assets of from $41,000 in 1975 dollars to $7,850. This group held a little less than 41 percent of total wealth. Below it, however, was the approximately 40 percent of wealthholders which in the south as in other sections of the country held little property. Probably because there were fewer free laborers in the towns to bring down the average, the average net worth of the bottom 40 percent was higher than in other sections, ranging up to $5,100; however, the lowest 10 percent had an average indebtedness of $450, and the lowest 40 percent of wealthholders collectively had only 3.4 percent of total wealth.

With their broad acres, imposing mansions, and numerous slaves, large planters set the mode of gracious living. The loneliness of isolation among black slaves fostered gregariousness and a tradition of hospitality that became proverbial. Plantation mansions, built to accommodate many guests, were the scene of frequent parties, which sometimes stretched out to a week of lavish entertainment. Both sexes studied conversation as an art and cultivated their ability to dance. Gentlemen gambled at cards and horse racing, and rode to the hounds after the English manner. An English traveller commented that many of their mansions "would make no slight figure in the English counties" and that "in most articles of life a great Virginia planter makes a greater show, and lives more luxuriously than a country gentleman in England, on an estate of three or four thousand pounds a year." Beneath the apparent frivolity and leisure of plantation life was a utilitarian core of duties involved in administering its economic and human activities, but the outward face of planter culture was aristocratic in its dedication to luxury and gracious living.

Aristocratic style was carried even further by lowland South Carolina planters, who acquired their wealth in the 30 or 40 years before the Revolution as large-scale rice culture developed and indigo planting was introduced. Aided by favorable British legislation, they made fabulous profits. Charleston, where planters spent most of the year to avoid the heat and fevers of their plantations, was renowned for the elegance of its upper-class society. With greater wealth than most Chesapeake planters, the nouveaux riches South Carolina planters outdid them in ostentatious consumption.

Whether slavery, with its degradation of labor and its emphasis upon a single crop, retarded the economic development of the south was a question seldom raised in colonial times. That it profited individuals was demonstrated by the fortunes accumulated by large slaveholders. English travelers, who had an eye out for profitable investment in America, generally agreed that the best place to invest in an agricultural estate was the slave plantation, always provided that one had enough capital to operate on a big scale. Yet there were strains upon the plantation system, particularly in the two decades before the Revolution, that undermined its prosperity. Tobacco, like every other cash crop in America, was grown by soil mining methods; hence, unless planters had large reserves of unused land, the productivity of their plantations tended to decline. Overproduction of tobacco kept prices low, allowing only a small margin of profit. Planter income was further eroded by the virtual monopoly of British merchants over every phase of marketing the crop in England and returning English commodities. It was commonly complained that the British merchants combined to keep tobacco prices down in the colonies, while they charged excessively for goods brought from England. As a result, there were limits to the income even of large plantations. Many planters in Virginia and Maryland turned to growing wheat and other crops, but without spectacular success.

They tried to sustain themselves by large-scale land speculation. One thing, however, that they tried only as a last resort was to live within their incomes. Luxurious consumption was so obligatory among their class that to preserve their status they continually spent more than their plantations earned. "Within these 25 years," wrote a Virginian in 1766, "£1,000 due to a Merchant was looked upon as a Sum immense and never to be got over. Ten times that sum is now spoke of with Indifference and thought no great burthen on some Estates. Indeed in that series of time Prosperity is more valuable & many Estates have increased more than ten fold. But their Luxury & expensive living have gone hand in hand with the increase in wealth."

By the time of the Revolution, Virginia and Maryland planters owed over £2 million to British merchants. The debt passed from father to son along with the plantation. Jefferson, in a well-known phrase, described the Virginia planters as a "species of property annexed to certain British mercantile houses." The relationship was not wholly uncomfortable for the planters. Since they had assets in land and slaves, they were good credit risks and could therefore depend on being able to borrow money to support their customary style of living in lean years. Happily, British merchants seldom foreclosed. Once a planter owed him money, the merchant was fairly certain of having all the planter's business, and the loan returned an interest that in the course of time equaled the principal. In any case, the forced sale of a planter's estate entailed losses for the merchant and made him no friends in the colony. Thus, out of mutual convenience, British merchants continued to lend and planters borrowed until the debts mounted to the point where, in prevailing circumstances, they could not be paid.

These debts were owed by small as well as large planters. From the 1740s on, Scottish merchants had transformed the Chesapeake tobacco industry. Up to this time the trade in tobacco had been handled mainly by consignment: English merchants brought their ships up the rivers alongside the docks of large plantations; they took away tobacco on consignment, transported it to England, sold it for whatever it would bring; they usually invested part of the proceeds in goods ordered by the planters, which they brought to America on the next voyage. They took their profits in the form of charges for freight, insurance, commissions on every transaction, and the markup on goods sold to the planter. The larger planters with whom they dealt frequently acted as intermediaries for smaller planters in the neighborhood. This procedure changed, however, with the advent of the Scots, who were more enterprising than their English predecessors. The Scots set up general stores everywhere in the Tidewater and Piedmont, employing resident factors who all year long sold merchandise on credit to planters big and small. The factors took payment in tobacco at harvest time and sent large-scale shipments back to the mercantile firms they represented. As Jefferson said, the planter elite of Virginia was indebted; however, the overwhelming number of debts owed to British merchants were those of middling and small planters. Planter indebtedness after mid-century may be seen as reflecting the surge of British economic growth, the greater availability of British credit, and, as scholars have noted, the tendency of expanding British enterprise to invade the internal operation of the colonial economy.

The role of economic factors in precipitating the Revolution in Virginia and Maryland can only be conjectured. Although one of the first acts of the Revolutionary government of Virginia was to suspend payment of private debts to British merchants, it is too much to say that debts were a primary factor in turning the Chesapeake planters toward revolution; the situation was not that simple. Nevertheless, declining economic prospects had made the planter elite a restless and discontented class, creating an inherently dangerous situation for Britain when disputes arose with the colonies.

CHAPTER IV

Combustible Material, Human and Ideological

Agrarian Discontent

As the disputes broke out that led to the Revolution, several colonies experienced internal convulsions that threatened to end in open warfare and in one case did. These crises were an intensification of sectional controversies that were endemic in the colonies generally, disputes between small farmers living on the frontier or elsewhere in isolated subsistence farming areas and the merchants and planters of older and more commercially advanced sections. Since common farmers opposed the colonial elite, an element of class conflict was also involved. Disputes ranged over a predictable field of issues. Paper money emissions always gave rise to conflicts of interest; creditors, usually backed by appointed governor and council, tried to keep down the amount issued, while the assembly, the elected body and usually the stronghold of paper money forces, could be counted upon to sponsor a larger quantity. Frontier defense was a perennial issue; in colonies with an exposed Indian frontier, the westerners were often aggrieved by what they considered the refusal of protected easterners to provide men and money for defense. Frontiersmen also resented exorbitant fees collected by public officials. In the various colonies, sectional interests were involved in land policy, taxation, and representation in the legislature.

A few episodes are worth recounting to indicate the substance and nature of east-west antagonisms. In Pennsylvania an outbreak occurred in 1764, on the eve of the Stamp Act controversy. Although by this time Germans and Scotch-Irish living in the interior counties made up two thirds of the colony's population, they had only a third of the delegates in the assembly. The Quakers held political control by denying proportionate representation to the non-Quaker counties, meanwhile fighting the governor for political domination of the province. One of the chief issues was the refusal of Quakers to support the defense of the frontier against Indian depredations during the French and Indian War (1754–63). Threatened with being expelled from the assembly by the British government, the more pious Quakers resigned; but other Quakers and their allies retained their influence over the assembly, which for the duration of the war resisted military appropriations, using approval of such legislation as a bargaining counter in contests with the governor. The chief victims of this controversy were the Scotch-Irish frontiersmen who, apart from the defense issue, despised the Quakers on religious grounds. As Presbyterians, they considered Quakers no better than atheists. Furthermore, the frontiersmen were in debt to the Philadelphia merchants and disliked them for this reason. To cap things off, the merchants in the course of the fur trade supplied Indians with rum and weapons.

Matters came to a head when, in 1763, an Indian outbreak, Pontiac's Conspiracy, swept over the frontier and the assembly failed to pass military appropriations. Driven to desperation, the frontiersmen avenged themselves upon a tribe of "tame" Moravian Indians living within the settled area, who, they had reason to believe, had acted as spies for raiding parties. They killed as many of the tribe as they could find. When they heard that the Quakers had taken another tribe to Philadelphia for protection, a body of frontiersmen, "Paxton's Boys," their numbers variously estimated at 700 and 1,500, marched upon the city. As they advanced, it was rumored that some of the city's inhabitants were prepared to help them in the assault. The governor proclaimed the riot act in force; arms were issued to citizens willing to fight and fortifications were hastily thrown up. Many Quakers were seen bearing muskets and daggers.

As Paxton's Boys approached the city, they were met by a delegation of prominent citizens, including Benjamin Franklin, who urged them to eschew force in favor of petition. Since the governor had taken over the city's defense, an attack would have been tantamount to rebellion; hence the frontier leaders allowed themselves to be pacified. They sent a petition to the assembly demanding protection against the Indians and equal representation for the western counties in the legislature. The assembly voted money for defense but ignored the other demand. On the eve of the Revolution, Pennsylvania was a divided province, torn by hostility between seaboard and backcountry.

A more violent conflict occurred in the Carolinas. In South Carolina it originated in the failure of the legislature, controlled by the eastern section, to provide courts and local government for the western counties. This neglect exposed the backcountry to pillage by lawless and degenerate bands, which stole cattle and horses, abducted young women and scoffed at the law. The virtuous inhabitants had no organized forces to protect property and to keep the peace. They suffered further from the fact that prosecutions at law were tried two or three hundred miles away at Charleston, to which it was hard to transport criminals for trial and where juries composed of townspeople frequently set the criminals free. Even to collect debts or defend themselves against lawsuits, westerners had to undertake the long and expensive journey to Charleston and an even more expensive stay in the city while they awaited the dilatory processes of justice. As a result, they were victimized by all sorts of sharpers.

The westerners at length formed "Regulator" associations to keep order. In a petition to the legislature in 1768 they threatened, after stating their grievances, to march on Charleston if refused redress. The legislature complied with their demands so far as to institute courts in the backcountry, but at the same time took steps to put down the Regulators. Because the Regulators tried and punished people in vigilante fashion, the governor sent several forces against them, and some bloodshed occurred.

With the establishment of courts, the Regulators' main object was accomplished, and they disbanded. However, their demand for equal representation went unheeded. With two thirds of the white population, the backcountry had only 6 out of 50 delegates in the assembly. No reforms were made until the Revolution, when the backcountry was given 40 seats out of a total of 184.

In North Carolina antagonism between east and west culminated in a pitched battle. The backcountry harbored a democratic and motley population of Scotch-Irish, Germans, Highland Scots, Swiss, English, and Welsh farmers, most of whom had come down from western Pennsylvania and Virginia. Although the upland counties had a majority of the white population, the legislature was controlled by the older plantation counties, each of which sent five delegates to the assembly as opposed to two each for the upland counties. The backcountry inhabitants had other grievances. Most of the best land had already been granted to easterners. Westerners had to pay heavy poll taxes, which were levied without regard for the meager cash incomes that they derived from subsistence farming. Money of any kind was scarce, and during the economic depression after 1763 people in the backcountry could get little for what they had to sell. Their farms were sold for nonpayment of debts or taxes and bought up by speculators at rock-bottom prices.

Superimposed upon these hardships was a system of exploitation based on the political hegemony of the eastern counties. Local government in backcountry North Carolina was more corrupt than anywhere else in America. Appointed justices of the peace and sheriffs, along with clerks, registers, and "tricking attorneys" formed a coterie in league with eastern planters. This "court house ring" milked the farmers by charging excessive fees, by fraudulent suits at law, and by collusion between local officeholders and land speculators. In addition, a good share of the taxes collected in the west never reached the provincial treasury, lodging instead in the pockets of the collectors. It appears that in the western counties the protestors were generally the poorer settlers, who held less than average wealth in land and slaves than their opponents, who held more than average.

Riots broke out in the 1750s in protest against large land grants to speculators, who ejected squatters and demanded high rents or high prices in selling land. An association was formed in 1766 to oppose suits for the collection of debts against farmers and to put an end to such abuses as the charging of extortionate fees by public officers, the collusive sale of debtor property to speculators at public auction, high taxes, and the embezzlement of taxes by the officials who collected them. The protest gathered momentum in 1768, when the inhabitants of Orange County formed an association to regulate government and vowed to pay no more taxes until previous taxes were accounted for. When their leaders were jailed, a party of Regulators several hundred strong stormed the jail and released them. A petition delivered to the assembly the next year stated their grievances. They wanted taxation according to ability to pay, an emission of paper money, regulation of fees, discontinuance of large land grants to individuals, and a reform of court procedure, including trial of cases before local juries. When no reforms were forthcoming, the Regulators lost all confidence in the legislature, and in 1771 widespread violence broke out as they closed local courts and assaulted hated officials. The legislature responded by declaring them outlaws, to be killed on sight. The British governor raised a force of eastern militia, marched into the backcountry, and at Alamance Creek encountered a party of 2,000 poorly armed men who, it seems, had come to parley rather than fight When, however, they refused to comply with the governor's order to lay down their arms, he ordered his force to attack. At the battle of Alamance Creek, many of the Regulators fled at once; others held out for a few hours before surrendering.

The defeat crushed the Regulator movement. Several hundred took an oath of allegiance, thereby escaping the death penalty, but thousands fled to the high mountain valleys, where they became the first settlers in what is now the state of Tennessee. During the Revolution, many ex-Regulators sided with Britain out of resentment against the eastern planters, who now carried the banners of American patriotism.

There were similar disturbances in the middle and northern

colonies, notably in the Hudson River valley where farmers challenged the dominance of great landed families, such as the Livingstons and the Van Rensselaers, who had received enormous land grants early in the century. These aristocrats preserved their thousand- and ten thousand-acre estates through the generations by never selling land, only leasing it to tenants. They had feudal rights, which they exercised over their tenants, requiring labor service and other humiliating exactions. Long simmering resentment of tenants and small farmers erupted in 1765, when anti-rent riots broke out in Westchester County and spread quickly to the northern counties. The rioters formed their own government and their own military forces, electing a Dutchess County small farmer as their leader. Although their main enemies, the great landlords, were beyond their reach, they destroyed landlord property, drove away officials sent to evict them from their farms, and set up popular courts which held trials and inflicted punishment upon people who opposed them. When rioters were jailed, armed bands released them. By 1766 there were 2,000 rioters under arms, and every jail between New York City and Albany had been opened. "Levellers" they were called by their opponents, after the radical sectarians of the Puritan Revolution.

Unable to suppress them with the militia, the governor called upon the British general, George Gage, for assistance. The rioters were put down by British troops, with the full approval of New York City patriots and Sons of Liberty who were unable to perceive any resemblance between the rioters' cause and their own. However, ex-rent-rioters resumed the struggle during the Revolution, when many of them became Loyalists, hoping that after Britain won, the estates of their landlords, most of them prominent American patriots, would be confiscated and distributed among loyalist tenants.

Farther north, armed conflict occurred over land rights as a result of conflicting grants by New Hampshire and New York. Both colonies laid claim to territory in what is now the state of Vermont. In 1764 the crown awarded the area to New York, and New York immediately began parceling out grants to influential persons, overriding the rights of settlers already on the land who derived their titles from New Hampshire grants. The settlers organized to resist New York and outside speculators. Again, it was small farmers against moneyed men and high officials who had the government behind them. The frontiersmen formed their own military force, established popular courts to suppress and punish opponents, and drove out would-be settlers with a New York title. So resolutely did the "Green Mountain Boys" defend their right to the land that New York legislated the death penalty for "riot and treason," but neither this nor any other New York law could be enforced in Vermont. The controversy lasted into the American Revolution, when the Green Mountain Boys established an independent state under a model democratic constitution, but New York's land claim and its influence upon other states dissuaded Vermonters from trying to join the Union. Early in the 1780s, when it appeared that Congress might award the area to New York, the Vermont leader Ethan Allen took the precaution of opening conversations with the British.

The sectional conflicts that broke out in the Carolinas, Pennsylvania, New York, and northern New England exhibit broad similarities. Agrarian rioters were easily aroused against constituted authority leagued with eastern, elite interests. A readiness to form their own governments and obey them betokened a sense of separate identity. The rioters were armed and resorted without hesitation to violence and defiance of law. Although their leaders were often land speculators, the theme and to a large extent the substance of conflict was the opposition of common men to the elite.

The Urban Crowd

Although a wide distribution of property existed in the colonies, the lowest 40 percent of the population, as we have seen, had almost no property and the lowest 10 percent was in debt. This should not surprise us because, apart from the unequal distribution of wealth that has always characterized human societies, at least since neolithic times, pre-industrial societies did not produce much above subsistence, and the lower classes, who got least, were exposed to absolute, as opposed to relative, want. They experienced real hunger and cold. It should also be kept in mind that statistics on property ownership can be misleading if not properly interpreted. The colonies had a high birth rate and therefore a predominantly young population, along with a relatively high degree of social mobility. Many propertyless individuals were doubtless young adults starting out in life, and their lack of possessions did not signify the existence of poverty as the permanent condition of individuals. This would be true of a proportion of wandering agricultural laborers and tenant farmers in the countryside.

Similarly, in the cities, the seamen and fishermen who constituted the largest segment of propertyless urban laborers were usually young men off the farm, almost never over 30 years old, who returned to the farm after a few years of seafaring. Many other urban laborers were apprentices and journeymen who might be expected to become masters or to leave the city eventually and set up shop in neighboring villages or in the secondary towns growing in the interior. Meanwhile, however, such laborers shared the lot of the dock workers, carters, day laborers, semiskilled craftsmen, apprentices, and servants who made up the city's permanent labor force. Although well paid by contemporary English standards, they could still afford no more than bare necessities. Ordinarily, they did not own enough property to qualify for the suffrage in city elections. They had one great advantage over laborers in Europe, an abundance of food, which was always available and cheap; there were no famines in the colonies. Nevertheless, they faced the near certainty of being unemployed part of the winter when ice and cold reduced shipping and the economic activity of the city slackened. Unable to lay up savings from their meager pay, they could never conserve for the future and in winter often had to depend upon charity for food and firewood. Although the colonial economy rose to higher levels after 1750, laborers did not share in the gains; they suffered instead from inflated prices and housing shortages.

Although most of them could not vote, urban workers were a political force. They had no influence upon government in a regular and legal way, but in irregular situations they acquired political power because they had physical strength and a taste for using it. Except when British troops were at hand, and that was rarely, the only force available to colonial authorities for suppressing large-scale disorders was the militia. Urban workers made up a considerable part of the militia; if they rioted, and it was typically they rather than the middling or better sort who did so, they could be put down only by the determined action of the rest of the community. If, on the other hand, rioting workers had widespread support, no governor dared order out the militia to suppress them.

In an age before government or law were thought of as representing, except in an abstract sense, the interests and opinions of the common people, riots expressive of popular will were accorded a certain legitimacy. In America, as well as in European countries, they were a recognized species of political action, alongside of and in addition to government. Their legitimacy depended upon the degree to which they reflected a consensus. Justifiable riots were by tradition directed against outsiders in support of local rights and privileges or against highly placed individuals within the community who were above the law. Riots executed the common morality against such targets as monopolizers and profiteers, prostitutes and bawdy houses, customs officers and tax collectors. Crowd action of this kind was not mere commotion. It was frequently connived at by government officers and by the better classes. The leaders of the crowd and some of its members were likely to be responsible men of middling circumstances, such as master mechanics and tradesmen. Demonstrations were purposive, often linked with larger political movements, and they were typically conducted with relatively little violence and property damage. In Boston, before the 1760s, the lower-class crowd acquired a quasi-permanent organization based on the annual observance of certain holidays, notably Guy Fawkes Day, when, besides smoking up the town with enormous bonfires, the north-end mob and the south-end mob capped the day's festivities by staging a prearranged pitched battle. These battles became ever more violent.

Rioting in American port cities tended to increase in the decades before the American Revolution. One reason was that urban laborers, as we have seen, were hard pressed as a result of overcrowding and rising prices. They were also distressed by the economic depression following the French and Indian War. The depression merged with the controversy with Britain in which the colonies for political reasons tried to cut off imports from the mother country. Every nonimportation argreement threw a large number of laborers out of work.

Urban laborers were nevertheless staunch supporters of the resistance to Britain. They had particular reasons to hate the British. The single grievance they felt most deeply was impressments: British naval officers backed by a force of sailors from warships in the harbor were accustomed to searching seaport towns for men to force into the British navy. Once seized by the press gang, a common man was doomed to prolonged servitude under barbarous conditions. In 1747, when a British admiral launched wholesale impressments in Boston harbor, the town erupted in two days of rioting. The rioters took control of the town and compelled the governor to secure the release of men taken in the press. Many other instances occurred in New England and New York in which impressments set off riots, British cruisers were fired upon or seized and burned, and British officers captured by mobs. Impressments were resented by all Americans, but as Governor Thomas Hutchinson of Massachusetts informed the Privy Council in England, "the lower class were beyond measure enraged." Less critical as an issue but still deeply resented by urban workers was the competition of British soldiers as laborers. Wherever troops were stationed, as at Boston and New York, soldiers were allowed to supplement their pay by working for private employers, and they accepted low wages, sometimes less than half the going rate. American workmen were bitter that their own people would hire British soldiers this way, but that did not prevent their hating and despising the soldiers, rough, lower-class men whom they jostled in taverns and in the street.

In the turmoil that led to the Revolution, laborers in colonial cities were linked politically with the class immediately above them, the enfranchised artisans and shopkeepers. Led by their political allies, they became the striking arm of the patriots. It was symptomatic of the trend of events that at the time of the Stamp Act the Boston mobs left off fighting their Guy Fawkes Day battles to become a "patriot militia" and riot in a higher cause. This higher form of rioting was legitimate under accepted norms because it was waged in defense of local rights. All classes of the community supported it. From the standpoint of the patriot leadership, the problem was to keep the crowd under control and channel its violence in the service of the cause. As resistance to British measures continued, the problem increased because the crowd showed a propensity to follow its own bent and inflict itself upon people of wealth and status.

Religion and Populist Revival

The sectarian fires of the Reformation still smoldered in 18th-century America. Religious differences were more keenly felt than they are today, and religion served more generally as a standard for determining right and wrong in public affairs. In the years before the American Revolution an explosion of religious fervor, the Great Awakening, swept over the country, generating in the common people an intensity of moral judgment that animated the resistance to Britain.

Religion had long been a divisive rather than a unifying factor in colonial relations with the mother country. The great majority of Americans were Dissenters, who adhered to Protestant faiths other than Anglicanism, the official religion of England. Some American churches, moreover, nurtured a tradition of old struggles against English kings and bishops. The Congregational churches founded by Puritans fleeing England still held the allegiance of the overwhelming majority of New Englanders. The middle colonies were a conglomerate of Quakers, Presbyterians, Baptists, Lutherans, and other German sectarians. Anglicanism had most adherents in the south, but even where it was strongest, as in Virginia and Maryland, it claimed less than 30 percent of the inhabitants. America was a melting pot of creeds as well as nationalities, and insofar as religion tends to cement allegiance to government it worked against rather than in favor of Britain.

The divisive effects were accentuated by the fact that American churches were locally controlled and self-governing, either by individual congregations or by local synods. In religious matters Britain had little control. This was true even of the Anglican church, which was nominally under the jurisdiction of the bishop of London but in fact was dominated by southern planters who controlled the salaries of pastors and their tenure in office. Pastors had to be ordained in England; hence few Americans entered the clergy, and since appointments in the colonies were not esteemed by English churchmen, the pastors who came over were frequently second-rate men, content to be congenial appurtenances of the planter elite. Southern planters were almost as concerned as Dissenters with preserving local control of churches.

The age of enforced religious uniformity had passed, both in England and America, but it had left a residue in an established church; that is, an official church supported by public taxation. In New England, except for Rhode Island, local Congregational churches were supported by town taxes which everybody had to pay, regardless of religious affiliation. By the time of the Revolution, however, adherents of other faiths were winning the right to have their taxes applied to the support of their own churches. Elsewhere, in Rhode Island, most of New York, and in New Jersey, Pennsylvania, and Delaware, church and state were unconnected, religion was a private matter, and, apart from Catholics, all denominations were on an equal basis. The Anglican church was established in the southern colonies and in part of New York, but except in Virginia only a few parishes existed;

most of the inhabitants either had no church at all or supported non-Anglican churches.

Except in New England and the eastern counties of Virginia, church establishments were fragile because there was no majority religion. For the same reason, religious freedom was in most colonies a substantial fact, even for those who were indifferent to religion altogether. Toleration owed a good deal to radical Protestant tenets under whose auspices some of the colonies had been founded. From its inception Rhode Island had allowed complete freedom of worship to all Protestants. In the Quaker colonies of Pennsylvania and Delaware nobody was ever penalized for religious reasons. Britain's influence was also cast on the side of religious freedom, if only because Anglicans were a minority in most colonies; under the English Toleration Act of 1689, which Parliament adopted after nearly a century of strife, Dissenters of all sorts had been given the right to conduct public worship. Catholics did not share in these benefits, and Dissenters were themselves excluded from voting and holding political office. Nevertheless, religious disabilities of all sorts were relaxed in Britain during the 18th century as the nation moved toward general toleration.

The same tendency, spurred by growing secularism and rationalism among the educated upper class, occurred in the colonies. Catholics were usually prohibited from voting or holding political office, but there were only a few thousand of them, mainly in Maryland, and they were allowed to practice their faith. Jews were generally left undisturbed. Except in New England, where non-Congregationalists were only grudgingly accepted, and in Virginia, where local authorities sometimes harried militant Baptist preachers, Protestants of any denomination suffered little or no repression.

By mid-18th century, Anglicanism, long dormant as a proselytizing faith, began to stage a recovery, notably in the middle and New England colonies, the stronghold of Dissenters. A powerful missionary organization in England, the Society for the Propagation of the Gospel in Foreign Parts, which had the backing of the government, tried to reinvigorate the church in America by sending over educated and dedicated men, not to convert Indians or blacks, but to reclaim Dissenters. More important in stimulating the advance of Anglicanism, however, was its appeal as an upper-class institution. As American society, particularly in the cities, became less parochial, successful men tended to identify themselves with the sophistication and social connections represented by the Church of England. Its membership increased in Boston, New York, and Philadelphia, and it partly captured Yale College. The trend alarmed other religionists, especially New England Congregationalists, because it extended British influence and, if it continued, raised the prospect of an Anglican establishment in all the colonies. This fear gained credibility as a result of frequent proposals advanced in Britain and recommendations of the Society for the Propagation of the Gospel that a resident Anglican bishop be set up in America. With the backing of crown and Parliament, a resident bishop could be expected to strengthen Anglicanism and encroach upon other denominations. Although Britain never acted upon the idea, apprehension that it would do so was an irritant factor in Anglo-American relations.

The Great Awakening, a "tidal wave of religious fervor," arose during the 1730s and rolled on with little or no abatement until the Revolution. It was the counterpart of a religious revival that occurred at the same time in Britain and on the Continent. Its effects upon American development are still not fully understood, but in a subtle yet fundamental way it propagated democratic attitudes, not only in matters of religion but in government and public affairs. The Awakening appears to have originated in response to a spiritual void created by the decline of religious observance into formality, by the absorption of the clergy into the manners and values of the social elite, and by an astonishing neglect to organize churches in newly settled areas that, as the country expanded, left great numbers without religious service. Existing churches lost touch with the emotional needs of the common people.

Doctrinally, the Awakening repudiated secular and rational ideas that had crept into the churches, reasserting old doctrines of original sin, predestination, and election. But the Awakening was first of all a popular revolution in the churches, and emotion, not doctrine, was the crux of its message. It said that religion was a matter of the heart, not the head, and that simple, ordinary men were more likely to be touched by the divine spirit than were the sophisticated upper class or an educated clergy which was dead to spiritual values. Although the Awakening had its share of educated and elite leaders, it was anti-intellectual in spirit and rejective of authority, preaching the spiritual worth of the common man. It was spread by evangelical preachers who cultivated a popular, exhortatory style, sometimes called the "holy whine," which was calculated to arouse emotion and play upon it. The greatest evangelist of the movement and of the age was George Whitefield, who came from England to tour the colonies several times, preaching to thousands and leaving them with an awakened sense of the terror and ecstasy of religious experience. The popular style, the distinctive feature of the Awakening, was sometimes carried to excess by evangelists who deliberately tried to provoke their listeners into hysterical fits, which were interpreted as a sign of God's presence. The movement also gave rise to much lay preaching; self-appointed ministers roamed the country and competed with the regular clergy, whose members they sometimes denounced as "letter-learned Pharisees" unfit, as never having experienced conversion, to occupy their positions. These tactics disrupted most of the churches and split the Congregationalists, the Presbyterians, and the Baptists for a time into opposing branches. "New Lights" saw in the Awakening a providential upwelling of religious spirit which deepened conviction and filled the churches. "Old Lights" regarded it as spurious, subversive of order, and in bad taste.

The Awakening vastly increased church membership and the influence of religion in all aspects of American life. It brought in a new religion: Methodism, an evangelical offshoot of Anglicanism, which grew rapidly after the Revolution, particularly in the southern backcountry. New Light colleges were founded, including Princeton, Brown, Rutgers, and Dartmouth. The evangelical style became typical of American religious observance, as distinguished from the practice of Anglicanism and other "high church" denominations. As the first intercolonial movement in America, the Awakening had a broadly unifying effect, forging bonds between the evangelical elements of churches in different colonies. Its most far-reaching effect, however, was psychological. It was the first populist movement in the country at large, and it eroded some of the foundations of a deferential society. By emphasizing simple, untutored capacity to experience religious emotion as the sign of election, the Awakening democratized salvation and elevated the common man to equality with his social superiors in his intrinsic worth as an individual and in the legitimacy of his moral judgment. The Awakening imbued masses of people with an intense, moral earnestness which led them to view public questions in terms of ethical standards which they presumed to intepret more truly than did their social superiors. Like the Puritans of old, who were the scourge of kings, they did not hesitate to judge their rulers. This psychological temper contributed heavily to the popular movement that rose with the Revolution. Unlettered mechanics and back-country farmers would probably not have been stirred very much by constitutional issues or abstract conceptions of natural law which interested the elite. They fought Britain because they regarded the measures of the mother country as an evil and a threat to the realization of a higher ethical order which they believed Providence had ordained when it revealed the New World and sent settlers to America. When it came, the Revolution was preached as service to the Lord against the forces of evil. Writing to the British foreign office, an observer quoted an American preacher as saying that "the Man, who was able in this Country to wield a Sword and did not endeavor to stain it with the Blood of the King's soldiers and their Abettors, would be renounced by the Lord Jesus Xt at the Day of Judgment." The observer added: "Your Lordship can scarcely conceive, what Fury the Discourses of some mad Preachers have created in this Country." Speaking of the migration of Puritans out of England in the 17th century, a modern British historian comments that it "merely postponed and moved to another continent, the final struggle with authority that was determined in England itself in the seventeenth century. A peculiarly seventeenth-century atmosphere envelops much of the dispute between Great Britain and the American colonies after 1763."

The Enlightenment

The religious revival of the times harked back in spirit to the Reformation, but a countervailing intellectual movement, which expressed the secular tendency of modern thought, was gaining ground. The Enlightenment marked a definite break from the past in its view of the universe and its conception of man, society, and religion. During the 16th and 17th centuries, the emergence of modern science had engendered an approach to knowledge which rejected theologically oriented philosophies in favor of inductive generalization and controlled experiment. All men of science were deeply stirred by the realization that beneath the variability of nature was an underlying order. The science of the age reached its apogee in the work of Sir Isaac Newton, whose *Principia Mathematica* was published in 1687. Its impact can hardly be exaggerated. The poet, Alexander Pope, wrote:

> Nature and Nature's laws lay hid in night:
> . God said *Let* Newton *be!* and all was Light.

The law of gravitation synthesized much of what was then known about the physical universe, defining in a single equation the orbits of the planets around the sun as well as the movement of bodies on earth. Earth and the heavens appeared as an integrated system, whose operation could be comprehended by man and stated in mathematical terms.

Educated people who were aware of scientific discoveries and their implications were obliged to recast their view of the universe to accord with the assumptions underlying physical science. These assumptions were that the universe is governed by natural law, and that, since the universe is uniform, the laws operate the same way in all its parts. All events proceed by cause and effect, the same causes producing the same effects everywhere. Moreover, natural law and the relations between cause and effect can be fathomed by human reason: man's ability to understand and control nature is therefore boundless. In the Newtonian universe there is no place for miracles or the supernatural. God, regarded as the ultimate creator, is supposed to have no need to alter what He has created. Natural laws are also God's laws, and His purposes are implicit in their operation. The universe is therefore a self-regulating system. The favorite analogy was that of a clock: the Newtonian world-machine, having been wound up by the Creator, ticks off to eternity according to a predetermined sequence.

The view of the universe unveiled by science had in time to be reconciled with religion. Deism, the religion of the Enlightenment, was not a set creed or the faith of a particular denomination, but a body of religious ideas compatible with scientific knowledge. It had professed adherents, but it eventually crept into and modified, without destroying, the practices of many churches. Prominent American Deists like Benjamin Franklin, John Adams, or even Thomas Jefferson did not feel it necessary to disavow conventional religion. They accepted the idea of God as a first cause, a benevolent principle in the universe, but they rejected the prevalent theologies and the divine inspiration of the Bible. Nature, not what they regarded as the church's outworn creeds, was to them God's testament, revealing by its marvelous intricacy and indwelling law the existence of a supreme intelligence. The expanded vision of the universe afforded by science gave Deists a vast and, to them, nobler canvas upon which to trace the divine presence.

> Look round the world, contemplate the whole and every part of it; you will find it to be nothing but one great machine, subdivided into an infinite number of lesser machines, which again admit of subdivisions to a degree beyond what human senses and faculties can trace and explain. All these various machines, and even their most minute parts, are adjusted to each other

with an accuracy which ravishes into admiration all men who have ever contemplated them. The curious adapting of means to ends, throughout all nature, resembles exactly, though it much exceeds, the productions of human contrivance. . . . By this argument *a posteriori,* and by this argument alone, do we prove at once the existence of a deity and his similarity to human mind and intelligence. (David Hume)

Central to Deistic thought was the idea of natural goodness. Since God created the universe, all things in their original nature were presumed to be good—the physical world, man, and, because it was integral to man, human society. Evil was defined as a corruption of original nature, to which man and his institutions were susceptible. False education and passion, it was thought, blind man to a course of conduct in harmony with nature; unnatural institutions take root in society. The correction of evil lies in the rational adjustment of human behavior and social institutions to natural law. The touchstone is reason. "By taking thought a man can add a cubit to his stature." By his capacity to reason, man can understand and thereby make use of nature's laws, which are also God's laws. Reason truly gives man a god-like eminence.

"Deistic rationalism," as this constellation of ideas and attitudes is sometimes called, provided the conceptual framework for a good deal of social and political thought. John Locke's social contract theory starts, for example, with the premise that "natural" society exists before government and that this society is naturally good. In it men have natural rights, to defend which government is formed and, if the government abuses its trust, a natural right to revolution. Similarly, a state of nature is the first premise of the laissez-faire economic theory of Adam Smith, whose *Wealth of Nations* was first published in 1776. In its natural state the economy is self-regulated by supply and demand and by the free play of competition. Any interference disrupts this natural order and is harmful in its consequences.

It is evident that the notion of what is "natural" implied value judgments, that the thinkers and writers who used the word were claiming the sanction of a universal order for what they wanted to do. Indeed, the late 18th century witnessed great upheavals, starting with the American Revolution and ending with the French Revolution, which spread through the Western World. Everywhere, the Deistic rationalism of the Enlightenment provided reformers and revolutionaries with their slogans. Applying the test of "reason" to existing institutions, they did not hesitate to declare that absolute monarchy, the privileges of nobility, official churches, and economic monopolies were contrary to nature and should be abolished. War they attributed to the personal ambitions of rulers, a thing that would never occur if the people governed. There was, in fact, a millennial quality to their thought. Confident of the power of reason to grasp the essentials of things in a world which contained no unfathomable mysteries, they looked upon human improvement as a relatively simple problem that could be solved in a short time. By the removal of impediments to natural order, society would at once be regenerated and justice secured to all men.

Enlightenment ideas were only one of the intellectual currents of the times, and possession of them did not necessarily turn a man into a democrat or a reformer. By force of implication, however, they promoted the spread of democratic and humanitarian attitudes. The dominant theme of older religion-oriented thought about the human condition was that the improvement of it is an individual moral problem. Man is basically evil and, if reclaimable at all, is so only by God's grace or a personal search for salvation. A man's faults derive from his own nature. Deistic rationalism, on the other hand, held that man is basically good, that individual failings are the result of false education and corrupt institutions. The fault is in society. Belief in the fundamental goodness of man justified a society based on equality and universal suffrage. Emphasis upon environment thrust strongly in the direction of social reform. Even the lowest of men it was held, can be uplifted by the correction of social evils and by mass education which will enable all men to rightly employ the gift of reason.

In America, as in Europe, the Enlightenment was mostly an

upper-class affair. In late colonial times, the common people were scarcely touched by it. If they read at all, they did not get far beyond the Bible and, in any case, lacked the education to grapple with the new learning at first hand. Some of the ideas sifted down to them, particularly natural rights political theory, but their betters did not encourage the spread of Deistic ideas among the common people whom they regarded as too simple to harbor such unorthodox ideas without becoming morally unhinged. "Talking about religion," Franklin said, meant "unchaining a tiger; the beast let loose may worry his liberator." The general outlook among the common people remained more closely akin to the Great Awakening than to the Enlightenment.

Among the upper classes for whom higher education was a badge of status, however, the new learning was much in vogue. Natural science was still not so highly technical and specialized that amateurs could not contribute to it. Many gentlemen dabbled in science during their spare time, taking astronomical observations, collecting botanical and zoological specimens, investigating the causes of earthquakes, and writing to one another about their ideas. America produced a few scientists of international reputation, notably John Winthrop, who taught at Harvard, Dr. John Mitchell of Virginia, Cadwallader Colden, who was lieutenant governor of New York, John Bartram, a Quaker botanist, David Rittenhouse, an astronomer, and, most eminent of all, Benjamin Franklin, who gained renown for his discoveries in electricity. Such Americans were sometimes members of the prestigious Royal Society of London and contributed to its scientific publications. A wide interest in science was betokened by the founding of the American Philosophical Society at Philadelphia in 1769.

Ideally, an educated man possessed a knowledge of Latin and Greek, which gave him direct access to the classics of antiquity and the Renaissance. The writings of antiquity had an immediacy in the 18th century that can be understood only if one appreciates the fact that in many ways the experience of ancient Greece and Rome was more relevant than that of the Middle Ages: the commercial and secular orientation of life in antiquity was more akin to the 18th century than the medieval past and provided more meaningful material for reflection upon man and society. But a full education also required acquaintance with more recent Continental and English writers whose ideas were the intellectual currency of the educated upper classes in all western countries. Thus grounded, an man gained entry into the literary and scientific culture of his generation. Since learning was limited to the upper class, he became identifiable as a member of the elite and qualified to discourse with gentlemen on equal terms. Educated Americans, even though they lived on the outskirts of European culture, belonged to an intellectual community that transcended national boundaries and national prejudices.

Fashionable though they might be, the ideas of the Enlightenment were explosive, and potentially disruptive of colonial relations with the mother country. The test of reason exposed the abuses in British political and social institutions, and the idea of a natural order in society undermined the authority which tradition might otherwise have vested in them. British modes had no more legitimacy than the colonists were willing to concede to them. Finally, the right of revolution sanctioned by both natural law and the English constitution provided a ready-made justification for rebellion.

CHAPTER V

The Empire Divided

The Setting

The interpretation of the American Revolution set forth by the Declaration of Independence was that King George III was determined to destroy the liberties of the colonists, and that their resistance led to confrontations with the home government ending in war and independence. This interpretation has been considerably revised by 20th century historians, but single explanations, in any case, seldom account for events in real life. As the consequences of the Revolution unfold in time, its causes are seen to be numerous and of diverse potentiality. Like a wide river, the Revolution drew from many sources, its currents intermingling in a complex directional flow.

Events took place in a setting that predisposed what was to happen, and some historians regard the conditioning circumstances as the cause. Although the processes by which nations are formed are not susceptible to exact definition, the colonies by mid-century had by any reasonable standard begun to acquire the attributes of a nation: a large population, a complex society, and a sense of identity—of being different from the English. Their governments were long established, competent, obeyed, and accustomed to handling their internal affairs. Their growing economy strained at the bonds of British regulation. The colonies in their growth had collided with the development of Britain, which, in the preceding century, had risen to a "height of glory and wealth," in the words of a British historian, "such as no European nation had attained since the decline of the Roman Empire." British power threatened the maturing colonies with envelopment and assimilation. Thomas Paine wrote in 1776: "To know whether it be the interest of this continent to be Independent we need only ask this easy simple question: Is it the interest of a man to be a boy all his life?"

After the new king, George III, came to the throne in 1760 and France was expelled from North America at the end of the French and Indian War, the British government, not for the first time but under more favorable circumstances, tried to exert effective control over the colonies in several areas of imperial policy. The British program, whether executed by royal decree or acts of Parliament, invaded freedoms long exercised by the colonists which they regarded as their constitutional rights. They interpreted the ensuing disputes with Britain, correctly enough, in terms of constitutional relations with the mother country. But British authority impinged upon them in another form, which raised universalist issues and allowed them to play a more selfless role. Because they were overwhelmingly Dissenters in religion, bred in Commonwealth political ideas, and educated in the critical, antigovernment views of the "country party" in Britain, their cause was easily involved in the ideology of British politics and linked with the current effort to impute to George III the intent to overthrow the constitutional settlement of 1689 and, by corrupting Parliament, restore the personal rule of the Stuarts. As the struggle against the king waxed but then waned in Britain during the 1760s, it appeared to the colonists, and to many of their sympathizers in Britain, that Americans had become the last defenders of liberty. In this aspect, the American Revolution could be viewed as the latest phase, straight in line from Magna Charta, of the defense of English constitutional liberties. This is how America's elite leaders regarded it. They placed themselves among that company of heroes celebrated in history for their defiance of royal tyranny.

If this had been all the Revolution was, it would likely have been an elitist affair, more like the Glorious Revolution in England, with America's upper class established in its rule and existing social arrangements confirmed. The triumph of conservatism would by no means have been as complete as in Britain, for America's upper class was relatively democratic and progressive for its time. Nevertheless, many of its members conceived of the Revolution precisely in the terms mentioned here: as self-rule within or outside the empire, but with internal arrangements intact. The flaw in their thinking was that unlike the British aristocracy of 1689, the American elite, although it started the Revolution, lacked the strength to carry it off without bringing in the common people. That policy entailed risks, as Gouverneur Morris of New York observed in 1774, delivering himself of one of his memorable soliloquies: "the mob begins to think and reason. Poor reptiles! it is with them a vernal morning; they are struggling to cast off their winter's slough, they bask in the sunshine, and ere noon they will bite."

The divisions that arose among patriot leaders, not loyalists, but those who supported the cause all the way through, were, in fact, largely over the question of popular action. Conservatives wanted to contain popular action, and popular leaders, no matter how elitist themselves, saw the necessity of going along with it. Inviting in the common people, however, meant that concessions would have to be made in forming policy and in setting up institutions of government. It meant tolerating popular initiative, action in the street, and pressure on leadership from below. It raised a possibility that the Revolution would be like the Puritan Revolution, when the Saints took over and tried to substitute transcendental ideas of social justice for legalities as the basis of social arrangements—a foundation of sorts had been laid for this possibility by the Great Awakening. It was also necessary to subscribe to ideologies which were dangerous to the status quo, to utter slogans based on natural rights philosophy and the equality of man before God, slogans that once given legitimacy were certain to remain in the popular vocabulary. Finally, activating such elements as the urban crowd and unruly backcountrymen invited a struggle for succession to determine which groups and interests would dominate the new regime.

Sources of British Colonial Policy, 1760–1765

Through the first half of the 18th century the colonies basked in Britain's "salutary neglect," but a basic element in the relationship between colonies and mother country was altered when French possessions in North America passed into British hands. Hitherto the menace of the French in Canada had kept the colonies dependent on British military protection and had fostered loyalty to the empire. With the menace removed, the colonies could afford to be bolder in resisting British authority. "The people in general," wrote General Thomas Gage, "begin to be sensible, that they are not obliged to do, what they submitted to, in times of danger." Britain, on the other hand, no longer had to temper her policies in order to secure colonial aid in wars against France. The necessity for mutual accommodation was reduced.

The enlargement of the empire invited a reappraisal of policy. With the acquisition of French Canada and Spanish Florida, British possessions now stretched from the Atlantic Ocean to the Mississippi River and from Hudson's Bay to the Gulf of Mexico. They harbored foreign and hostile elements: French and Spanish nationals, and warlike Indians who had recently been enemies. They also presented new fields of economic opportunity: the rich fur trade of the interior, previously controlled by the French, and a vast agricultural frontier west of the Appalachians now open to settlement. The ministry took the position that the defense of this empire required a permanent garrison of regular troops, paid and supported by the home government. The necessary force was estimated at 10,000 men, whose maintenance would cost about £300,000 annually. Since the war had raised the British national debt to £130 million and taxes levied to support it were already so high that to increase them seemed out of the question, the ministry decided that the colonies should be made to bear part of the load.

Until the recent war, when British regular troops had shouldered the main burden of military operations, defense had been left to the colonial militia. From the British standpoint, the colonies were not to be trusted with responsibility for a greater empire. They had always shirked military obligations except those that served their own purposes. Although in their own view the colonies had exerted themselves to the utmost during the French and Indian War, British statesmen regarded their contributions as niggardly, wrung out of them only by the promise of reimbursement for their expenditures. British attitudes on this subject were confirmed by colonial behavior in 1764, when Pontiac's Rebellion swept away every British post in the northwest except Forts Pitt and Detroit. The only provinces willing to supply men or money were those struck by the attack; the others were indifferent. Hence the decision was made to put British troops in the colonies.

As Americans suspected, the official reasons did not constitute the whole explanation. Americans wondered why the expulsion of the French did not warrant a reduction rather than an increase of military forces. To them the idea that British troops were intended to protect them from Indians was a hollow pretense. Regular troops stationed in military posts had never been much help against Indians, who easily evaded and bypassed fortified positions. Moreover, as later became apparent, the kind of troops destined for service in America were European-style regiments, not rangers trained in Indian warfare, some detachments of which were actually withdrawn from the colonies at the close of the French and Indian War. Finally, when the troops arrived, most of them were stationed, not on the frontier, but near centers of population.

Colonial suspicions had a basis in fact. Mixed with the idea of strengthening colonial defense was the king's desire to maintain a larger standing army, an objective which was not unreasonable from Britain's standpoint, since France and Spain, who were Britain's chief rivals, had for the first time stationed considerable bodies of troops in their own West Indies possessions. As public opinion in Britain made it difficult to maintain troops in the home country, the king's purpose could be accomplished by keeping them out of sight in America and by making the colonies pay for them. A further consideration was reinforcement of British authority. Many British leaders thought that with the French gone Americans would try to throw off British rule.

One way of making the colonists contribute to the support of the new military establishment was to enforce customs regulations. It was no secret that duties were commonly evaded. An investigation disclosed that the levy upon enumerated articles transported from one colony to another had yielded only £35,000 in 30 years, and that the duty on imports under the Molasses Act had produced only £21,000 over a similar period. These were the principal British customs duties collected in the colonies. Such promiscuous evasion was from Britain's standpoint more outrageous in view of the colonists' flagrant trading with the enemy during the late war. Although British forces in America had been short of supplies, New England merchants had sold goods to the French army. Even more galling to the British was the large wartime trade between the colonies and the French West Indies. Wanton misbehavior of this kind stiffened the ministry's determination to enforce the laws.

Customs revenues, however, could raise no more than a fraction of the sums needed, and it was the momentous decision of the British government to secure the remainder by levying taxes on the colonies. This was something new. Parliament had never hesitated to legislate for the colonies or to lay duties upon their exterior commerce. But trade regulation was one thing, taxation quite another. Although in theory Parliament recognized no limit to its power to tax the colonies, the power had never been exercised. Always before, when Britain had tried to get money from the provinces for imperial purposes, the various legislatures had been allowed to raise it themselves. From Britain's standpoint the results had been meager, and there was now no confidence that the colonies would voluntarily support a military establishment. Accordingly, it was decided to levy taxes. The only question was the form that they should take.

Joined with military and revenue problems was the need for a coherent policy with regard to the trans-Appalachian west. The land was Indian country and before 1763 had been the focus of

Anglo-French rivalry. As long as it was in French hands, Britain had encouraged colonial expansion into the region, but this now appeared less desirable. The advance of settlers threatened to touch off expensive wars with the Indians and to disrupt the fur trade, now a lucrative British activity. British statesmen also thought it preferable to confine the population to the coast within reach of British commercial regulations, rather than to allow it to dissipate into the interior where trade would be hard to control. Such considerations suggested the need for definite policies administered by the home government. Hitherto, the colonies had been given virtual free rein in handling Indian affairs, regulating the fur trade, buying land from the tribes, granting it to their citizens, and pushing territorial claims beyond the mountains. As it appeared that the west would fall to Britain, the ministry entertained the idea of restricting settlement until the Indians could be conciliated and then permitting occupation of the west to proceed under British rather than colonial regulation.

Considered at large, Britain's reinvigorated colonial policy had four main objectives: (1) to keep a standing army in America; (2) to regulate western expansion and Indian affairs; (3) to enforce the Navigation Acts, with the twofold aim of making the laws effective and increasing customs revenue; and (4) to raise money in the colonies by parliamentary taxation. This experiment in imperial policy was undertaken by a weak, coalition ministry headed by George Grenville, a man of undistinguished ability. Like most Englishmen then in the ministry and in Parliament, he was insensitive to the changes that had taken place in the empire, unaware of any need to revise previous concepts, and accustomed to regard colonial affairs as subservient to British interests and party politics.

The Grenville Acts

The Grenville ministry's first act was the Proclamation of 1763, a royal decree forbidding settlement or the purchase of Indian lands west of a line drawn along the crest of the Appalachians. The object was to check colonial expansion and to create a buffer zone between settlers and Indians until some form of government could be extended over the west and treaties made with the tribes. Henceforth, Indian trade was to be regulated by royal officers and the right to purchase tribal lands reserved to the crown. In 1765 two royal commissioners were appointed to license the fur trade and to negotiate treaties leading to the cession of tribal lands. The same year the Privy Council ordered the governors of Virginia and Pennsylvania to evacuate settlers who had moved beyond the Proclamation line.

The Proclamation deprived the colonies of authority in western affairs and vested it in the British government. Some colonies which had no western claims were not affected, but others, including Virginia, the Carolinas, Georgia, and New York, were hard hit. In the past they had freely promoted land speculation by their citizens, sanctioned the private purchase of Indian lands, and granted large tracts to individuals. With the French out of the way, they had looked forward to exploiting the further reaches of the west, but after the Proclamation their schemes could no longer be managed under local auspices. Virginia was the greatest loser. The colony laid claim to the present state of Kentucky and the entire region northwest of the Ohio River. A group of Virginians organized as the Ohio Company had launched a colonization scheme near Pittsburgh in an area also claimed by Pennsylvania. The Ohio Company had received a grant of 200,000 acres from the crown in 1740, but its efforts to develop the land were halted by the French and Indian War. As the Ohio associates were preparing to revive their project at the end of hostilities, the Proclamation transferred jurisdiction over the area to the crown. In the lobbying that then went on in London, the Virginians lost out to rival land companies, and eventually the claims of Virginia and all the northern colonies to the region northwest of the Ohio were invalidated by the Quebec Act of 1774, which incorporated the territory into the province of Quebec. Britain thus implemented its decision to make colonial expansion subservient to British interests. The Proclamation line was not final, but western settlement was to be permitted only under British auspices. In the years before the American Revolution, British ministers also entertained the idea of creating a large Indian reserve in the northwest, closed to settlement and set aside for the fur trade.

In 1764 Parliament gave notice of its intention to restrain the colonies in a sphere not organically related to defense and revenue but of vital importance to the colonies. Through most of the 18th century, as already noted, the Board of Trade had tolerated colonial monetary practices. A stiffer policy had been inaugurated with the passage of the Currency Act of 1751, which prohibited land banks and the enactment of legal tender laws in New England. When the French and Indian War opened, the colonies were permitted to issue paper money just about as they pleased in order to raise money for the war. But in 1764 Parliament enacted new restraints. The Currency Act of that year applied to all the colonies, including those of New England. Its major provision was to forbid their making paper money legal tender. Thereafter, the Board of Trade not only enforced the law, but put up stronger resistance to paper money legislation of any kind.

Most colonies regarded tender laws as necessary to preserve the value of their currency. They deeply resented British interference, especially as a postwar depression, coupled with the steady withdrawal of bills issued during the war, created a general shortage of money. They succeeded in making some headway against the restraints by continuing to issue paper money, although it could no longer be legal tender, and by establishing several new land banks. It was evident, however, that British policy was narrowly geared to protecting the interests of a few British merchants and that colonial needs were held in small esteem.

That Britain was bent on subordinating the colonies became abundantly clear with the passage of the Sugar Act of 1764. It was a revenue measure, but it was also a determined effort, long overdue in British opinion, to enforce the Navigation Acts. The Sugar Act extended and amended the Molasses Act of 1733, which had been designed to force Americans to buy molasses from British West Indies rather than from the French islands.

From the moment of its enactment, the Molasses Act had been evaded by customs officers, by American merchants, and by residents and public officials of the British West Indies alike. The rum industry of New England had grown up on smuggled molasses. Under the Sugar Act the duty on foreign molasses was reduced from six to three pence a gallon, but the entire machinery for enforcing the Navigation Acts was tightened. The act prescribed elaborate new regulations covering the shipment of goods in or out of the colonies. It required affidavits, bonds, and licenses at every turn, for nonenumerated as well as enumerated articles. Lacking such official papers, vessels were liable to seizure upon entering a British port or when within two leagues of any British colony. Under an act of 1763 naval patrols had been assigned to American waters. The Sugar Act also established new procedures for the trial of customs violations. Previously, trials had been held within the jurisdiction where seizures had taken place, either in common law courts that employed juries or, at the election of the prosecutor, in Vice-Admiralty courts in which the decision was given by judges. In practice, most cases tried in the colonies were conducted in common law courts, whose juries seldom convicted. Under the Sugar Act the prosecutor was authorized to remove trials to a new Vice-Admiralty court to be established at Halifax, Nova Scotia. Finally, the act gave customs officers virtually free rein to do what they wished without penalty. They were exempted from suit for damages arising out of illegal seizures. In all the colonies the new regulations were regarded as legal harassment, but they aroused most resentment in New England, where molasses and other products smuggled from the West Indies were of major importance in overseas commerce.

Except for the revenue-raising features of the Sugar Act, which drew little attention, parliamentary acts and royal decrees up to this point affected only particular segments of colonial society and were within the acknowledged scope of British authority. However, the Stamp Act passed in March 1765 struck all the colonies, every class of American citizens, and invaded rights which the colonists had long regarded as inviolable. It became the symbol of oppression.

The Grenville ministry introduced the bill into Parliament only after mature consideration. It was recognized as an innovation, since Parliament had never before levied taxes on the colonies. Petitions from America and the advice of colonial agents in London had made it clear that there would be strong opposition. But the ministry had no confidence in any alternative, and Parliament approved the bill without much dissent. It required revenue stamps to be placed on newspapers, pamphlets, cards, dice, papers involved in court proceedings, wills, academic degrees, licenses, permits to sell liquor, and a variety of other legal and commercial documents. The stamps were to be sold in America by royal agents, and paid for in specie. Their sale was expected to raise from £60,000 to £120,000 annually. The money was to be remitted to Britain and held as a fund to discharge "the necessary expense of defending, protecting, and securing the said colonies and plantations."

The Stamp Act seemed designed to unite the colonies in opposition. It struck the most vocal and influential elements of the population: merchants, printers, and lawyers. It joined the staple colonies of the south with the commercial north. By threatening to draw hard money out of the country it alarmed both merchants and planters. Such considerations, however, were but incidental to the constitutional issue that it raised, an issue which all Americans instantly perceived. The Stamp Act was a menace to representative government. The degree of self rule that the colonists had achieved, their "liberties," depended upon legislative control of taxation. If, as in the present case, Britain managed to secure revenues to support its officials without recourse to colonial money grants, the means of legal resistance to any British measures would be undermined, and king and Parliament could rule the colonies as they pleased.

The dispute over the Stamp Act revealed a wide gulf between colonies and mother country. In its entirety the British program abridged the whole range of privileges which the colonies had long enjoyed, asserting the priority of British over American interests in the regulation of maritime trade, the occupation of the west, and the conduct of government. The British regarded the program merely as the enforcement of existing law and the reduction of the colonies to a proper subordination to the mother country. The colonies, however, had grown beyond the status assigned to them by British law and constitutional theory. They saw the British program as a broad invasion of their rights and a portent of future oppression.

The Stamp Act and Popular Resistance

The 12 most populous colonies were for the first time united on a single issue. Nearly every important leader opposed the Stamp Act, and the common people were in advance of their leaders, forcing them to ever more radical positions. Mass meetings became an ordinary procedure, and, since liberty was every man's concern, all men voted at these meetings without regard for property qualifications. Resistance to the act was a powerful educative force, impelling the common people to examine the postulates upon which government rested and to take an initiative in public affairs which had hitherto been left to the elite. Mass protest, confrontation, and violence became acceptable modes of political action. The Stamp Act provoked a general uprising, led by the elite, but manned by a united people.

The colonies wavered indecisively in 1765, waiting for the act to go into effect, uncertain whether to resist and, if so, by what means. The Old Dominion at last gave the signal. In Virginia, the outstanding popular leader was a young firebrand, Patrick Henry, who had found the key to popularity in bold assertion of American rights. A backcountry delegate of inconspicuous family, he had been catapulted to fame by his oratory and his fervid denunciations of Britain, becoming a darling of the people and, most exceptionally for a man of no family, a powerful figure in the assembly. Addressing the House of Burgesses, he delivered the famous phrases that compared George III with previous tyrants of history who had met their proper fate—Caesar, who had his Brutus, and Charles I his Cromwell—and said he hoped that some American would be found to stand up for his country.

When the Speaker cried out that he was uttering treason, Henry apologized, but he nevertheless introduced a set of inflammatory resolutions. He said that the Virginia legislature alone had the right to tax the inhabitants. With the resolutions containing this sentiment even his most conservative colleagues could agree. But Henry went on to urge defiance of British authority, saying that Virginians were not bound to obey the Stamp Act, and that anyone who urged the contrary should be deemed an enemy to the province. Henry's oratory did not persuade the legislature to adopt his extreme propositions, which were beyond what most responsible American leaders would agree to at this time. Only the resolutions concerning self-taxation were approved, but the full set of resolutions was published in newspapers all over the country as the Virginia Resolves. The Old Dominion, which included a fifth of America's people, seemed to have pointed the way.

A popular upheaval swept the colonies. Before the Stamp Act went into operation on November 1, 1765, every stamp distributor was forced to resign his office. Patriot committees confiscated the stamps upon their arrival. With stamps unavailable, business was soon resumed in open defiance of parliamentary law. Meanwhile, in order to bring pressure upon the British government, merchants signed pledges not to import British goods until the act was repealed. In October, the Stamp Act Congress assembled at New York, the first major intercolonial meeting ever held at the volition of the colonists themselves—an ominous portent for the future of British rule. The Congress addressed petitions to the king and Parliament, declaring that recent acts, particularly the Stamp Act, had a "manifest tendency to subvert the rights and liberties" of Americans.

Except for persons attached by interest or ambition to British official society, Americans of all classes were united. The gentlemen who attended the Stamp Act Congress represented the elite that normally governed the country. Prominent merchants and lawyers headed patriot committees elected by town meetings, and the passionate crowds that threatened stamp distributors in the southern colonies included members of the most eminent families. Everywhere, the popular tumult convincingly demonstrated that the people were behind their leaders. Nevertheless, later divisions in the patriot movement were foreshadowed. Although the upper classes took the lead, resistance to Britain could only be sustained by drawing the common people into the cause. Extralegal activities such as the coercion of stamp distributors, the enforcement of nonimportation agreements, and the intimidation of British sympathizers opened a field for action by the middle and lower classes. In Boston, as in New York and other towns which were the early centers of resistance, popular agitation showed a disturbing tendency to vent itself against wealthy, prominent men who could be singled out as lukewarm in their devotion to American liberty.

Leaders who appealed to the people and advocated strong measures sprang into prominence. In Boston, which was to play a crucial role in bringing on the Revolution, Samuel Adams entered upon his notable career. Born into a well-to-do family but a failure in business, he got into local politics by cultivating the support of the shopkeepers and tradesmen as opposed to the wealthier merchants and British placemen. The developing conflict with Britain enabled him to shape the course of great events. He, like Patrick Henry, represented a new species of political leaders who solicited the people and manipulated popular sentiment to achieve their ends.

When news of the Virginia Resolves reached Boston, it touched off mob violence. The targets were prominent men identified with British administration, notably Thomas Hutchinson, lieutenant governor and chief justice of the colony, long hated by the people for the policies he had sponsored in the colony's domestic affairs. The mob threatened his life and laid waste his mansion, one of the costliest residences in town. Not a single person, private or acting in an official capacity, raised a hand to interfere as the mob spent the entire night systematically demolishing the structure. Although the leader, an intrepid shoemaker named Ebenezer Mackintosh, was known to authorities, they were afraid to put him in jail. The stamp distributor, Hutchinson's brother-in-law, whose house had also been destroyed, resigned in terror. Thenceforth, during the Stamp Act crisis, the streets were ruled at night and sometimes during the day by what the British governor described as a trained mob, recruited by such men as Samuel Adams and acting under orders. At its head were the "Sons of Liberty," a standing organization dedicated to direct action and uncompromising support of the patriot position. The chain of command, according to the governor, reached up to the leaders of the town meeting and Boston's delegates to the provincial legislature. The mob supported the patriot cause, and hence its excesses were condoned by public opinion. A few persons of quality who first countenanced violence began to wonder whether they had not "raised the devil and could not lay him again."

Governor Bernard said that on the night Hutchinson's mansion was wrecked, 15 houses had been marked for destruction by the mob in what he called "a war of Plunder, of general levelling and taking away the Distinction of rich and poor." A merchant wrote that rich men in Boston were leaving their valuables in the homes of poorer friends who were above suspicion of having British sympathies. While there may have been an element of truth in these remarks, they were calculated to place the rioting in the most unfavorable light. As William Gordon, the first historian of the Revolution, wrote in 1788, it was a mistake to assume that the "dregs of the colonies" were responsible for the riots. Besides the lower classes, he wrote, the mobs included respectable men of middling status; moreover "merchants, assemblymen, magistrates, etc., united directly or indirectly in the riots, and without their influence and instigation the lower class of inhabitants would have been quiet."

In New York City events took a somewhat similar course. A mob quickly forced the resignation of the stamp distributor, but the governor of the province seized the initiative by impounding the stamps and placing them in nearby Fort George, which he had fortified with artillery. Although the Sons of Liberty did not attack the fort, they surged through the streets night after night hunting down British adherents and burning their houses. They hanged people in effigy, demanded that the governor hand over the stamps to them, insisted that merchants and lawyers resume business illegally without using stamps, and promised to give protection to those who did so. Since the city was headquarters of the British army in America, the Sons of Liberty suspected that the British commander, General Gage, would use troops to enforce the Stamp Act, beginning in New York. They therefore formed an alliance with Sons of Liberty in Connecticut, and hundreds of armed citizens of that colony swore to come to the aid of New York patriots if they were attacked. Patriot groups in upper New York province, Long Island, and New Jersey also pledged military assistance. As in Boston, the New York Sons of Liberty appointed a committee of correspondence to arouse kindred spirits in other colonies, with the result that Sons of Liberty were organized in all the colonies. They compelled stamp distributors to resign, enforced nonimportation agreements, and tried to bring about resumption of business without stamps. In this crusade, newspapers played a crucial role by hammering away at British measures and denouncing people allegedly disaffected to the patriot cause.

The Stamp Act was a dead letter. As news spread of what had happened in Boston and New York, patriots elsewhere were moved to commit acts of equal audacity. A Rhode Island mob wrecked the houses of British apologists and compelled the stamp distributor to resign. In Connecticut, a mob hunted down and captured a recalcitrant stamp distributor, exacting a public reading of his resignation. The Maryland stamp distributor fled to New York, where he was captured on Long Island and forced to resign. In Pennsylvania, when the Quaker-dominated legislature refused to take a strong stand against the Stamp Act, a mass meeting presented an ultimatum to the stamp distributor, who promised not to enforce the act. In all the southern colonies except Georgia, popular demonstrations compelled stamp distributors to surrender their offices. The governor of Georgia solemnly commented: "The flames spread through all the Continent, and one colony supports another in their disobedience to superior powers." The people of the colonies had defeated the Stamp Act before it could go into operation.

Natural Rights

In opposing British policies, Americans were united by interest and sentiment; they were further welded together by adherence to political ideas that in 1776 were all but universal in the colonies. These ideas were drawn from antimonarchical and anti-statist doctrines thrown up by the English revolutions of the 17th century, when England was for a short time a republic, and from the continuing criticism poured out upon the British governmental system by a variety of British writers who were avidly read in America. The criticism expressed in these writings was reinforced by the struggles of the colonists themselves against British governors. Although not fully sensed or articulated before 1776, the experiences of the colonists and the elements of the British tradition that they sorted out and chose to accept had already contributed powerfully to what Jefferson later described as the ineradicable republicanism of the American mind.

Looming large in their abstract political thought was the natural rights theory as set forth by John Locke and elaborated by more radical British writers. Men have natural rights to life, liberty, and property. In order to protect these rights, they enter into a contract with one another to institute government. In actuality, governments have many historical origins, usually mere conquest, but beneath any legitimate government is an implicit social contract—the agreement of the people to accept, or at least acquiesce in, the authority of government in order to secure protection for their natural rights. When a government abuses its trust and becomes destructive of the ends for which it was created, the people have a right to overthrow it.

The right to revolution was regarded as one not to be exercised lightly but only as a last resort. Defenders of monarchical privilege and the status quo often argued that a social contract, once made, was inviolable, and that the acceptance which the people extended to government at its inception—say, to the government of William and Mary after the English Revolution of 1689—was forever binding and could never be withdrawn. Americans rejected this idea. By the time of the Revolution, some of them were reading radical English theorists who declared that every individual born into a society has a personal right to accept or reject the existing government. But whatever the refinements of social contract theory as Americans understood it in 1776, its general effect was to assert that sovereignty lies not in government but in the people, that this sovereignty is irrevocable, and that the people have a continuing right to determine the legitimacy of any existing government.

Natural rights doctrine was coupled with profound anti-statism. Americans distrusted government as a matter of principle, an attitude inherited from writers in the English parliamentary tradition and abundantly confirmed by their observations of the monarchical states of the Old World, including Britain. Such slogans as "power corrupts" and "eternal vigilance is the price of liberty" bespoke a conviction that all government has an inveterate tendency to become tyrannical, that power has such an exquisite appeal that, having savored it, all men will seek to increase it and will end by abusing it. It was held that the principal source from which violation of private rights is to be expected is not the people, who have a rational common interest in the preservation of their rights, but the government. The science of politics, as understood in America, was chiefly concerned with checks upon power.

The monarchies of Europe, including Britain, clearly demonstrated the inimical tendency of government: centralized authority, vast and corrupt bureaucracy, standing armies, and heavy taxation. The alternatives which Americans opposed to this recognizable pattern of evils was the supremacy of local government, directly elected by the people, limited in functions, economical, too poor to be a source of corruption, administered by people like themselves, and weak enough to be resisted. Part of the definition of liberty was reliance upon a militia, a citizen army composed of amateurs, rather than on professional soldiers who were regarded as likely instruments of despotism. Liberty also required the supremacy of the legislature over the executive, an idea reinforced by conflicts between colonial assemblies and

British governors: all power was dangerous, but it was most safely given to an elected legislature disciplined by frequent elections and girded about by limitations upon its authority. Finally, although the colonists had little reason to ponder the subject before the Revolution, their conceptions of liberty were also served by their methods of public and private finance. Unlike the British system with its corruption and funded debt, colonial paper money and land bank loans did not enrich private individuals, they were not a source of official corruption, they did not administer to business profits, and they allowed American governments to function without accumulating large, permanent debts.

As Americans confronted the central power of the empire, they were inspired by an image of themselves and their society as superior to the people and institutions of the Old World. Many of their Puritan ancestors, regarding themselves as "sifted seed" of the Lord, had come to the colonies with a sense of mission, intent upon constructing life upon higher ethical principles. Many others, fleeing repression, had migrated to the new country in search of a more just society. In spite of the inevitable gulf between the ideal and the reality, colonists of all classes believed in the virtue and rectitude of Americans and American society as contrasted with the decadence of the Old World. They were not alone in entertaining this concept. The idea of the innate virtue of unspoiled nature, an intellectual cliché in the 18th century, had propagated among Europeans the same Arcadian vision of America. With the disruption of a parochial society brought about by colonial wars and by increasing wealth and social inequality, particularly in the cities, much had happened to cast doubt upon America's self-image. To many colonists, as the pamphlet literature of the time discloses, the British program, with its projection of British influence and sponsorship of the Anglican church, threatened to destroy American virtue and absorb the colonies into the British social system. Resistance, in a sense, was an instinctive effort to thrust back the Old World.

The Theoretical Defense of American Rights

The colonists denounced the Sugar Act and the Stamp Act on grounds of expediency, saying that they simply could not pay such high duties. They also said, in disregard of the fact that the revenue from the taxes was to be spent mainly in the colonies, that the drain of specie would ruin the American economy. Britain was already getting rich from the Navigation Acts and the profits of American trade. Parliament should take care lest it kill the goose that laid the golden eggs.

The argument moved to higher ground in the dispute over constitutional issues. Colonial spokesmen were not yet prepared to embrace the heady doctrines of natural rights, whose implications were open-ended and quasi-revolutionary. They relied instead on legalistic arguments which assumed the continuation of the status quo and were more calculated to appeal to a British audience. Americans, they said, possessed the rights of Englishmen, which had not been forfeited by emigration. These rights included trial by jury, now suspended by the use of Admiralty courts to enforce the Sugar Act. Above all, they included self-taxation, a right exercised without question since the first settlements, but now violated by the Stamp Act.

American spokesmen did not at this time deny Parliament's right to legislate for the colonies or to lay duties upon American commerce in the course of regulating trade. But the Sugar Act, they held, was designed not to regulate trade but to raise money, and the Stamp Act was purely a revenue measure. Both acts invaded their right of self-taxation, without which they would have no means to protect their persons or their property from governmental abuse. They referred to their condition under such a regime as "slavery." The remedy was not representation in the British House of Commons, which few colonists thought practical. Their position was that they should be taxed only by their own legislatures.

Such arguments were easily countered by British exponents of ministerial policy. Notwithstanding charter grants or long usage, they replied that colonial governments had no sovereign powers such as were implied by control over taxation, that their powers were not comparable to those of Parliament but to those of English towns, whose privileges existed only by grace of the sovereign authority and were revocable. Against the complaint that Americans were being taxed without representation, British spokesmen advanced the principle of "virtual representation," an idea cherished by English conservatives who used it at home in defending rotten boroughs and inequitable representation against demands for parliamentary reform. The argument rested on the premise that delegates to the House of Commons represented all classes of the population—i.e., country gentry, yeomanry, urban middle classes, etc.—rather than geographical areas. Hence they spoke for the interests, not of their constituents particularly, but of such classes throughout the realm of Britain and the king's dominions. Under this concept, Americans were "virtually" represented in Parliament, as much so, it was said, as most of Britain's inhabitants who either did not have enough property to vote or who lived in towns unrepresented in the Commons. Ministerial spokesmen argued further that there could not in logic be a division of sovereignty within the empire such as was implied by American claims to the right of self-taxation. There had to be one supreme head. Since the Glorious Revolution of 1689 that head had been Parliament, which had indivisible sovereignty over the empire and the right to legislate in all cases whatsoever.

From a constitutional standpoint there was much to support the British argument, but however tenable in theory it ignored de facto changes in the empire which had occurred during the century and a half since the colonies were founded. As some English realized, the Americans in practice exercised the right of taxation, their legislatures had acquired a large measure of self-rule, and the people were so accustomed to direct representation that they thought anything else an infringement of their liberties. They had grown so apart from Britain that the idea of their being virtually represented in the Commons, even if virtual representation were admitted in principle, was absurd. In sum, they had so long possessed the rights for which they now contended that they considered them the normal order of things, part of the English constitution.

America's "Friends" and the Repeal of the Stamp Act

The American cause had numerous sympathizers in Britain, who saw in it a reflection of their own struggle for liberty. With the accession of George III a constitutional crisis had developed in British politics. His Hanoverian predecessors had allowed royal prerogatives to slip into the hands of powerful Whig nobles who formed ministries, initiated policy, and consolidated their power by lavish dispensation of governmental patronage in return for political support. Upon gaining the throne, George III determined to restore the constitutional position of the monarch in the British system of government. Taking his cue from the Whig nobles themselves, he built up a following in Parliament by dispensing patronage. With more offices to bestow than any private person, he had an advantage in the contest, and to a degree unknown in previous decades Parliament fell under royal influence. Old party divisions between Whig and Tory, which for some time had been indistinct, now ceased to have meaning. The struggle was between the "king's friends," won over by conviction or bribery to support the monarchy, and the leaders of the opposition. The latter group was headed by Whig nobles whose status had declined under the rejuvenated monarchy. They interpreted the king's bid for power as an attempt to circumvent the Revolution of 1689 and restore the personal government of the Stuarts.

Colonial resistance to the Stamp Act at once became the leading issue in British politics. The aristocratic Whigs took up the American cause, which furnished ammunition to attack the king's handpicked ministries and a "corrupt" House of Commons which, said the Whigs, was no longer an independent branch of government but subservient to the monarchy. Edmund Burke, one of their leading spokesmen, portrayed the

Americans as standing in the long line of British heroes who had
defended liberty against royal tyranny. William Pitt, not in
principle opposed to a vigorous monarchy but an arch foe of
a prostituted Commons, declared: "I rejoice that America has
resisted!" To aristocratic Whigs the Americans became brothers-
in-arms. Ultimately, as the colonists were to discover, there
was a point at which this comradeship dissolved. Champions of
Parliament against the king, the aristocratic Whigs were also
staunch advocates of parliamentary supremacy over the empire.
They agreed with Americans that the king was out to destroy
the English constitution. But when the question became one of
parliamentary rights as opposed to the rights of colonial legislatures, they deserted the Americans, unable to accept a limitation
of Parliament's authority in the matter of taxation or anything
else.

A much closer affinity existed between Americans and the English Dissenters and parliamentary reformers. These groups,
although affiliated in politics with the aristocratic Whigs, were
more radical in their ideas. They were critical of Parliament, not
because it was corrupted by the king, but merely because it was
corrupt and not representative of the nation. A movement for
parliamentary reform arose in Britain during the 1760s, coinci-
dent with the disputes with America. It had a numerous following among Dissenters who, since they did not adhere to the
Church of England, were excluded from public office. The movement drew heavily from the middle and lower classes of towns
clustered about London, where electoral processes were more
democratic than elsewhere in Britain. It enlisted the manufacturing districts of northern and western England, which had few
or no delegates in the Commons. Whereas the aristocratic Whigs
stood for the existing parliamentary system with its rotten boroughs and inequitable representation, provided only that it was
shorn of undue royal influence and dominated by the aristocracy,
the reformers attacked the system itself. They wanted to adjust
representation to population and make Parliament responsive
to the will of the nation. These ideas, which were democratic in
tendency and subversive of class privilege, closely resembled

those held by most Americans. In London coffeehouses and the intellectual clubs which were such a prominent feature of 18th-century urban life, Benjamin Franklin and many other Americans engaged in heartfelt communion with English reformers. Throughout the resistance to Britain, Americans believed that they were making common cause with liberals in England, and they interpreted their own revolution as an incident in the historic defense of English constitutional rights.

The furor aroused by the Stamp Act in both Britain and America induced Parliament to repeal the act only six months after it went into effect. Among all the colonists' "friends" in Britain, their best advocates proved to be merchants and manufacturers who testified to the ruinous decline of trade and depression of British manufactures brought about by colonial nonimportation agreements and testified also to the inability of British merchants to collect payment on debts estimated at £7 million. The ministry was also sensitive to the fact that American resistance was so uncompromising that the act could not be executed without military force, which was likely to invite the intervention of Britain's late enemies, France and Spain. Clearly, the Stamp Act was not worth the risk, and it was repealed in March 1766. To signify that the repeal was a matter of expediency and indicated no surrender of parliamentary authority over the empire, the ministry, now headed by Whigs who were sympathetic with the colonies, sponsored the Declaratory Act. It asserted that Parliament had "full power to make laws and statutes of sufficient force and validity to bind the colonies and people of America, subjects of the Crown of Great Britain, in all cases whatsoever." If the colonists had been attentive, the Declaratory Act would have had an ominous ring, but in exulting over what they considered a complete victory they chose to disregard it.

The Townshend Acts

Anglo-American disputes were not allowed to rest. In March 1767, only a year after the repeal of the Stamp Act, Chancellor of the Exchequer Charles Townshend introduced into Parliament another set of measures designed to tax the colonies and enforce the Navigation Acts. The revenue features consisted of new duties on tea, glass, lead, painters' colors, and paper. In objecting to the Stamp Act, colonial spokesmen had distinguished between internal taxes, collected within the country, and external taxes laid on goods at ports of entry. Their argument was that duties on external commerce had a regulatory function, which was within Parliament's authority, whereas internal taxes had no purpose but raising revenue and were therefore in their nature an invasion of American rights. Townshend proposed to get around this objection by levying revenue taxes in the form of duties on external commerce. The income from these duties, as well as from the duty on molasses, which after its reduction to one pence a gallon in 1766 had become productive, was to be applied to the general support of the British administration of the colonies. The passage of the Townshend Act so soon after the repeal of the Stamp Act disclosed that the British government was determined to free its officers in the colonies from dependence on legislative money grants.

A repressive tendency was also exhibited by the suspension of the New York legislature. In 1765 Parliament had passed the Quartering Act—another device to compel the colonists to support British troops. Besides requiring colonial governments to provide barracks or other quarters, it stipulated that they must supply the troops with certain articles and provisions. Not a single colony complied fully with the act, but from the British standpoint the chief offender was New York. Because routes to Canada and the northwest ran through its territory, the province harbored a large number of troops. When the assembly refused to provide more than part of the supplies required by the law, Parliament suspended further sessions of the legislature until the Quartering Act was observed in full. The assembly continued to meet and pass laws, thus in part nullifying the effect of the suspension; nevertheless, it was apparent to colonists in New York and elsewhere that Parliament would recognize no limits to its authority and was capable of sweeping aside the cherished rights of Americans with a single stroke.

Equally menacing in its implications was the elaborate machinery set up to enforce the Navigation Acts. In 1767 Britain reorganized the American customs service, placing it under a resident board of commissioners at Boston. The number of customs officials was increased, accounting procedures were improved, and Vice-Admiralty courts set up to try cases at Halifax, Boston, Philadelphia, and Charleston. Writs of assistance—i.e. blank search warrants which could be filled in with the names of any suspects—were authorized and customs officers exempted from suit for illegal seizure. Additional requirements were added to the multiplicity of licenses, bonds, writs, and penalties already imposed upon American merchants, who were increasingly exposed to extortion by customs officers. The new regulations were an impediment even to legal trade, but in the British view they were successful; for the first time the customs service in the colonies produced a revenue above the cost of collection.

It was by this time apparent that British troops in America were not being deployed along the frontier, but near the settled areas. This fact was consistent with suspicions which the Americans had always entertained that the troops were intended to suppress the people rather than fight the Indians. In 1768 troops were stationed in Boston. When Massachusetts held a special convention to protest, its action was interpreted by Parliament as a move toward independence. Some of the king's ministers urged him to try to find evidence of treason and deport Massachusetts leaders to England for trial.

Americans, thoroughly alarmed by the Townshend Acts, which were undisguised revenue measures, were almost as dismayed by the suspension of the New York legislature. Patriots were more divided, however, than in 1765. Merchants, now enjoying a period of prosperity, had no wish to damage business by a resumption of nonimportation. Remembering the mob violence of the Stamp Act crisis, they and other substantial citizens were apprehensive of resorting to extralegal measures which would revive it. But years of blundering British statesmanship created a hard core of animosity in the American people which no mere rational consideration could dissolve. A new generation of political leaders had risen, who based their careers upon exploiting and manipulating popular hostility to Britain in opposition to older leaders whose political fortunes were tied to cooperation with the mother country. Moreover, in the fight against the Stamp Act, an embryonic intercolonial organization had sprung up consisting of legislative and city committees of correspondence, now easily reanimated, and radical Sons of Liberty organizations established in coastal cities and towns. With the examples of previous struggles and British retreats before them, Americans were more practiced in resistance. British attitudes had also stiffened. Both the ministry and Parliament showed more disposition to use force and to regard the dispute with the colonies as a test of British sovereignty.

No intercolonial congress was held but, in spite of the growing disposition among conservative leaders to avoid provocative acts, the colonies in the end stood together. When the Massachusetts legislature addressed a circular letter to the other colonies, stating the familiar objections to taxation without representation and inviting them to send petitions to the king, Parliament formally censured the colony, and the British minister in charge of colonial affairs demanded that the other colonies repudiate its action. Spurning these appeals, one assembly after another, either in regular session or in unofficial meetings held after they were dissolved by the governor, endorsed Massachusetts' position. Virginia adopted a circular letter of its own, proposing a united stand of the colonies against "measures which they think have an immediate tendency to enslave them."

Meanwhile, the popular party, the Sons of Liberty, and, in some cities, the mob worked to revive the nonimportation agreements which provided such agreeable scope for extralegal action and had proved so effective against the Stamp Act. Although opposed by most merchants, nonimportation agreements spread from New England to the middle colonies and as far as South Carolina, gradually closing ports to British importations, which in one year dropped from £2,500,000 to £1,635,000.

Although British merchants were not now champions of the American cause, the resistance gave the ministry the opportunity to realize that the new duties were a mistake even in terms of Britain's own interest, for they operated, especially in conjunction with nonimportation, like a protective tariff to foster the growth of colonial manufactures and reduce dependence on British imports. The duties were repealed in April 1770, except for the short-sighted and provocative retention of the tax on tea, which was kept on in order to sustain the principle that Parliament could tax the colonies. The more ardent American patriots tried to keep nonimportation going until even that duty was repealed, but popular support waned, and the resistance collapsed.

British Troops and the Boston Massacre

Violence in word and deed were nevertheless making enemies of the colonies and mother country. Amidst all the controversies, Britain's single most provocative act was probably the stationing of troops in the colonies, particularly near centers of population where they served as a constant warning of Britain's willingness to crush resistance by force. Americans, moreover, had inherited a long anti-military tradition, in which professional soldiers were the veritable symbol of royal despotism.

In New York, headquarters of the British army in America, the presence of a British garrison generated constant tension and conflict between soldiers and the Sons of Liberty. At one point the Sons of Liberty undertook a campaign to close all shops and homes in the city to soldiers, trying thereby to force them out. The focus of confrontation, however, was a liberty pole erected at the time of the Stamp Act; the soldiers twice tore it down and the Sons of Liberty rebuilt it. In January 1770 the soldiers destroyed a third liberty pole, cut it up, and deposited the pieces at the entrance to a nearby tavern frequented by the liberty boys. The next day more than 3,000 people gathered to denounce this provocation and pass resolutions that nobody should employ soldiers as workers and that they should be confined to barracks in the evening. The soldiers refused to submit to these restrictions, and a series of incidents ensued, culminating in bayonet attacks by soldiers upon civilians in which several people were wounded and one killed. Civilian mobs retaliated, chasing the soldiers to their barracks. To put an end to the situation, General Gage ordered troops confined to barracks when off duty (although they were still permitted to work out). The Sons of Liberty proclaimed a victory and built a new, mammoth liberty pole which was still standing when British troops occupied the city during the Revolution.

A more momentous battle occurred between troops and townspeople in Boston. In 1768 the British ministry had stationed troops in the city for the avowed purpose of controlling the people. Before the arrival of the troops, there was wild talk of armed resistance. This was given up but, although the troops were sufficient to infuriate the people, they were not numerous enough to maintain order. The people were incensed by the arrogance of British officers and the thieveries and rapes committed by soldiers. They assaulted "Bloody Backs" and "Lobsters" with sticks and pelted them with stones. Soldiers beat up townspeople, clubbing them with their muskets. On one occasion a customs officer fired into a threatening crowd, killing a 12-year-old boy. Encounters were instigated by reckless patriots, who welcomed incidents that would deepen public antagonism toward Britain. Boston was a powder keg. On Beacon Hill a tar barrel was planted, whose firing was to summon the countryside to the city's aid in event of a general engagement. Many of the inhabitants looked forward to "fighting it out" with the troops.

Affairs reached a climax on the night of March 5, 1770, when fights broke out all over the city between townsmen and soldiers. Mobs roamed about, and the ringing of church bells brought more people into the streets. One mob gathered before the customs house, threatening the life of a sentry who had previously struck a young apprentice with his musket during an argument. As the mob increased to 300 or 400 people, the sentry was joined by a troop of eight soldiers sent to his rescue. The mob, however, would not let the soldiers escape to the guardhouse. Counting on the fact that the soldiers were under orders not to fire their muskets, the mob hurled stones and chunks of ice and pressed in against their bayonets, daring them to fire. Finally, one of the soldiers, knocked to the ground by a thrown club, rose to his feet and fired his musket. In the confused skirmishing that followed, the other soldiers fired into the crowd and stabbed with their bayonets against their assailants, who struck back with clubs and threw stones. As the mob scattered, it left three men dead on the spot; two others later died of their wounds. Running from the scene, people shouted "Townborn turn out!" Drums began to beat, summoning the militia, and a vast armed mob gathered to avenge itself upon the troops in the city. For hours there was danger of a bloodbath, which was averted only by the promise of the governor, delivered to an enormous crowd, that the soldiers who had fired the shots would be brought to trial and punished.

The aftermath of the Boston Massacre was discreditable to the patriot cause, as testimony taken at the trials of the soldiers revealed the complicity of patriot leaders in precipitating violent incidents. Whatever their sympathies, moreover, many Americans were shocked at the serious turn of affairs and inclined to look askance thereafter at intransigent statements of American rights. Indeed, an interlude of relative calm followed the repeal of the Townshend Acts. The ministry gave up for the time its effort to tax the colonies, preferring "to let all contention subside, and by degrees suffer matters to return to their old channels." Responsible American leaders tried to keep the peace. Years of controversy had left a residue of easily awakened hostility toward Britain but had also crystallized the differences between popular leaders, who expressed and cultivated that hostility, and conservatives who wanted to avoid an open break.

Tea Party and the Intolerable Acts

Despite hopes for peace, the controversy was renewed in 1773 by the passage of the Tea Act, a measure only distantly related to previous disputes. It was designed to aid the East India Company by exempting it from the provisions of the Navigation Acts requiring tea bound from India to the colonies to be landed first in Britain and sold there at public auction. The company was now allowed to ship directly to America and to sell through its own agents. In sponsoring the act, the ministry had no thought of giving offense, but the colonists perceived another violation of their rights. American merchants regarded the act as creating a monopoly and as a precursor of other acts which would confer special privileges upon individuals. Popular leaders saw in it a veiled attempt to induce Americans to drink dutied tea and thereby acquiesce in parliamentary taxation; even with the duty paid, the East India Company tea would now be cheaper than the smuggled Dutch article widely consumed in the colonies. The fact that the company chose for its agents men who in the past had been apologists for British policies added political implications to the situation. In truth, the quarrel with Britain had gone on so long that the colonists were quick to perceive grievances and to resist.

Well-tested modes of opposition were revived. In Philadelphia tea shipments were returned to England; in Charleston they were stored in a warehouse. As usual, however, the provocative incident occurred in Boston. When three tea ships entered the harbor, the inhabitants of Boston and nearby towns held a mass meeting, demanding that Governor Thomas Hutchinson issue clearance papers to permit the ships to return to Britain without landing the tea and paying duties. Hutchinson refused because the procedure was unlawful. When 20 days had elapsed—the time during which a ship could remain in the harbor without paying duties—a second mass meeting requested his final answer. When the meeting was informed of his refusal, Sam Adams, who was acting as moderator, gave a signal. A party of "Mohawks," citizens attired as Indians and with blackened faces, walked down to the dock, and, while a large crowd watched, dumped £10,000 worth of tea into the harbor.

The Boston Tea Party invited retaliation from the British government, which had long regarded the town as a nest of rebellion. Successive encounters with colonial disobedience had thinned the ranks of American sympathizers in Britain. There were few men in the ministry or in Parliament who did not now believe that the time had come to enforce British authority. On the assumption that only Massachusetts had to be dealt with and that the province could be isolated and punished as an example to the others, Parliament passed the Coercive Acts, known in the colonies as the "Intolerable Acts." One of these changed the form of government in the colony. The upper house of the legislature was made appointive, as in other royal colonies, rather than elective. Henceforth, all justices of the peace were to hold office only at the pleasure of the British governor. Except for routine elections, town meetings could not take place without his permission. Public officials accused of murder in the prosecution of their duty could be removed to other colonies or to Britain for trial. Military commanders were authorized to requisition houses and other buildings for the use of troops. Boston harbor was closed to seaborne commerce, except for imports of food and fuel, until the tea was paid for. The inhabitants were thereby cut off from their means of livelihood. Finally, although not one of the Coercive Acts, the Quebec Act, which was passed at this time, was considered by New Englanders as evidence of Britain's ulterior purposes. In its adjustment of relations between Britain and the newly conquered French province, the Quebec Act was an enlightened piece of legislation, but the colonies regarded it as a threat to themselves that Britain set up a government without an elected representative body, established in effect the Catholic church, and extended the boundaries of the province to include all the territory north of the Ohio River and westward to the Mississippi.

Boston merchants wanted to pay for the tea, but were overruled by the inhabitants, who chose to meet British repression head on. Attempting to involve other colonies in its cause, the patriot organization sent out appeals for aid and requested a boycott of British goods. Throughout America popular opinion rallied behind the beleaguered colony. Many conservatives, fearful of reopening the disputes, would gladly have left Boston to its fate, but they did not dare admit such sentiments. When it was proposed at town meetings held at New York and Philadelphia to call an intercolonial congress, they supported the idea, trusting that a high level meeting would be controlled by moderates. Popular leaders also agreed to a congress, hoping to widen the resistance, rescue Boston, and present a united front to Britain.

The First Continental Congress

When the First Continental Congress met in Philadelphia on September 5, 1774, it was at once evident that the delegates were not of one mind. Conservatives such as Joseph Galloway of Pennsylvania wanted to pursue American aims by legal methods and to find a basis for reconciliation. At the other end of the political spectrum were popular leaders such as John and Sam Adams of Massachusetts and Richard Henry Lee of Virginia, who were determined to assert American rights without compromise, rally the people, and resist by force if necessary. In the jaundiced view of Galloway, they already aimed at independence:

> One [party] intended candidly and clearly to define American rights and explicitly and dutifully to petition for the remedy which would redress the grievances justly complained of—to form a more solid and constitutional union between the two countries, and to avoid every measure which tended to sedition, or acts of violent opposition. The other consisted of persons whose design, from the beginning of the opposition to the Stamp Act was to throw off all subordination and connection with Great Britain; who meant by every fiction, falsehood, and fraud to delude the people from their due allegiance, to throw the subsisting governments into anarchy, to incite the ignorant and vulgar to arms, and with those arms to establish American independence.

Galloway, who shortly became a loyalist, was exaggerating when he imputed to popular leaders a conscious desire for independence, but he correctly sensed their determination to settle the dispute only on America's terms and to throw off sub-ordination to Parliament. Nine years earlier, at the time of the Stamp Act, no American leader had denied Parliament's right to legislate for the colonies except in the matter of taxation. But years of contention had forced Americans to reflect more deeply upon their constitutional relation with Britain, and by 1774 such colonial spokesmen as John Adams, James Wilson, and Thomas Jefferson argued that Parliament had no right to legislate for the colonies at all. In their view, each of the colonial legislatures was equal to Parliament, with similar powers to legislate for its own people, and the colonies were bound to the empire only by their subordination to the crown. England, that is, was subject to Parliament, but the colonies were outside the "realm" of England, and were part of the king's "dominions," over which Parliament had no authority. Benjamin Franklin wrote: "The sovereignty of the Crown I understand; the sovereignty of Britain I do not understand . . . We have the same King, but not the same legislature."

In a supreme effort to settle the dispute on a constitutional basis, Galloway advanced a plan for colonial union. It provided for a central government consisting of a council of delegates elected from each province, presided over by a governor-general appointed by the crown. It was to have power to levy taxes and legislate in such general matters as defense, Indian affairs, and western lands. Its acts were to be subject to veto by Parliament, and it in turn would have a veto over parliamentary acts concerning America. Although Galloway's plan had its drawbacks, it resembled schemes for colonial union previously advanced by Britain and afforded a basis upon which to negotiate a permanent settlement of the Anglo-American controversy. For these very reasons, however, it was unacceptable to the popular leaders. It entailed closer ties with Britain, recognition of Parliament's right to legislate for the colonies, and a curtailment of the powers and independence of the provincial governments. It was precisely what the Lees and the Adamses were determined to prevent.

Victory in the end lay with the popular party, mainly because it had the support of the common people. The turning point was the introduction of resolutions adopted by a town meeting in Suffolk County, Massachusetts, and carried to Philadelphia by Paul Revere, dispatch rider for the patriot organization. Taking high ground, the Suffolk Resolves declared that the Coercive Acts should not be obeyed and strongly implied that they would be resisted by force. A further declaration was that all trade with Britain should be suspended. The introduction of the Suffolk Resolves placed the issue squarely before Congress either to endorse the radical enthusiasm of the people or, by refusing, show a readiness to yield to British pressure. Congress adopted the Resolves and thereby committed itself to the popular program, the chief feature of which was the Association—a nonimportation, nonexportation agreement with teeth in it. Citizens were obliged to sign a declaration neither to import British goods nor to consume goods on which duties had been paid. Those who refused to abide by the agreement were to be exposed as enemies to their country and ostracized by all patriots. Soon after adopting the Association, Congress took another bold step by sanctioning resistance to the Coercive Acts by force and by pledging the support of all the colonies to the people of Massachusetts. Galloway's plan of union was quietly dropped, and all reference to it erased from Congress's journal. Thus the first Congress disdained compromise and refused any solution except on America's terms.

No prominent leader yet spoke openly of independence, but the Declaration of Rights which Congress passed in October 1774 took a position so radical as to make a settlement of the dispute nearly impossible under British conceptions of empire. On the basis of natural as well as constitutional rights, it denied the authority of Parliament to legislate for the colonies, asserting the right of Americans to rule themselves, subject only to the negative of the king. Out of regard for the mutual interest of both countries, the Congress expressed its willingness to accept parliamentary regulation of the colonies' external trade. However, the Declaration set forth a list of acts and measures, including the Coercive Acts, to which Americans refused to submit and whose repeal was the condition of any reconciliation. It concluded with an implicit warning that if peaceful resistance did not get results, the colonies would take up arms.

War and the Overturn of Government

By sanctioning the use of force, Congress gave a spur to violence, and it was soon forthcoming. On the night of April 18, 1775, a force of British regulars moved out of Boston, which had become a garrison town. Its object was to destroy patriot military stores at Concord, about 20 miles distant. On the way, the troops exchanged what proved to be the opening shots of the Revolution with a body of militia gathered in the village of Lexington. The Americans fled, leaving a few dead behind, but before the regulars covered the remaining miles to Concord, the first detachments of "minute-men," newly formed companies of alerted militia, began to arrive along the British line of march and to fire upon the troops from behind cover. The British destroyed what stores they found at Concord, but, as they started back toward Boston, militia companies converging from nearby towns thickened along the road. The British troops retaliated with frequent sallies, bayoneting any man they could catch. Fighting was savage, with heavy casualties on both sides; as the day wore on the tired regulars were in danger of being overwhelmed. The arrival of reinforcements from Boston probably saved them from capture. Lord Percy, leader of the relieving force, wrote: "whoever looks upon them as an irregular mob will find himself much mistaken . . . Nor are several of their men without enthusiasm . . . for many of them concealed themselves in houses, and advanced within ten yards to fire at me and other officers, although they were morally certain of being put to death in an instant."

This prolonged skirmish was followed by the battle of Bunker Hill. After the encounter at Lexington and Concord, patriot forces gathered in great numbers in the hills about Boston, penning the British forces in the city. On the night of June 16, an American detachment of 1,600 men invested the heights above

Charleston, a hamlet located on a peninsula across the harbor from Boston. The British reacted instantly but, disdaining tactical maneuver, the commander, General William Howe, in what has been described as "an armed expression of contempt for the opposing militia," landed a force on the beach and attempted to carry the heights by frontal assault. Twice the British were repulsed by aimed fire, but on the third attempt they took the hill, driving the colonists in headlong retreat off the peninsula to the cover of their own lines. Colonial losses were 100 dead, 267 wounded, and 30 taken prisoner. The British suffered 1,054 casualties, a high proportion of them officers. It is estimated that one-eighth of all British officers killed in America during the Revolution fell at Bunker Hill. The battle raised patriot morale, for it proved that the raw colonial militia could fight British regulars.

War spirit flamed through the colonies. During the preceding months the patriots had been making military preparations. In October 1774 Massachusetts formed her companies of "minutemen." In Virginia Patrick Henry predicted the outbreak of war and urged Virginia to prepare. "The first gale that sweeps from the north will bring to our ears the clash of resounding arms," he reputedly said in a speech to the legislature in March 1775. The choice was now between war and slavery, and he had made his decision: "Give me liberty or give me death!" The Virginia convention thereupon appointed a committee to procure arms. Everywhere, patriots collected weapons and ammunition, laid up stockpiles, and drilled the militia. As news of Lexington and Concord spread, excitement rose. A mob broke into the arsenal in New York City and handed out weapons to the people. Volunteer companies from other colonies marched to the siege of Boston. Waverers were silenced, and American leaders who still hoped for reconciliation were forced by popular opinion to support military action. Never again during the Revolution was enthusiasm so high as in 1775 and 1776. An observer in Boston wrote to an English correspondent: "they are all determined to die or to be free. It is not the low idle fellows that fight only for pay but men of great property are common soldiers who say they are fighting for themselves and posterity." In a spirited "Declaration of the Causes and Necessity of Taking Up Arms" issued on July 6, 1775, the Second Continental Congress avowed its determination:

> We have counted the cost of this contest and find nothing so dreadful as voluntary slavery. . . . Our cause is just. Our union is perfect. Our internal resources are great, and, if necessary, foreign assistance is undoubtedly attainable. . . . We most solemnly, before God and the world declare, that . . . we will in defiance of every hazard with unabating firmness and perseverance, employ . . . [our arms] for the preservation of our liberties, being with one mind resolved to die free men rather than live slaves.

The outbreak of war brought about the dissolution of legal governments and the transfer of power to patriot organizations. As the existing colonial legislatures responded to Massachusetts' appeal for aid, endorsed the resolutions of Congress, or undertook military preparations, British governors dissolved them. The void was filled at the local level by a network of committees formed to enforce the Association. The active patriots elected delegates to extra-legal provincial congresses which passed laws, voted money for supplies, took command of the militia, suppressed loyalists, and appointed committees of safety to direct military operations. These bodies were effective agencies of government. In some provinces they had the support of the overwhelming majority of the people. In areas where loyalists were numerous or many people were indifferent, they held the dissidents in check by sheer force and energy. Thus government passed into patriot hands, and the drift toward revolution was accelerated. The same tendency was inherent in the actions of Congress once war began. In coping with practical circumstances —designating the forces at Boston as a "Continental" army, appointing Washington to command, requesting troops from other colonies, issuing paper money, suppressing loyalists, and negotiating with the British military command—Congress step by step assumed the functions of government.

The Failure of British Policy

In the course of a decade of contention the constitutional ideas of Americans had been constantly tested. By 1774, as we have seen, they had advanced to a demand for equality with Parliament under the crown. This idea, which anticipated the development of the British empire in the next century, was not one which many Englishmen were able to grasp in 1776. Aristocratic Whigs would admit no abatement of parliamentary sovereignty over the empire. A few Dissenters boldly championed America's cause even after the outbreak of war, but most of America's former "friends" thought the issue was now simply whether the colonists would submit to British authority. Neither British merchants nor the ministry was much concerned about the Continental Association, for it had little effect upon the British economy. Although British exports to the colonies dropped to virtually nothing in 1775, they increased by more than a million pounds over the same period to the Mediterranean and the East Indies. Except for a handful of Dissenters and radical Whigs, public opinion was solidly against the colonies. The historian Edward Gibbon wrote to a friend in 1774 that if the Angel Gabriel spoke in behalf of America he would not be heard.

Backed by a solid phalanx in Parliament, the North ministry was determined to bring the colonies to their knees. A feeble gesture toward compromise was thrown out in 1775 when Parliament adopted Lord North's motion for conciliation. Any colony that would guarantee financial support of the British military and civil establishment was assured that no parliamentary taxes would be collected within its borders. This proposal was unacceptable, even to American conservatives, but any effect it might have had was destroyed by a succession of British acts based on the premise that the issues were to be resolved not by compromise but by force. In August 1775 the king declared the colonies to be in a state of rebellion. In a speech to Parliament in October he accused them of taking up arms to gain their independence. Parliament passed the American Prohibitory Act which declared Americans to be outlaws and subjected their vessels to capture by British cruisers "as if the same were the ships and effects of open enemies." Finally, in January 1776, Britain contracted with the rulers of Hesse-Cassel and Brunswick for the services of 18,000 German troops. They were originally destined for Ireland to replace British troops which were to be sent to the colonies. However, when the Irish protested, the Germans were dispatched to America. These mercenaries had a reputation for brutality, and when news arrived that Britain was so ruthless in her intentions as to unleash them on the people of the colonies, the break with the mother country became all but irreparable. The prospect of the colonies' rejoining the empire voluntarily receded, and the issue became total defeat or independence.

Independence Declared

As the Second Continental Congress met in May 1775, many of the questions that had come before the first Congress had been settled by the outbreak of war. The major question now was whether the colonies should strike for independence. A significant step was taken in that direction when Congress, in reply to British outlawry of American commerce, opened American ports to vessels of foreign nations, thereby repudiating the Navigation Acts. By January 1776, a declaration of independence was openly discussed. It could be recommended as the means of sweeping away false notions that were obstructing the war effort. Popular leaders such as John and Sam Adams thought it perfectly clear that the old relationship with the mother country could never be restored. They wanted to dispel illusory hopes of reconciliation in order to concentrate the whole force of the country on the struggle that lay ahead. A declaration of independence held out the practical advantages of allowing the colonies to obtain recognition of their belligerent status by foreign nations, of being able to proceed legally against loyalists, and of claiming for captured Americans the usual rights of prisoners of war rather than the summary punishment or execution customarily meted out to rebels. Most important, however, it promised to bring France into the war. Congress had been unofficially informed by agents of the French government that, if independence was the goal, France would render aid. Although France was the traditional foe of the colonies as well as of Britain, Americans were in no position to refuse assistance from any quarter.

The idea of taking such an irrevocable step caused people to examine their deepest convictions. Among all classes of the population there were many who still had a residual loyalty to the mother country, reinforced by tradition and cultural values, identification with British official society in the colonies, economic ties with the empire, or simple fear that the rebellion would fail, that heads would roll, and that property would be confiscated. In the middle colonies many conservatives were afraid that a separation from Britain would lead to political upheaval and civil war within America. Without the protection offered by the British connection, the Quaker, mercantile oligarchy that dominated Pennsylvania feared aggression from the Scotch-Irish, Presbyterian backcountry. "I see, and I see with fear and trembling," wrote the conservative Gouverneur Morris of New York, "that if the disputes with Great Britain continue, we shall be under the worst of all possible dominions; we shall be under the domination of a riotous mob. It is to the interest of all men, therefore, to seek for reunion with the parent state." Moved by these and other considerations, the legislatures of New York, Pennsylvania, Maryland, Delaware, and South Carolina instructed their delegates in 1775 to vote against any motion for independence brought up in Congress.

Nevertheless, the pressures behind independence continued to grow. In January 1776, Thomas Paine published *Common Sense,* one of the most effective political pamphlets of all time. To those who said America could not win he replied that she could not lose if the effort was made. Deprecating ties of sentiment and tradition, he described British government and society as corrupted by Old World evils from which America now had a chance to shake free. He held up the vision of creating for the first time in history a society based upon rational principles of justice and freedom. Against Quakers and other conservatives who feared democracy, he argued that men were naturally moral and that property was safe in the hands of the people. Paine's pamphlet was read everywhere in the country. It converted many to the desire for independence.

Led by North Carolina's action on April 12, 1776, one colony after another instructed its delegates in Congress to sponsor a declaration of independence. Popular leaders in Congress grew increasingly impatient with conservatives, now led by John Dickinson of Pennsylvania, who still spoke of reconciliation. On May 15, after messages arrived from North Carolina and Virginia instructing their delegates to propose independence, Congress adopted a critical resolution: all colonies whose governments were not "sufficient to the exigencies of their affairs" should form new governments deriving their authority from the people. This was an open invitation, particularly to the people of Pennsylvania, to overthrow governments holding out against independence. On June 7 Richard Henry Lee of Virginia was given the honor of moving that "these United Colonies, are, and of right ought to be, free and independent states." John Adams seconded the motion. Fighting a defensive battle, conservatives managed to defer consideration of independence until July 1, although Congress, in anticipation of an affirmative decision, appointed a committee headed by Thomas Jefferson to draft a declaration.

Opponents of the measure argued that, although the colonies could probably never be reunited with England, a declaration of independence was premature. The middle colonies were "not yet ripe for bidding adieu to the British connexion." Hasty action would throw them into civil war, or else they would withdraw their support from Congress. It would be better to form some plan for a central government first. This would allow time for the middle colonies to come around to the idea of independence. To declare independence before the country had actually formed a union, contracted foreign alliances, and prepared itself to fight would merely expose it to ridicule and accomplish nothing but a show of spirit.

The advocates of independence knew that they could not act

unless the colonies were united. But they argued that even in the dissenting colonies the people, if not their delegates to Congress, were enthusiastic for independence. Further delay would be suicidal. Unless independence was formally declared, foreign powers would not give aid. A declaration should have been made months before and foreign alliances contracted. In any case, the colonies were already independent; a declaration would only announce an established fact.

During the interval before July 1, when the question was taken up again, the delegates of New York, Maryland, and Pennsylvania wrote to their legislatures asking for instructions. The replies were still equivocal. In Pennsylvania, however, the situation was changed by the overthrow of the old colonial government. The popular party elected a provincial convention which seized power, began drafting a new constitution, and issued instructions to Pennsylvania's delegates to Congress permitting them to vote for independence. Delaware and New Jersey revised their instructions. Finally, just as Congress was preparing to debate the issue, a special messenger arrived with a resolution of the Maryland convention instructing for independence. Virginia, meanwhile, had declared independence without waiting for Congress.

On July 1 Congress was still not unanimous. Many of the delegates were not positively instructed by their legislatures and were therefore free to follow their own judgment. Pennsylvania and South Carolina voted in the negative, Delaware was divided, and the New York delegates withheld their vote. On July 2, however, South Carolina shifted to the affirmative for the sake of unanimity. Caesar Rodney, a newly elected delegate from Delaware, arrived after riding all night to swing the vote of that province. By not voting, John Dickinson and Robert Morris gave independence a majority of the Pennsylvania delegation. New York's delegates still refrained from voting on the ground that they had not yet received specific instructions from their legislature. Nevertheless, the decision for independence was carried without a formal negative and could therefore be proclaimed as unanimous. The Declaration of Independence in its final form was agreed to on July 4. The copyist had it ready in early August, when it was signed by delegates then attending Congress.

The Declaration of Independence, drafted in its final form by Thomas Jefferson, spelled out the conception which most Americans had of their revolution as an incident of the eternal struggle to preserve liberty against the tyranny of government, a struggle going back to the barons of Magna Charta, and to the defense of English rights against the Stuarts in the century in which America was founded. Once again, as Jefferson later expressed it, the tree of liberty had to be watered by the blood of patriots and tyrants, this time by Americans. Reciting a long train of "abuses and usurpations" which, as the colonists had come to believe, disclosed a deliberate conspiracy on the part of George III and his corrupt ministers to "reduce them under absolute Despotism," the Declaration asserted that it was not only the right but the duty of Americans to throw off allegiance to such a government. In his invocation of natural rights philosophy, however, Jefferson went beyond the legalisms of the English political tradition to utter principles that became the official creed of the United States and, in later times, the inspiration of successive generations of humanistic reformers. "We hold these truths to be self-evident, that all men are created equal, that they are endowed by their Creator with certain inalienable Rights, that among these are Life, Liberty, and the pursuit of Happiness." This phrase scarcely mirrored existing reality, but it committed the new nation to the highest political ideals of the age.

CHAPTER VI

War and Diplomacy

The War on Land: Strategy of Survival

The war of American Independence bears some resemblance to wars of colonial liberation of the 20th century in the fact that the people were active partisans in a struggle against a foreign power. Probably the decisive factor in the entire war was patriot control of the militia, the standing military organization of the colonies. Control of the militia, gained before the fighting started, enabled the patriots to suppress the loyalists, intimidate the lukewarm, and draw forth the resources of the nation on their side. Wherever the enemy was not actually present the militia dominated the country. The British were never able to overcome this advantage.

A Continental army came into existence in the summer of 1775 as Congress assumed responsibility for supporting local forces engaging the British in New England and New York. In response to urgent appeals from Massachusetts, Congress authorized the recruitment into "the American continental army" of six companies of riflemen in Pennsylvania, Maryland, and Virginia, which were to join the forces besieging the British at Boston. The next day George Washington was appointed commander, and during the next two weeks Congress proceeded to create a military organization, appointing the higher field officers and a staff to take charge of commissary, quartermaster, payroll, and hospital functions of an army of 20,000 men. Two million dollars of paper money was issued; part of it was sent up to General Washington at Boston and to General Philip Schuyler, who had been put in command of American forces in New York. In these early days, while Congress was creating a military establishment, there was no clear distinction between the Continental army and forces raised by provincial governments. On June 26 Congress declared that it would consider any body of troops of up to 1,000 men raised by provincial governments as an "American army" and provide for its pay.

This casual procedure soon gave way to a more highly organized system which was followed for the duration of the war. Congress called upon each state to enlist its quota of men for the Continental army. The recruits served in separate units under their own officers up to the rank of colonel. Congress appointed the general officers. The Continental army, consisting of various state *lines* plus certain specialized corps not attached to any state, was the basic military force, reinforced as events required by state militia. As the war moved into different states, Congress requested the governors to call out the local militia to fight with the Continental army. When the fighting shifted to another area, the militia was sent home. The states also maintained forces for local defense.

American attitudes toward war profoundly affected the nature of military operations. Imbued with strong antimilitary traditions, the people were hostile to anything that savored of military professionalism. With European examples in mind, they considered professional soldiers as the dregs of society and their officers as arrogant scions of nobility. They cherished the idea of an amateur army, such as their own militia, which could be drawn from the people and at war's end returned to the people without becoming a menace to public liberty. A man fighting for his home and in a just cause they thought more than a match for any mercenary who fought for pay or plunder. Hence, they took care to avoid anything to propagate military traditions or the growth of a military class. One consequence of this was a general dislike of long-term enlistments which might keep a man so long in the army as to turn him into a professional soldier. State governments were extremely reluctant to draft men for military service, preferring short-term enlistments, for 9 or 12 months, solicited by the offer of a bounty. The Continental army therefore consisted largely of amateur soldiers. Discipline was lax, and in any case hard to impose upon men who often had little reverence for superior rank. Soldiers and officers were frequently of the same social class, and in New England the recruits usually elected their own officers.

Whether in the long run this militia concept of war served the Americans ill or well is a debatable question, but it slowed the development of trained forces able to stand up to British regulars in pitched battle. Americans were accustomed to the use of arms, and they fought bravely, but Continental troops, to say nothing of unseasoned militia, seldom had the fortitude to sustain a British bayonet charge. Officers, like the men under them, were for the most part amateurs, without experience in commanding large bodies of troops. Gradually the Continental army acquired a hard core of veterans and discipline improved. Washington survived his early mistakes and gained experience. Such officers as Nathanael Greene, Benedict Arnold, Daniel Morgan, and Anthony Wayne became good combat generals. Through most of the war, however, the basic inferiority of the American forces precluded seeking battle on anything like equal terms. American commanders pursued a Fabian strategy of harassing the enemy and trying to exploit his errors. General Washington thoroughly understood that the war could be lost in a single battle but that as long as his army was intact the British could not win. Washington's aide, Alexander Hamilton, articulated the strategy: "Our hopes are not placed in any particular city, or spot of ground, but in preserving a good army, furnished with proper necessaries, to take advantage of favorable opportunities, and waste and defeat the enemy by piecemeal."

For Britain it was the wrong kind of war, fought under conditions that did not allow its army to realize the elements of superiority it possessed over the Americans. British troops were unaccustomed to wilderness encounters, in which combat plans foundered in rough terrain and action took place in dense forests where one could see only a short distance. The difficulties were compounded by evasive American tactics, the avoidance of pitched battle. "The manner of opposing an army that avoids facing you in the open field," wrote Lord George Germain, "is totally different from what young officers learn from the common discipline of the army." British strategy was to force Americans into battle on open terrain and on roughly equal terms; it rarely succeeded. The British also lacked mobility. Troop movements were slowed by heavy artillery, baggage and supply trains, and by a numerous crowd of camp followers. The individual grenadier marched with a 60-pound pack on his back, besides carrying his heavy musket. At the level of general strategy, too, the British command has been charged with committing blunders. The war office in London never laid out an overall plan for the war in America and resolutely followed it up by putting available military resources into its execution. Troops were spread out in occupation of territory rather than concentrated against the main American armies. Although before France entered the war, naval superiority allowed the British to strike swiftly at any point along an enormous coast, they seldom found ways of exploiting their advantage.

Whatever may be attributed to error, Britain's chief problem, however, was space. Cut off from free access to the countryside, the army had to get nearly all of its provisions from Britain or Ireland and fight at the end of a supply line 3,000 miles long. Everything transported was exposed to accident, delay, and spoilage. In an age of sailing ships and uncertain conveyance either by land or by sea, the mere organizing of transport for these supplies was an almost insuperable problem. When fighting moved into the interior of America, the supply lines grew even longer and more vulnerable to attack, and although the British forces could march almost at will, they were "tethered by their supply lines to the coast." The vast space of the country, on the other hand, was America's ally, giving its armies endless room to retreat. Moreover, the country had no nerve center, no citadel, whose capture would end the war. The British could prevail at any point, but they could not control the countryside beyond their own lines. The Americans were able to overcome disaster and rise to fight again, whereas the British, fighting in hostile territory, lost an army when they suffered a major defeat. As long as the Americans kept their forces in being and the people supported them, as long in fact as they retained a will to resist, the British could hardly achieve a military decision.

The British cause also suffered from an ambivalence of purpose. Although public opinion in Britain rallied behind the war effort, many Englishmen thought and continued to say publicly that it was hopeless to attempt to recover the colonies by force. As Britain's traditional enemies, France and Spain, joined the conflict, the idea grew that the war against the revolted colonies was the wrong war. The ministry could not persuade Parliament to commit powerful military forces to America. The ambivalence of the home government extended to commanders in the field. General William Howe, the first commander-in-chief, who had many chances to capture Washington's army, was distracted by the fact that he had come to America under instructions to negotiate peace. He, as well as some other British generals, realized that if the rebellion were put down they would still have to live with the colonials and come to terms with them. Moreover, British officers were at first contemptuous of American soldiers, regarding them as "a set of upstart vagabonds, the dregs and scorn of the human species." Benjamin Franklin quoted a British general as saying in 1774 that with a thousand grenadiers he would march from one end of America to the other "and geld all the Males, partly by force and partly by a little Coaxing." Such bluster came easily to the British because they thought the rebellion would be quickly put down by a show of force; indeed, loyalists represented the patriots as an extremist minority and most of the people as faithful to the mother country. British commanders fought, therefore, with insufficient energy and failed to follow up their early victories by butchering the American survivors; they eschewed the use of terror which their military superiority gave them. When the British captured Fort

Washington in 1776 and loyalists urged General Howe to turn the 3,000-man garrison over to the Hessians to be massacred, Howe refused. Some British officers advocated a harsher policy; one military captain argued in 1775 that "the good people of England" should "lay aside that false humanity toward those wretches which has hitherto been so destructive to us . . . they must permit us to restore to them the dominion of the country by laying it waste, and almost extirpating the present rebellious race. . . ." King George himself said there was "more cruelty in protracting the War than in taking such Acts of vigour which must bring the crisis to the shortest decision." Nevertheless, British policy continued to fall between conquest and reconciliation.

The War at Sea: Privateers and Ships of the Line

Although in disrepair at the outset of the war, the British navy was overwhelmingly superior to any force the Americans could muster. The colonies had always relied upon British naval protection and thus had no heavy fighting ships, whereas for two centuries Britain's navy had been its chief weapon. In contests with other maritime powers, Britain had grasped the substance of later 19th century doctrines of naval warfare which stressed the importance of command of the sea, defined as the ability to concentrate in any vital area a force superior to the enemy. The emphasis was on big ships with heavy fire power. The 74-gun frigates which were Britain's ships of the line had the same fundamental importance to naval power that the armored dreadnaught was to have in the 19th century. Lighter ships were no match for such monsters and of little use in a trial of strength. The virtuosity of Britain's seamen and the willingness of its people to bear the enormous expense of a big navy had made Britain the world's foremost naval power. Unchallenged in American waters until 1778, British squadrons blockaded the coast, intercepted merchant vessels, convoyed supply ships, and transported armies almost at will. The maritime strength that enabled Britain to fight from across the ocean was a primary factor in the war.

Congress never for a moment entertained the notion of building a fleet that could compete with Britain's navy on equal terms. Although a few vessels were brought into service as Continental ships of war, the United States relied almost entirely on privateers. Before armored, steam-powered battleships came into use during the 19th century, fighting ships were not so highly specialized that ordinary merchant vessels could not be converted to military uses by the mounting of additional guns on them and the strengthening of their crews. It was the universal practice of governments in time of war to license private individuals to prey upon enemy commerce. As a business venture, privateering was a highly speculative but often lucrative enterprise. Owner, captain, and crew shared in the sale of captured ships and cargoes. A lucky voyage might yield an enormous return. There was, of course, the risk of being captured. But no misgivings deterred seafaring Americans, and hundreds of their privateers soon roamed the seas, hovering off the British West Indies and even the English coast itself. Massachusetts alone licensed 958 privateers during the war, and Congress issued 1,697 commissions. In the single year 1778 an estimated 10,000 Americans were serving on such vessels. Actually, there was no clear distinction between privateers and ordinary merchantmen: all ships went to sea armed and, when their captains saw a weaker vessel under enemy colors, they tried to capture it. Since Britain also commissioned a multitude of privateers, the ocean was the scene of a vast confused struggle, in which vessels were frequently taken, retaken, and taken again before reaching port.

Americans had the advantage in the melee. As will be noted later, they were permitted to operate out of French ports close to the channel coast of England. The primary factor, however, was that more British than American merchants vessels sailed the seas and were exposed to capture. Estimated British losses during the war amounted to £18 million, with the taking of 2,000 vessels and 12,000 seamen. American captures were so numerous that cargoes taken and sold in American ports were an important source of goods for the economy, and the profits of privateering bulked large in national income. The inhabitants of Providence, Rhode Island, for example, were said to have gained £300,000 from privateering and shipbuilding in a single year, a sum double the property value of the entire town in 1774. Privateering did not, however, overcome the advantage that Britain derived from naval superiority. Britain kept its supply lines open throughout the war and supported the movements of its army. For lack of adequate bases on the American coast, the royal navy was never able to maintain a complete blockade, but it took a constant and heavy toll of shipping.

Sources of Internal Disunity: Blacks and Loyalists

Two large segments of the American people were potential allies of Britain and therefore a serious danger to the patriot cause. One was the half million black slaves in the south, who presumably could be induced to flee or to rebel against their masters. Early in the war, the last royal governor of Virginia, Lord Dunmore, probed this source of American weakness by offering freedom to slaves who joined his forces. His policy was followed by British military commanders throughout the war. Blacks were a military asset—not as soldiers for, out of deference to slave-holding loyalists, the British hesitated to give them arms —but as laborers in all the work of military transportation and fortification. Their employment released soldiers for combat. They acted as spies and as guides in unfamiliar territory. More important, the southern economy rested on slave labor and would have been ruined by slave defection on a large scale. Alert to this threat, southern patriots increased the number of patrols, evacuated blacks from war zones, and inflicted the death penalty on those caught fleeing to the enemy. Their efforts did not prevent a large number from escaping to the British lines, but the body of the black population remained dutiful, and the mass desertions or uprisings that would have crippled the American war effort did not occur. Many blacks, in fact, joined the patriot forces as laborers, guides, seamen, and soldiers. All the Continental battalions raised in the northern states had a sprinkling of blacks, and Rhode Island raised a separate black battalion.

Slaves served in the Continental army in place of their masters, and consequently, as a captured Hessian officer observed, "No regiment is to be seen in which there are not Negroes in abundance; And among them are able-bodied, strong, and brave fellows." However enlisted, slaves who served out their term in the Continental army gained their freedom.

The attitude of southerners did not permit full utilization of the black's military potential on the patriot side. Early in the war Congress rejected the idea of inducting slaves into the Continental army. By 1779, however, enlistments were so short and British operations in the south so menacing that Congress recommended to South Carolina and Georgia that they raise black troops for their own defense, enlisting slaves as well as free blacks by purchasing them from their owners. In spite of the danger from the British invasion, the legislatures of neither state could be persuaded to adopt the proposal. The South Carolina council, in fact, was so indignant at the idea that it entertained a proposal to open peace negotiations with the British. Of the southern states, only Maryland authorized slave enlistments.

A more serious threat to internal unity was the existence of numerous British sympathizers, particularly in the middle states and the south. Some were active loyalists, numbering, according to the best estimates, about 128,000 adult males, who with their families constituted 513,000 persons or slightly under 20 percent of the population. An estimated 100,000 fled to the British during the war or departed with them at the evacuation. They furnished men for a number of battalions, but, whether discouraged by the contempt in which British officers held all colonials or whether they expected Britain to do the work for them, loyalists contributed little to British arms, despite their numbers. In any case, British commanders frittered away this potential source of manpower. In the early stages of the war, they thought they could do without the loyalists and made little effort to recruit them. Loyalists were kept out of regular British regiments and obliged to form separate battalions which were accorded an inferior status in the British military organization. The number of loyalists actually serving in the British army increased only gradually from 1,000 in 1775 to 2,300 in 1776 and 4,410 in 1777. After France entered the war and Parliament refused to increase British troop strength in North America, the war office tried to base strategy upon hoped-for loyalist support, particularly in the south. The number of loyalists in British service mounted to 7,400 in 1778, to 9,000 in 1779, and to about 10,000 thereafter. But it was too late. The loyalists had lost whatever initiative they might once have possessed, and were usually unable to defend themselves against the patriots without the help of British regulars.

Active loyalists were on the whole less dangerous to the patriot cause than the much larger number of British sympathizers who stayed in place, nonresistant but hostile and ready to collaborate with the enemy whenever he gained the upper hand. The strength of pro-British sentiment was evident in the warm reception extended to British occupation forces in New York City and Philadelphia. Later in the war, when the British invaded the south, their presence brought many loyalists out in the open. The struggle in Georgia and the Carolinas then became a civil war waged with all the venom and atrocity typical of such conflicts.

The Disaffected and the Strategy of Popular Leadership

Apart from persons in varying degree loyal to Britain, a considerable but undetermined number were just disaffected, without real commitment to either side, but for reasons indicated below, hostile to the patriot cause, particularly in the early years of the war. Their main interest was to avoid fighting, and they were not willing to make sacrifices for either side. In preparing the colonies for war in 1775, the patriot committees tried to compel farmers, who up to this time had taken little part in the resistance, to leave their fields and serve in the militia. These farmers were at the same time suffering economic losses as a result of Congress's prohibition of exports. Many obeyed the patriot committees, but others refused. "It is better," one wrote, "for the poor people to lay down their arms and pay the duties and taxes laid on them by King and Parliament than to be brought into slavery and to be commanded and ordered about as they are." The people who wanted to stay out of the war tended to side with Britain, not out of loyalty, but because the British asked nothing of them and required no military service. A Continental officer wrote: "It appears that a majority of the people [in Delaware] are disaffected and Would I believe afford the enemy every aid in their power except service in the field which the greater part want spirit to do."

Disaffection was widespread on the eastern shore of Delaware, Maryland, and Virginia, where loyalists were able for a time to sustain an open show of force, aided by British supplies. The patriot militia was unreliable in some areas and could not be trusted to suppress disturbances. Groups of armed blacks were rumored to be plotting insurrection, encouraged in their plans by whites. In places where disaffection was too strong to cope with, the patriot leadership ignored it, abandoning any effort to control the situation or demand anything of the people. Farther south, in the Carolinas, disaffection had a pre-existing foundation in the animosities left over from the recently suppressed Regulator movement. The Regulators were still hostile to the easterners who now led the patriot cause, and the authority of the early patriot governments hardly extended to the back country.

Something similar occurred in eastern Long Island, where, throughout the war, the people who stood by the British were in the unique position of being supplied with British arms from nearby New York and protected by the British fleet. These people, too, were evidently less loyalist than merely disaffected to the patriot cause, wanting to stay out of the war. How many others elsewhere in the country would have been of the same mind if shielded by British military force is an open question. In most areas they had no choice; their allegiance was dictated by the patriot militia, which could be and was sent in from outside to quell opposition to patriot governments.

In order to preserve their alliance with the common people, lure the disaffected away from the British, and keep the new Revolutionary governments going long enough to establish their legitimacy and authority, popular leaders had to adopt "popular" policies, which were sometimes distinctly adverse to the interests of America's upper classes. It is not especially significant that in the beginning, the war was financed by emissions of paper money; there was no alternative. It is significant, however, that for the first three or four years, none of the new state governments levied direct taxes. The people went virtually tax-free. In fact, the patriot governments were not secure enough to risk their authority by trying to collect taxes. When taxation was eventually resumed, patriot leaders in the southern states, in order to hold small planters and farmers to the cause, were forced to alter the inequitable tax systems of colonial times that relied chiefly upon regressive poll taxes as the chief source of revenue. A greater resort to land and property taxes shifted much of the burden to larger planters. Finally, in an effort to uphold the value of paper money, state governments throughout the country adopted tender laws which made depreciated paper currency acceptable at face value in payment of private debts. These laws nearly eliminated payments on existing land leases and went far toward cancelling other kinds of debts. They benefitted tenant farmers and debtors at the expense of large landholders and creditors. Private indebtedness was universal in America before the Revolution; the tender laws steadily wiped it out.

In the end, the British probably did more to lose the support of the disaffected and the loyalists, however, than the patriots did to win it. The British were incorrigible in displaying open contempt for Americans, even, as we have seen, of the loyalists who fought for them. Loyalists also learned by bitter experience that British protection was a delusion; when the British army came around, they revealed themselves, only to be left stranded and exposed to their enemies when the redcoats marched away. Equally detrimental to the British cause was the fact that the British forces never rose above the role of an army of occupation. The officers could not control their men, who insulted, abused, and pillaged Americans, regardless of whether they were loyalists or patriots. It is true that American troops committed their share of depredations on the civilian population, and they as well as the British resorted to impressments. The British, however, often just seized what they wanted, whereas American impressments were conducted most of the time with a show of legal process and at least the promise of repayment. Probably the underlying fact was that wherever British rule prevailed it was a military occupation, whereas American authority was enforced by a civil government. Nevertheless, it is not surprising, since the British troops were foreigners and from a large, conquering nation, that they were apparently less respectful of civilian rights than the Americans. In eastern Long Island, for example, the British occupation taught most of the inhabitants to welcome the return to American rule at the end of the Revolution. Even at Yorktown, when the conquered British regiments laid down their arms, a French observer wrote that throughout the whole ceremony the British were insolent: "Above everything else they showed contempt for the Americans." The British by their behavior did much to forfeit their potential support in America.

Problems of Manpower, Organization, and Money

Presumably a nation of 2.5 million people fighting on home ground was a match for the British forces assigned to the country, and yet it was difficult for the nation to exert its strength. After the initial burst of ardor in 1775 and 1776, enthusiasm for military service cooled rapidly. Men were reluctant to enlist, particularly for long-term service in distant places. The states seldom if ever raised their quotas of troops for the Continental army, and the regular forces under Washington's command sometimes dwindled to the point of extinction. Desertion was frequent and occasionally on a large scale. Apart from simple unwillingness to serve, the shortage of troops owed something to the fact that America's small-farmer economy required the labor of most of its male population to keep it going.

A further difficulty was lack of arms and equipment. The war cut across normal trade channels which had previously supplied America with cloth, tools, and a wide variety of manufactures imported from Britain. In the early stages of the war, especially, there were often critical shortages of imported goods necessary for the army. The British blockade and occupation of coastal cities such as New York and Philadelphia multiplied the problems of supply and transportation. As the war progressed, shortages were partially made up by increased local manufactures and by an elaborate organization of overseas trade through neutral countries. Ever larger quantities of British goods passed from Europe to the French, Dutch, and Spanish West Indies and thence to the United States. John Adams reported in 1781 that British customs receipts had steadily increased as a result of the recovery of American markets by roundabout trade.

Even when both men and arms were available, however, defects in governmental organization obstructed their use. Congress was restrained in the exercise of power by the general aversion of the people to centralized authority. With no coercive power over the states, Congress had to rely on the voluntary and often disjointed cooperation of 13 state governments. Members of the Congress shared the prevailing distrust of power; hence in organizing Continental administration they kept the executive functions in their own hands, refusing to delegate them. Business was conducted by transient committees and boards, and Congress had to act as a body on matters of small detail. Not until 1781 was the system improved by the creation of departments headed by single executives.

Overshadowing all other problems were those of financing the war. Unable to borrow sufficient money either at home or abroad, Congress resorted to issuing paper money—$20 million by the time independence was declared. The emission of paper money was the usual method of war finance, as we have seen, and had worked fairly well in colonial times. Although Congress could not levy taxes, it pledged the faith of the United Colonies for the redemption of the money and requested that the states withdraw it by taxation.

In the early stages of the war, state governments, which were only just beginning to establish their authority, were reluctant, as we have seen, to tax their supporters. Also, enemy occupations and the disruption of trade crippled their normal revenue systems. As a result, few taxes were collected, or could be, before 1779, by which time Congress had been driven to emit huge amounts of paper currency. The expenses of this war were high beyond comparison with anything known in colonial times. Added to the effects of a positive rise in prices was the toll exacted by the profiteering of merchants and farmers who sold goods to the government and by waste and fraud on the part of Congress's purchasing officers. A member of Congress lamented: "The Avarice of our people and the extravagant prices of all commodities, joined with the imperfect management of our Affairs, would expend the mines of Chili and Peru."

Since none of the currency that Congress issued was withdrawn by state taxes, the volume in circulation became enormous, and by the fall of 1776 Continental currency began to depreciate in value. In January 1778, 4 dollars exchanged for 1 dollar in hard money, a year later the rate was 8 to 1, and by January 1780 over 40 to 1. Despite ever larger emissions, Congress derived less and less real income from the emissions and was forced to issue progressively larger amounts. By the spring of 1778 Congress was spending currency at the rate of about a million dollars a week. By the end of 1779 the total amount issued was $226 million. At this point Congress decided to cease emissions in the knowledge that further additions to the currency would reduce its value to the vanishing point and provide no substantial income to support the war.

The nation itself was prosperous, enjoying an economic boom, but Congress was frequently without funds and at last was wholly unable to meet even the most pressing emergencies. The army felt the effects as it went without equipment, without pay, and often without sufficient food. Lack of funds hindered the war effort at every turn.

Campaigns in 1776 and 1777

The military operations of the Revolution fall into three phases. The first, which was extremely critical for the United States, extended from the beginning of the war to the surrender of General Burgoyne at Saratoga in October 1777. The British had their opportunity to crush the rebellion before the patriot forces had learned to fight or the nation saw any prospect of victory. The second phase began with the victory at Saratoga, which transformed the war into an international conflict, but then a stalemate ensued for nearly three years, in which Britain fought with limited forces in America and the patriots, as yet not actively supported by their French allies, were too feeble to make any headway. The main campaigns were in the southern states, which were partially overrun by the British. The third and final phase began and ended in 1781 with the combined American and French attack upon Yorktown, assisted by French naval forces. This campaign led to the capture of Cornwallis and assured American independence. The definitive treaty of peace was not signed until September 1783, but, except for desultory skirmishing in the deep south, the war ended at Yorktown.

In the year 1776 the American cause was constantly on the verge of disaster. Soon after Congress declared independence, the British attacked New York City with a superbly equipped and disciplined army of 32,000 men supported by a fleet of 10 ships of the line, 20 frigates, and hundreds of transports, manned by 10,000 seamen. It was the largest expeditionary force ever sent out from Britain. Opposing it under General Washington were some 28,500 raw and poorly armed troops, of whom only about 19,000 were effective. Expecting to draw Washington's army into combat and destroy it, the British commanders, General William Howe and his brother, Admiral Richard Howe, who commanded

the fleet, brought with them a British offer of peace on the basis
of submission.

Although the American army was inferior to the enemy,
Washington separated his forces, leaving part of them on Manhattan Island and placing the rest on Long Island, which was
entirely surrounded by waters controlled by the British fleet.
The blunders committed by Washington and his officers were
enough to ensure defeat. As the British landed on Long Island,
the American forces took positions along Brooklyn Heights, outnumbered over four to one. Instead of a frontal assault, as at
Bunker Hill, the British executed a flanking movement, en-
circling the American positions. Most of the Americans, fighting
hard, managed to break through and gain the fortifications at
Brooklyn. But their position was still desperate as the British
started siege operations and their naval vessels on the East River
threatened to cut off retreat. Under cover of night, Washington
managed to withdraw his troops across the river to Manhattan
Island and thus avoid disaster. The American forces were too
few, however, to defend the island, and in a series of engagements
in which he barely escaped capture, Washington moved north
from Manhattan Island to the mainland, crossed the Hudson
River, and fled into New Jersey with the enemy in hot pursuit.

Probably the only thing that saved the Americans at this time
was the dilatoriness of General Howe, who although an excellent field commander was slow to move between battles, unwilling to take risks, sparing of casualties among his own troops
and perhaps more intent upon negotiating peace than upon an-
nihilating the foe. Deep in New Jersey and with winter at hand,
Howe gave up the pursuit and put his army into winter quarters.
Washington gained a reprieve, but his army was discouraged and
dwindling in numbers. "These are the times that try men's
souls," wrote Thomas Paine, who was with the army. "The summer soldier and the sunshine patriot will, in this crisis, shrink
from the service of their country; but he that stands it *now*,
deserves the love and thanks of man and woman."

Patriot hopes were suddenly restored by the remarkable victory at Trenton. Renewing the fight even in the cold of winter,

Washington obtained reinforcements and with a force of more than 6,000 men was strong enough to attack small Hessian garrisons at Trenton and Bordentown. The attack upon Trenton was brilliantly executed. Crossing the icy Delaware River on the night of December 25, he fell upon the unsuspecting Germans at dawn. A third of the garrison escaped but, after a brief struggle in which American losses were negligible, the remaining 1,000 Hessians surrendered. For a time it seemed that the victory would be dearly bought, for British forces converged upon Washington and he was in grave danger of being surrounded. In a skillful maneuver, however, he disengaged his army from a British force that held it at bay, marched around the enemy, and after a hard fight with three British regiments at Princeton, gained the hills at Morristown, where he went into winter quarters. News of the victory at Trenton "flew upon the wings of the wind—and at once revived the hopes of the fearful, which had almost fled! How sudden the transition from darkness to light; from grief to joy!"

The Americans by this time had been thrown back in an attempt to invade Canada. In May 1775 a party of 300 Vermonters under Ethan Allen surprised and overwhelmed the garrison at Fort Ticonderoga, winning control of Lake Champlain and opening the invasion route to Montreal. General Richard Montgomery captured the city in November and chased a handful of British defenders down the St. Lawrence River toward Quebec. Meanwhile, a small army under General Benedict Arnold had pushed its way through Maine up the Kennebec River, enduring terrible hardships and the loss of over half of its original force from sickness and desertion before reaching Quebec, where it joined Montgomery's men outside the fortress walls. It was now December, and the combined American forces numbered only 1,000 men, somewhat less than the defending British troops, who had recently been reinforced. A protracted siege was impractical in the winter's cold; the city had to be carried by assault if the campaign were not to be given up. The desperate attempt was made on December 31. Montgomery died in the savage fight, and Arnold was severely wounded. Although the American army was nearly cut in half, Arnold wanted to renew the attack; however a British fleet arrived with a force of regular troops. The Americans had to retreat along the St. Lawrence river to Montreal and eventually out of Canada. The campaign failed; nevertheless, it won valuable time by diverting British strength from the colonies.

The first year of fighting had ended. The American forces were still in existence. They had suffered repeated defeats, but had shown their mettle. The valor of the Americans at Quebec won universal admiration. Washington's generalship during the retreat through New Jersey commanded respect and gave encouragement to patriots. Despite many opportunities, the British had fumbled the chance to end the war quickly. As the next year's campaign opened, their prospects were less hopeful than at the beginning.

The paramount British strategy in 1777 was to mount an invasion from Canada along the line of Lake Champlain and the Hudson River. The plan called for General John Burgoyne, with a force of 9,500 men, to move southward along the lake and river route to Albany, there to be joined by Colonel Barry St. Leger with 9,000 regulars, Tories, and Canadians, traveling to that point from Lake Erie. The combined forces were to link up with General Howe's army in New York, which was to render assistance if needed. The execution of this plan would have given British control of the route to Canada and cut New England's land communication with the rest of the country.

Whether this strategy, if successful, would have contributed to Britain's winning the war is doubtful, but the way it was executed led to disaster. General Howe was not much concerned with helping Burgoyne, who was his rival. He had his own scheme for taking Philadelphia, even though the commitment of his troops to this venture meant that he would not be able to assist Burgoyne if called upon. The British War Office in London was scarcely in a position to judge the situation. Like its commanders in America, it underestimated the dangers that Burgoyne was likely to encounter in his line of march. It gave half-hearted sanction to Howe's scheme, and Howe set out for Philadelphia, leaving Burgoyne to his own resources.

Howe easily captured Philadelphia. Embarking from New York with about 15,000 troops in July 1777, he landed at the head of Chesapeake Bay and marched northward toward the city. Eleven thousand Continentals and militia under Washington attempted to bar the way. At Brandywine Creek, Washington risked a general engagement, but after suffering a thousand casualties, as compared with half that number for the enemy, his army fled in confusion. While Washington stood helplessly by, the British entered Philadelphia on September 27. Washington attacked their defenses at Germantown, but again his forces were routed. After maneuvering impotently near the city until December, he took up winter quarters at Valley Forge, about 20 miles away.

Burgoyne, meanwhile, had proceeded from Montreal toward Albany. The campaign got off to a promising start when Fort Ticonderoga surrendered without a fight, opening the way down the Hudson River Valley. Albany was only 70 miles away. But Burgoyne's progress was slowed by a long artillery train, lack of horses, poor equipment, excessive baggage, and the general crowd of women and other camp followers who accompanied the army. The Americans who lurked in the forests did everything possible to retard his advance, felling thousands of trees and diverting streams across the wagon road he followed. Burgoyne at times gained no more than a mile a day, while the Americans were steadily reinforced by the arrival of Continental troops. More ominous for Burgoyne, however, was the steady gathering of the New England militia, which converged in large numbers to fight it out in defense of home and country. Burgoyne's own reinforcements failed him. St. Leger, trying to reach Albany through the Mohawk Valley, was delayed by the subborn defense of Fort Stanwix, which gave time for American reinforcements to come from the Hudson River. St. Leger than met such hard combat at the battle of Oriskany that his Indian allies threatened to desert and he had to retreat. Meanwhile, Burgoyne's army was pounded in a series of vicious engagements, in which the Americans inflicted heavy casualties and took numerous prisoners. Depleted in numbers and hemmed in on all sides, his forces came to a dead stop. Burgoyne knew that there was no chance of relief from New York, and on October 17, 1777, he surrendered to General Horatio Gates with his entire army.

France Enters the War

Victory at Saratoga resulted in a formal alliance with France. On the strength of secret assurances from the French government, Congress early in 1776 had sent Silas Deane to Paris to get military supplies. Arrangements for French aid, however, had already been made in unofficial conversations between Arthur Lee, who was then residing in London, and the talented adventurer Caron de Beaumarchais, who espoused the American cause and urged the French court to intervene in the war. The French foreign minister, Vergennes, had long pondered ways of exploiting Britain's quarrel with its colonies, and the French court was disposed to seize the present moment. Uncertain how long the colonies would continue to fight, however, the court decided to preserve formal neutrality and thus avoid an open break with Britain. Accordingly, the French government, avoiding official action, set up a private commercial firm to aid the Americans. This was headed by Beaumarchais, financed with government money, and furnished with weapons from government arsenals. Assisted by Silas Deane, Beaumarchais busied himself shipping supplies to America. They began to arrive in 1777 and were of vital importance in the campaigns of that year. France also opened its home ports to American privateersmen, who used them as bases and enlisted French money, vessels, and seamen in raiding British commerce. The British government was closely informed of all these activities, but tolerated them in order to avoid forcing France into the war.

In December 1776 Benjamin Franklin went to France as American political commissioner. His primary mission was to negotiate a treaty of alliance. Already internationally known as a scientist and philosopher, Franklin was well versed in high-level diplomacy and possessed a worldly charm and wit that interested the French court and captivated the French people. As a symbol of the American Revolution to cultivated French society, no better man could have been chosen, but even his talents failed to persuade the court to enter the war until it had more assurance that the Revolution would succeed. France was also restrained by the indecision of its European ally, Spain. Although eager to recover Gibraltar, which Britain had seized in 1704, the Spanish court was no friend to republics, particularly the United States, whose westward expansion would menace the Spanish empire and conflict with Spain's own territorial ambitions. When Spain did not respond to French proposals for joint war upon Britain, France refused to enter the contest alone.

The turning point was the capture of Burgoyne. This impressive victory had a profound effect in Britain, where the war had never been entirely popular. Many Englishmen had long urged that it be given up in the belief that America could not be subjugated or that, if it could, the colonies would never be reconciled to British rule. Burgoyne's capture pointed up these arguments, as well as the imminent possibility that France would openly join the United States. The ministry decided to make peace overtures in the hope of forestalling a Franco-American alliance and of restoring the empire. Parliament repealed the Coercive Acts and the duty on tea. A commission headed by Lord Carlisle was sent to the United States, equipped with funds for bribery and instructions to accept all the demands that the Americans had made in 1776. The Carlisle Commission was not authorized, however, to consent to independence or to the withdrawal of British forces then in the United States, and any agreement it made had to be ratified by Parliament. The terms which it offered conceded most of what Americans had once demanded, but by 1778 most patriots had lost all trust in British integrity and, with the French alliance in prospect, would accept nothing less than complete independence. On May 4, 1778, a month before the Carlisle Commission reached the United States, Congress ratified the alliance with France.

The treaty pledged France to continue the war until American independence was established. Neither party was to lay down its arms or conclude a separate peace without the consent of the other. France renounced any claim to her former colonies in Canada and the northwest. Both parties guaranteed the possessions of the other in the New World as they would exist at the close of the war. Accompanying the military alliance was a commercial agreement providing for trade on a mutually favorable basis. In June 1778, soon after the treaty was signed, France declared war on Britain, and a year later Spain entered the conflict. The Spanish government at first tried to bargain with Britain, offering neutrality in exchange for the return of Gibraltar. When Britain refused the offer, Spain signed a war pact with France. In 1780 still another European power, Holland, came into the fray when Britain declared war on it.

The entry of these European powers transformed the American Revolution into a major international war. Thenceforth, Britain was not free to concentrate its forces against the United States. Compelled to defend its possessions in all parts of the world, Britain also had to guard its own coast against invasion. Since its antagonists were all naval powers, the British fleet was extended to the limit of its resources. Britain lost command of the sea in American waters and could not maintain an effective blockade. Its convoys were subject to attack. After 1778 a French naval squadron under Count d'Estaing operated continuously in the West Indies and along the American coast. No longer could Britain transport and supply its troops at will, and there was constant danger that a French fleet would isolate one of its armies in some remote place on the continent, cut off its relief, and expose it to capture.

The War in the Doldrums, 1778–1780

After the alliance with France, Americans expected to deliver hard blows, but instead the war languished for nearly three years. In 1778 the presence of d'Estaing's fleet gave the allies temporary naval supremacy on the American coast, but they

were unable to dislodge the British from New York City or
expel them from Rhode Island, which the British had occupied
a year earlier. D'Estaing finally sailed to the West Indies in disgust, not to return until 1781. During this interval the United
States got small loans from France, but not large-scale financial
or military assistance, and its own efforts faltered. With the
depreciation of Continental currency, Congress sank into poverty and then into penury. The state governments assumed
primary responsibility for supporting the war, but they also had
run through their currency and were without funds. In the general collapse of paper money, the war was increasingly supported
by impressments.

The army was badly supplied and feeble in numbers. As the
war dragged on inconclusively year after year, military officers
became thoroughly embittered. The country seemed incapable
of striking a blow in its own behalf. Patriots had taken courage
when France entered the war, believing that America could not
then be conquered. There was danger now that the Revolution
would fail out of mere frustration.

It was fortunate for the Americans that after Saratoga the
scale of British military efforts in America declined. Having to
cope with enemies in other parts of the world, the British government would not give General Henry Clinton, successor to
Howe, enough troops to defend New York City and at the same
time operate against Washington's army on any better than
equal terms. Clinton's strategy, therefore, was to harass the
Americans by destructive raids and to confine aggressive military
operations to the south, where relatively small forces could be
effective and loyalists could be expected to rally to the British
standard. It was an indecisive strategy, scarcely calculated to
force a military decision, but it was at first strikingly successful.
The British invaded Georgia in the fall of 1778. Within a month
the state was under British control. Beating off counterattacks,
the British marched into South Carolina and laid siege to
Charleston, which was defended by General Benjamin Lincoln.
On May 7, 1780, Lincoln surrendered with his entire garrison
of 5,000 men and a valuable stock of munitions. It was the worst

American defeat of the war. The British then invested South Carolina, raising numerous loyalists, who joined them in the fight.

American resistance in the Carolinas was kept alive by guerrilla bands, which raided British outposts and supply lines under such intrepid leaders as Francis Marion and Thomas Sumter, and then retreated into the swamps to elude pursuit. In August some 3,000 Americans led by General Horatio Gates challenged a British force under Lord Cornwallis at Camden, South Carolina. The Americans, mostly militia, fought well for a time but were outmaneuvered and scattered by their more experienced enemy. Gates distinguished himself in the precipitous flight by riding 60 miles on horseback before nightfall. This humiliating defeat opened North Carolina to invasion, while in Virginia British detachments raided the coasts of Chesapeake Bay and the Tidewater. As the campaigns of 1780 closed, the British were confidently preparing to roll up the south clear to the Potomac River.

Victory at Yorktown

Britain's prospects were not as bright as they seemed. Unable to control the countryside, the British could not prevent the Americans from regrouping to fight again. Ominous for the future were the circumstances reported by a British officer after the capture of Charleston: the city and surrounding area were pacified, he wrote, but "there is such a fund of hatred and animosity in the hearts of the people as time only can extinguish. The men being prisoners do not dare to speak out, but the women make full amends for their silence; they amuse themselves by teaching their children the principles of rebellion, and seem to take care that the rising generation should be as troublesome as themselves." Trouble beset the British when, in October 1780 a force of 1,100 loyalists was set upon by 900 North Carolina backwoodsmen, who followed them to King's Mountain and in a single hour slew 224 and captured the rest. This encounter dampened the ardor of North Carolina loyalists and rescued the backcountry from enemy attack. Not long afterward, in January 1781, the British suffered a damaging setback at the Battle of Cowpens. General Daniel Morgan, a frontier fighter leading a force of Continentals and militia, was caught with his back against a river by British regulars under General Banastre Tarleton. Morgan deployed his men with great skill, withstood the British charge, and then routed the enemy with a counterattack. The battle was fought along conventional lines by numerically equal forces. With only small losses, Morgan's men killed, wounded, or captured at least 600 men, over half of the opposing army.

Throughout 1781 the British position in the south deteriorated. Cornwallis, operating in North Carolina and Virginia, was now opposed by General Nathanael Greene. Although in his entire military career Greene never won an important battle, he was an able commander and managed to check Cornwallis at every point. Driven from the field at the battle of Guilford Court House, he nevertheless inflicted losses that obliged Cornwallis to retire to Yorktown. Greene then assailed the remaining British forces in South Carolina and Georgia. Although victory, as always, eluded him, his attacks sapped enemy strength and, as the British weakened, patriots rose everywhere and expelled them from post after post. By midsummer of 1781 the British forces, now consisting mainly of loyalists rather than regular soldiers, had been pushed back into the coastal ports of Charleston and Savannah. British reverses in the southern campaigns set the stage for the final battle of the war.

When Cornwallis took up defensive positions at Yorktown, Virginia, his security rested squarely on the power of the British navy, for Yorktown was on a peninsula. Without relief by sea Cornwallis was vulnerable to entrapment. The Americans and their French allies had long hoped for just such an opportunity. They at last had their chance to execute a combined naval and military operation. Its success depended not only upon concentrating land forces against Cornwallis but upon gaining naval superiority off Yorktown. The military elements required for the campaign were widely dispersed. Washington with an army of about 10,000 men, including 5,000 French troops under Rochambeau, was before New York City, rather hopelessly trying to find a way to drive out a superior British force. In Virginia a small army under Lafayette was shadowing Cornwallis. In the West Indies a French fleet sailed under command of Admiral De Grasse, who had instructions from his government to cooperate with Washington.

When De Grasse sent word that he was ready to take his fleet to the Chesapeake, the elements of the combined operation were quickly assembled. Washington gave up the attack upon New York in favor of trapping Cornwallis, and notified De Grasse of the plan. The admiral promised to arrive on schedule, carrying, besides his crew, 3,000 French regulars from the West Indies. A French squadron sailing from Rhode Island was to join him at the Chesapeake. As the scheme got under way, Washington disengaged 7,000 of his troops before New York so skillfully that they were south of Philadelphia before the British had any idea of their destination.

The British reacted swiftly but blundered in executing their countermeasures. A British fleet under Admiral Rodney had been keeping watch over De Grasse in the West Indies but, when De Grasse sailed for the mainland, Rodney sent only inferior forces in pursuit. After proceeding to New York and picking up what ships were there, they attacked De Grasse in Chesapeake Bay, but were beaten off. Cornwallis was isolated. By land he was besieged by Lafayette's forces, strengthened now by the 3,000 French regulars brought by the French fleet. Before he could escape, Washington's army came up. Cornwallis was surrounded by an overwhelming force of 16,000 veterans, half of them French, besides thousands of militia who blocked the roads in every direction. The allies began regular siege operations, supported by an intense artillery bombardment. They pressed ever closer to his outworks and on the night of October 15 captured two advanced redoubts. Cornwallis's position became untenable. He tried to escape by crossing the York River but was halted by a storm. Finally, on October 17, he surrendered with an army of a little over 6,000 men. On the afternoon of October 18, 1781, the 3,200 rank and file still fit for duty marched out under their officers in good order and threw down their arms in large piles. According to tradition, their band played an old tune: *The World Turned Upside Down*

> If ponies rode men, and if grass ate the cows,
> And cats should be chased into holes by the mouse . . .
> If summer were spring, and the other way 'round,
> Then all the world would be upside down.

After the Yorktown debacle, Britain gave up the war in America. On March 4, 1782, the House of Commons resolved that it would consider "as enemies to his Majesty and Country all those who should advise or by any means attempt the further prosecution of offensive war on the Continent of North America, for the purpose of reducing the revolted Colonies to obedience by force." The North ministry, which had conducted the war, gave way to the Rockingham-Shelburne ministry headed by men who had been sympathetic to America. The British commander at New York was instructed not to take the offensive and, if heavily pressed, to surrender. Peace negotiations were soon opened with Franklin at Paris.

Foreign Entanglements and the Peace Treaty

The Revolution was for the Americans as much a triumph of diplomacy as of arms. Victory had been won by involving European powers in the American rebellion. Nevertheless, the situation had its perils, for the same self-interest that had brought France into the war could induce it to betray the United States in making the peace. The possibility was, in fact, imminent, for its ally, Spain, whom France was obliged to conciliate, had ambitions conflicting with those of the United States. Spain wished to confine the United States to the eastern slope of the Appalachians. During the war it had seized West Florida from the

British and gained de facto possession of the lower Mississippi Valley by constructing a chain of forts up the river as far north as Natchez. Having no wish to see the United States either independent or strong, it had withheld recognition of American independence, had refused to give substantial aid, and in 1780 had negotiated with Britain with a view to ending the war by truce which would have left Britain in possession of New York City and parts of the south. The French government had supported this proposal. In the bargaining certain to accompany a general peace negotiation, it was not unlikely that American interests would be sacrificed to the ambitions of its allies. The United States was chained to this predicament by its treaty with France, under which neither party could make peace without consent of the other.

The United States had previously taken a strong position with respect to peace negotiations. When Congress in 1779 sent John Adams to Europe, he was instructed to demand a western boundary at the Mississippi River, extending from its source as far south as the 31st parallel. Adams was to act in concert with the French government but in what he deemed essential to use his own judgment. Similar instructions were given to John Jay, who was appointed minister to Spain the same year. Jay was directed, in the event that Britain ceded West Florida to Spain in the peace settlement, to obtain a guarantee that Americans would have full right to navigate the Mississippi River to its mouth.

The powers were not ready to make peace in 1779, and in the dark days before Yorktown, Congress felt it necessary to conciliate France and Spain in order to obtain the utmost aid in winning the war. In June 1781 Congress appointed a peace commission consisting of Adams, Franklin, John Jay, Thomas Jefferson, and Henry Laurens. Its instructions were to insist only upon independence and in everything else to be guided by France. In a note dispatched to Jay earlier in the year, Congress advised him that in dealing with Spain he was to yield, if necessary, the right to navigate the Mississippi. In its weakness the United States prepared to bow to its allies.

The nation was rescued by the sagacity of its peace commissioners by the victory at Yorktown, which ended dependence upon France, and by the decision of the British ministry to open separate peace negotiations. Reconciled to the loss of its colonies, Britain was intent upon waging war against European rivals. In order to sow dissension among them and to detach the United States from the alliance, the ministry accepted Franklin's invitation to discuss peace terms. Preliminary conversations were followed by the appointment of a formal British commission. Franklin, who began the negotiations, was eventually joined by Adams and Jay, both of whom were darkly suspicious of America's allies. Adam's experience abroad had only increased his tendency to regard European courts as sinks of corruption and their sponsorship of the virgin American republic as calculated self-interest. His public declarations that America owed no gratitude to France had already earned him the dislike of the French court. Jay, although he may have started with different views, had become convinced during his stay at Madrid that Spain was hostile to the United States. Adams and Jay scarcely needed to instruct the worldly Franklin in the venality of courts. The American commissioners at first observed both the letter and the spirit of the French alliance. Although they negotiated separately, it was on the premise that whatever terms they arrived at would be incorporated into a general peace settlement that would include France and Spain. They were careful to keep Vergennes informed of their progress. As the negotiations progressed, however, France and Spain revealed unmistakable hostility to American aims. The commissioners finally cast off the shackles of the French alliance and concluded an agreement with Britain. Technically it was not a separate peace, for it was to become effective only when France and Britain came to terms.

The treaty recognized the independence of the United States. It required the complete withdrawal of British forces, with the added proviso that they were not to carry away slaves. The territorial provisions were generous. The United States gained possession of the western empire into which Americans had begun to move even before the Revolution. Although the British would not surrender Canada, as the American commissioners at first demanded, they showed little reluctance to accept the remaining American proposals. The northern boundary was fixed almost as it is today along a lake and river line running from St. John's River in Maine to the as yet unknown source of the Mississippi River. The western boundary was the Mississippi River south to the 31st parallel. The southern boundary followed the 31st parallel eastward to the Appalachicola River, thence to the head of the St. Mary's River, and down that river to the Atlantic. Free navigation of the Mississippi was guaranteed to both countries By a secret agreement the southern boundary was to be at the 31st parallel if Britain ceded West Florida to Spain, but at 32°28′ if Britain retained it. At John Adams's insistence, Americans were given the right to fish in Canadian waters and to use adjacent coasts for drying their catch. This condition was essential to the acceptance of the treaty by New England.

Britain had certain demands of its own. One related to prewar debts owed by Americans to British citizens. Public opinion in Britain was so strong on this point that the ministry was obliged to secure some promise of repayment. The treaty provided that no lawful impediments should be placed in the way of the recovery of debts. Another point on which strong British feeling existed related to the compensation of loyalists, who had entered claims against the British government for the losses incurred from the confiscation of their property by American states. Although Congress had no power to enforce its rulings upon the states, the treaty obliged Congress to "earnestly recommend" that the states make restitution to loyalists.

After the talks were concluded, the American commissioners waited until the agreement was signed by the British ministry, on September 30, 1782, then showed it to Vergennes. His chagrin was less than the commissioners had expected. Commenting upon the generosity of the terms, he ironically observed that Britain had not made peace, she had bought it. However, his reaction to the separate treaty was tempered by the fact that France itself was insolvent, tired of a war now going against it, and unwilling to make further sacrifices for the sake of Spanish ambitions. On January 30, 1783, France and Spain signed their own provisional articles of peace with Britain. The definitive treaties between the parties to the war were signed on September 3, 1783.

American diplomacy had ably exploited the international rivalries of the Old World, had avoided pitfalls, and had carried off the fruits of victory. The treaty conferred everything upon the new nation that it could reasonably have hoped to attain.

CHAPTER VII

Not without Effort:
Stresses and Strains
in Wartime Society

Conventional and Partisan Warfare

The Revolution was a civil war in that it involved an internal struggle between patriots and loyalists, but most of the time and in most parts of the country, it was relatively free of the atrocities characteristic of fratricidal war. Later, when they viewed the carnage of the French Revolution, Americans took satisfaction in having accomplished their own Revolution in a humane way. They were able to do so, however, mainly because the loyalists were so quickly reduced to impotence and, unless they joined the British, put out of the conflict. In the period before independence, when the avowed aim of patriot resistance was still the restoration of American rights within the empire, British sympathizers were cowed and isolated by mob violence. Their homes were looted and wrecked. They were stripped naked and dropped into vats of tar, whipped, beaten, ridden on rails, and shut into rooms where they were smoked by fires of green logs. A loyalist historian described the treatment meted out to a certain Dr. Beebe of Connecticut who had spoken too freely in favor of the crown. He was

assaulted by a Mob, stripped naked, and hot Pitch was poured upon him which blistered his Skin. He was then carried to an

199

Hog Sty and rubbed over with Hogs Dung. They threw the Hog's Dung in his Face, and rammed some of it down his Throat; and in that Condition exposed [him] to a Company of Women. His House was attacked, his Windows broke, when one of his Children was sick, and a Child of his went into Distraction upon this Treatment. His Gristmill was broke, and Persons prevented from grinding at it, and from having Connection with him.

After the formal separation from Britain, loyalists were kept under surveillance, restricted in their movements, imprisoned, banished, taxed at double or triple rates, forced to accept depreciated paper money, and fined for not serving in the militia, and the property of those who fled to the British or merely left their estates for no acceptable reason was confiscated. But there was no slaughter of loyalists; few reprisals occurred when American forces reoccupied areas after British evacuation, nor were there even many instances of individual murder, except in parts of the country where loyalists were strong enough to fight.

In those parts of the country, however, all rules of civilized warfare lapsed. Loyalists with their Indian allies raided exposed settlements on the New York frontier, inevitably committing massacres which provoked counter massacres by patriot forces. "The struggle on the Mohawk and Susquehanna," writes an historian, "became a war of savage, unsparing retaliation." In the Carolinas, General Nathanael Greene, commander of the Continental army, wrote: "the whigs and tories pursue one another with the most relentless fury, killing and destroying each other whenever they meet." Even in 1782, with peace in sight, he wrote that the country was "still torn to pieces by little parties of disaffected who elude all search and conceal themselves in the thickets and swamps . . . and issue forth . . . committing the most horrid murders and plunder and lay waste the country." These armed bands were not necessarily attached to either Britain or the United States; they pillaged and fought for themselves, or they changed sides according to who they thought was winning. Living in close proximity to one another, American and British adherents were so apprehensive of sudden raids that they took to "lying out," not daring to sleep in their houses and hiding in swamps at night. Apart from operations conducted by the main British and American armies, and sometimes even then, the war in the south degenerated into plunder and murder by both sides.

In most circumstances, however, the organized forces were governed by a code of military behavior which was observed by both American and British commanders. Officers on either side dealt with one another as gentlemen of honor. Although British officers could not always restrain Indians and Hessians, soldiers who surrendered were seldom massacred, either by the British or by the Americans, nor were prisoners murdered, starved, or tortured. Neither side complained much of the treatment of captured regular troops. What seems an extraordinary degree of communication and mutual accommodation took place between the opposing forces. Women joining their husbands, gentlemen engaged in private business, and officers on special missions received passes to go through enemy lines. Cartels were arranged to permit each side to send supplies to prisoners in enemy hands. Captured officers and soldiers were frequently and often quickly exchanged, although Washington was sometimes reluctant to exchange common soldiers because the men he got back were short-term enlistees, while the British he gave up were permanent soldiers. On one occasion, when a commission dispatched from England to a British officer at New York ended up in American hands at Philadelphia, Washington courteously permitted it to be forwarded.

An exception to humane treatment of prisoners was the confinement of captured American seamen on British prison ships in New York harbor, where from all accounts they suffered appallingly from filth, disease, and malnutrition. These seamen did not belong to the American navy; they had been captured aboard American privateers. They had little prospect of being released or exchanged. Under the military conventions of the time, Congress was supposed to pay their living expenses while in captivity, but there was no chance that Congress would ever have the money to do it. They might have been exchanged for British seamen captured aboard privateers, but such prisoners were all in state custody; Congress had none to exchange. The British commander in New York tried to induce Congress to exchange captured British soldiers for them, but Washington would never consent to such an unequal trade. The result was that most of the brave Americans held at New York who refused to enlist in the British navy, an inducement continually held out to them, spent years rotting in the prison ships, and if not dead were still there at the end of the war.

The amenities that usually governed the treatment of prisoners, however, are illustrated by arrangements made for the so-called Convention troops captured at the surrender of General Burgoyne. Under the agreement between Burgoyne and General Gates, the troops were to march to Boston and disembark for England under a pledge that they would not return to fight in America. The United States was to supply their provisions and transport and was to be compensated by Britain, at American insistence, in hard coin. On their march to Boston, the troops were cheerfully greeted by the inhabitants, but at Cambridge, where most of them were bivouacked, the people were hostile, and the British at first complained of crowded quarters and cold rooms. The officers, however, were permitted to rent quarters, duly paid for by Britain. The troops stayed around Boston for a year, at considerable expense to Britain, which was charged $370,000 by the United States for supplies over a single six-month period, a bill which the British considered exorbitant. A British vessel was allowed to unload a cargo of clothing in Boston harbor for the use of the Convention troops.

Suspecting that Burgoyne would fail to adhere to his pledge that the troops would not be returned to America, Congress violated the Convention agreement and found an excuse to send the troops to the Virginia backcountry. The evacuation began early in November 1778. The British commanders, fearing that the troops would suffer during the long winter march, asked Washington to order that the movement each day be by easy stages, that lodging be found in barns at night, and that ample provisions be furnished. Washington promised the officers to do everything possible. When the troops arrived at their destination near Charlottesville, British ships were given passports to bring money and supplies for the men into Hampton Road; from there the articles were transported to the troops by American vessels and wagons. During their long stay in the backcountry, the British and German soldiers cultivated vegetable gardens and the officers amused themselves by purchasing fine horses. From the time of their arrival at Boston, desertions had been frequent; many of the soldiers left their regiments to find work, to become indentured servants, or to join the American army. Maryland had a German battalion in its Continental line. Later in the war, the Convention troops were moved up to backcountry Maryland and Pennsylvania; some were quartered in Philadelphia. At the end of the war, only a minority of the Germans went back to their home country.

Raising the Continental Army

Enthusiasm for military service was higher at the beginning of the war than at any time afterward. In 1776 nearly 47,000 men served in the Continental forces, assisted by 26,000 militia. From then on enlistments declined, to 34,800 in 1777, 32,900 in 1778, 27,700 in 1779, 21,000 in 1780, and 13,291 in 1781. New England contributed proportionately more men than any other section of the country, 53 percent of total enlistments during the entire war. Southerners, who were distant from the early campaigns, more frequently served as militia after 1778, when the British invaded the south. Although the number of battalions in the Continental army ran as high as 107, at full strength more than 75,000 men, the numbers were mostly on paper. A congressional inquiry into the state of the main army in 1777 disclosed only 14,089 privates fit for duty. These soldiers were led by 1,247 commissioned officers and 1,584 noncommissioned officers, a ratio of one officer to every five privates. Manpower available for actual service in the field was further depleted by the universal practice of drawing men out of the ranks to act as servants for the officers, as assistants in the quartermaster and commissary departments, and as skilled workmen and functionaries at numerous military posts. Without money to hire civilians, military commanders had to use soldiers in a multitude of noncombatant services. Every winter, moreover, the fighting force virtually melted away as men's enlistments expired. On several occasions, as the war became inactive over the winter months, General Washington dismissed troops before the expiration of their enlistments because he did not have supplies to maintain them.

Although a number of specialized battalions, such as cavalry, engineers, and light troops, were directly enlisted by the Contiental government, the bulk of the Continental army was raised by the states and organized by state lines. Deeply reluctant to use coercion, the states relied upon voluntary enlistments, offering bounties which became progressively higher as the war continued. The bounties were additional to a land grant and a money bonus which Congress offered to those who would serve for the duration of the war. Short enlistments were the rule. From an early stage of the war Congress requested the states to enlist men for at least three years or the duration, but not many were willing to serve for a lengthy period; the states took what enlistments they could get, and Congress had to accept them.

Washington never ceased to complain that such men barely got used to camp life before their terms expired and they left for home. Under pressure from Washington, Congress ultimately asked the states to institute a compulsory draft, and some did so. The usual method was for the state government to require a town or rural district to deliver so many men for the Continental army. How they did it was their own business. Sometimes, when their own inhabitants showed no eagerness to enlist, they raised money by taxes to pay bounties high enough to induce somebody in the area or from elsewhere to volunteer. On other occasions, they paid the purchase price of an indentured servant to the master and gave the servant his freedom after service in the army. Frequently, slaves were procured for military service on the same terms. All these devices failed to produce more than a small corps of permanent Continental troops until the war was nearly over. At Washington's insistence, Congress demanded that the troops raised for the 1781 campaign be enlisted for the duration of the war. The main army at this time consisted largely of old men and boys who had enlisted for the bounty, but at least it was a permanent force.

Whatever its shortcomings, the creation in a short time of an army even marginally capable of standing up to British grenadiers was no mean accomplishment. The materials were in some degree at hand. Americans were accustomed from infancy to firearms and more skilled in using them than any other people. Backcountrymen knew how to live outdoors and to survive under harsh physical conditions, besides which they were often good shots. The main obstacle to molding an effective fighting force was lack of discipline. Americans regarded military drill as useless, and they often refused to obey orders or, if they did, delayed carrying them out. They were careless about firearms, discharging them in camp for trivial reasons. General Washington wrote in 1776: "seldom a day passes but some persons are shot by their friends." They neglected sanitation, refusing to wash themselves or clean their clothes, and they defecated where they pleased. As did American troops in the French and Indian War, they so fouled their own camp (to the disgust then of British officers) as to contribute heavily to illness and the spread of disease. They were frequently absent without leave or they deserted, often just to reenlist and get another bounty, although a few joined the British (whose own deserters often joined the Americans). They molested civilians; the vicinity of a camp was exposed to pilfering and vandalism. Drunkenness was a problem, both in and out of camp. There was, besides, the general crowd of camp followers, women, black and white, often with their children, who had no place to go when their men enlisted and who followed them into the army, where they were put on rations. Genteel observers were shocked by the spectacle of these women with "their hair flying, their brows beady with the heat, their belongings slung over one shoulder, chattering and yelling in sluttish shrills as they went and spitting in the gutters."

Washington understood that discipline could only be imposed by degrees on men unaccustomed to arbitrary authority. Even so, he acquired a reputation for being a severe disciplinarian. Public opinion in America would not ordinarily sanction the death penalty for infractions of military discipline, and it was rarely imposed. Whipping was the lesser penalty and it was heavily employed in all armies of the time. The British gave up to 1,000 lashes, the American army at first only 39, then 100. Washington found that 100 lashes would not drive hard-bitten malefactors to repentance, whereupon he asked Congress to sanction 500 so he would not have to invoke the death penalty to enforce discipline. He was not given that permission. Some of his officers, however, had another way: assisted by others, they simply beat the men up.

The behavior of soldiers in war has much in common at all times and places, but although Americans never developed a model army in terms, say, of the high standards of the French expeditionary force, whose troops never fouled their camps, never offended civilians, paid in hard money for what they took, and apparently never got drunk, the problem of discipline diminished after 1778. By this time the Continental army had acquired a core of seasoned veterans habituated to camp life and regulations. In the sense of military exercises, the achievement of discipline owed a great deal to the personality and experience of General Von Steuben, a former Prussian officer who had served as an aide to Frederick the Great. Von Steuben joined Washington's army early in 1778 at Valley Forge, where he at once began to drill cadres of men and send them out to train other men. As discipline improved, Continental troops became more manageable and dependable in the field. They never attained the unthinking obedience and ritualized maneuver inculcated into European armies. Indeed, the Continental army was notable for the independent judgment and iniative exhibited by private soldiers and noncommissioned officers in combat.

Whenever it occurred, combat was intense and brutal, and resulted in heavy casualties. The army, however, seldom engaged in actual fighting more than a few days a year and, except in the south, almost never during the winter months. On the other hand, if a man was wounded at all seriously or caught a malignant disease, it was likely to be the end of him. Until late in the war, sick and wounded men were treated in large hospital centers where they were exposed to teeming contagion. An army doctor wrote in 1781: "America has already lost more men from this course than from the sword of her Enemies." Not long afterward it was reported that 100 sick soldiers of the Maryland line adamantly refused to enter the Continental hospital. Eventually, the Continental medical department treated sick and wounded men as far as possible in small field hospitals, sending only those with chronic or incurable ailments to the main centers.

Until 1782 the Continental army was badly supported by the country. Washington wrote that the men starving at Valley Forge, leaving occasional bloody footprints in the snow for lack of shoes, would have been helpless against a British attack and unable to retreat for want of transport. The army was in even worse condition in 1780, when Washington wrote that the men had been "five or six days together without meat; then as many without bread, and once or twice, two or three days together without either." People would find it hard to believe, he wrote, that "in the same Army, there should be numbers of Men with scarcely as much clothing as would cover their nakedness and at least a fourth of the whole with not even the Shadow of a blanket, severe as the Winter had been." There was no American campaign in 1780. The main army was so feeble that Washington shortly gave up any hope of active operations.

Military pay was low: $6.60 a month for privates, running up to $8 for a sergeant, $20 for a captain, and $50 for a colonel, with additional allowances to officers for extra rations. As late as 1778, when the army was reorganized, the pay of privates remained the same, although officers got a little more. By this time the depreciation of Continental currency had made all salaries worthless. Both officers and men were paid in currency whose value had sunk to two and one-half cents on the dollar by 1780. In that year Congress could not pay the army even in paper money and asked the states to take over their salaries. It also asked the states to compensate the men for their losses in having received depreciated currency in the past. The states complied with these requests but, having little or no money themselves, they could only give their troops in the Continental line state securities which they had no money to redeem. Most of the securities ended up in the coffers of speculators, who bought them at huge discounts from impoverished soldiers and officers. Eventually, neither the states nor Congress could afford military salaries; the army went virtually without pay from the middle of 1780 until its discharge in the spring of 1783.

The loyalty displayed by the army in putting up with hardships and neglect was marvelous even to those who contributed nothing to its support. "Would that our boys had some of this!" was a common toast while raising the wine glass in Philadelphia. General Johann De Kalb, former brigadier general in the French army who joined the Continental army and died fighting to the last at the Battle of Camden, wrote: "No European army would suffer the tenth part of what the Americans suffer. It takes citizens to support hunger, nakedness, toil, and the total want of pay, which constitute the conditions of our soldiers, the hardiest and most patient that are to be found in the world."

Congress, nevertheless, was startled in January 1781, when the Pennsylvania line mutinied. Two officers and six enlisted men were killed when they tried to quell the revolt. The soldiers chose new officers from among themselves and marched away to take up defensive positions, holding General Anthony Wayne in custody. Even though many of the troops consisted of British deserters, they kept scrupulous discipline, plundering not a single inhabitant, and when two British spies came down from New York to persuade them to change their loyalty, they delivered the spies over for execution by American authorities. Their grievances were lack of pay and clothing, but their main complaint was that, having enlisted for three years or the duration of the war, they were being held in service beyond the three years. They considered their enlistments over and were the more indignant because state agents were offering large bounties for short enlistments which they could not take advantage of. Congress in great alarm appointed a committee which went to the mutineers' camp along with the president of Pennsylvania, who brought some hard money with him. In the subsequent negotiation the mutineers were satisfied and returned to their posts. A revolt occurred about the same time in the New Jersey line, but Washington managed to suppress it, hanging a few of the ringleaders. Washington and members of Congress were seriously afraid that these uprisings would spread to the entire army.

While the mutiny of the Pennsylvania line was the only significant challenge to authority offered by common soldiers, the discontent of the officer corps was a continuing problem. "We begin to hate the country for its neglect of us," warned Alexander Hamilton in 1780, at that time a lieutenant colonel on Washington's headquarters staff. The officers endured many of the same deprivations as the men, including lack of pay. They had the usual grievances characteristic of large organizations. They fiercely resented Congress's elevation of rivals to higher rank than themselves for what they considered political reasons, most particularly in the case of French military officers who were virtually assured of high commissions when they arrived bearing letters of recommendation from American agents abroad. The refusal or inability of the country to provide the men and money to make headway against the enemy infuriated the more zealous officers, making them feel the futility of their personal efforts. They were outraged, moreover, by the spectacle of men of their own social class getting wealthy in business while they themselves suffered in the field and spent their private resources for their own support. In 1778 Congress promised officers who remained in service for the duration of the war a bonus of seven years' half pay, but in 1780 Washington made it known that the Continental forces would soon be without officers unless they were given half-pay pensions for life. Although the idea affronted the antimilitary traditions of many Americans, who dreaded anything that might create a special military group or interest in the country, Congress had no alternative and, against the resolute opposition of the New England delegates, granted life pensions. The question of how and in what circumstances the pensions would be paid remained unsettled.

Merchants in Government and the
Deane-Lee Affair

Congress started the war as a policy-forming body without an administrative staff, but, as it took over the functions of a central government, it had to devise ways of coping with practical tasks such as supplying the military forces. Matters of this kind were first handled in an impromptu fashion by committees or individual members of Congress who were given money and instructed to buy supplies and deliver them to the army or navy. Such committees became permanent and, with the addition of hired members who were not delegates to Congress, evolved into boards of war, marine affairs, and the like. The outstanding feature of this procurement system was the employment of merchants who continued in private business while serving the government in an official capacity. There were reasons for this practice. In an age before business had become highly institutional, commerce was conducted by individual merchants dealing on a personal basis with other merchants. The only people who had connections and the expertise to cope with the multifarious details of purchasing commodities, packing them, and arranging their transport were merchants already engaged in such transactions. When employed by the government, they did not give up their private status; their relationship to the government was the same as if they had been commissioned by another businessman. Acting for the government, they freely employed their own partners, bought their own goods, used their own ships, and engaged in trade unrelated to official duties. They were compensated, not by salaries, but by commissions received on the money they spent. It should be noted that this prebureaucratic system had been employed by European governments a century earlier and still characterized some branches of French administration.

The advantage of this system was that, in the absence of any other arrangements, it got things done. Equipped with Continental paper money but with no other resources than their own zeal and ingenuity, Continental agents often performed their duties with skill and devotion to the public interest. Many times —and it was expected of them—they used their own money when they ran out of Continental funds, and the government fell heavily in debt to them. On the other hand, the system inevitably gave rise to a conflict of interest. The general public could not resist the suspicion that when merchants, as procurement agents, did business with themselves and made a profit on the transactions, they often sacrificed the public interest to their own. This charge was repudiated by the merchants concerned, who in terms of their own moral standards saw no ethical problem. "I shall continue," said Robert Morris, one of the greatest of them, "to discharge my duty faithfully to the Public and pursue my Private Fortune by all such honorable and fair means as the times will admit of."

Before the war ended, Congress launched formal investigations into the conduct of the chief officers in most of its executive departments, finding evidence of misbehavior in some cases and failing to find it in others. The investigations were in some measure the outgrowth of the scandals arising from the Deane-Lee affair, a controversy that engulfed Congress for several years and seriously affected national politics. The origins of this dispute went back to 1776, when Congress appointed Silas Deane, a Connecticut merchant, to purchase supplies in France. Upon arriving in France, Deane entered into contracts on behalf of the United States for supplies to be delivered by Beaumarchias, an unofficial agent of the French government. Under the contracts, Beaumarchais was to receive payment; however, another American, Arthur Lee, who had previously conversed with Beaumarchais in London, was convinced that the supplies were in fact a gift to Congress from the French court and that the contracts represented a conspiracy between Deane and Beaumarchais to defraud the United States. Lee was further outraged by Deane's furious pursuit of private business and the speculations on the London stock market which he carried out on the basis of inside knowledge derived from his diplomatic position as American representative at the French court. The Lees of Virginia were a politically influential family, and when Lee's denunciations of Deane were laid before Congress, they became a public issue.

The principal target of the Lees was not Deane, but Robert Morris, a Philadelphia merchant who rose to a commanding position in Congress and the Continental government. A man of wealth, great personal force, outstanding ability, and dedication to the American cause, Morris had been appointed head of the Congressional committee in charge of foreign procurement. In this position he built up a private mercantile empire upon the structure of Congress's commercial and diplomatic representation abroad. Most of the congressional agents in Europe and the West Indies were his business partners, including Silas Deane, and as chief of foreign procurement he conducted Congress's business jointly—and inseparably—with his own. The Lees accused Morris and his associates of systematically milking the funds of the United States. Because France was not yet an open ally, the committee which Morris headed operated in secret, even from Congress, and there was sufficient mystery about its affairs to afford room for allegations of corruption.

Probably the deepest significance of the Deane-Lee imbroglio, however, was its political aspect—a struggle for power in Congress. At the outset of the Revolution, the popular party which drove the country toward war and independence was most decisively represented by the delegates from Massachusetts and Virginia, the so-called Adams-Lee junto. This radical thrust was resisted by delegates from the middle colonies, most notably in opposing independence. Apart from its being a contest to determine which states should dominate Congress, this alignment extended to measures of internal policy, such as paper money, economic legislation, the assertion of congressional authority over the states, and the structure and command of the army. Morris, Deane, and Benjamin Franklin became the figureheads of the middle-state interest as opposed to the Adams-Lee alliance. The divisions not only permeated Congress but reached out to American representatives abroad, whom the fury of the controversy forced to take one side or the other.

The dispute gradually lost its momentum. Deane was recalled, and, when he could not produce documentary evidence to refute the charges against him, was sent back to France to get the necessary papers. He eventually disgraced himself in the eyes of Americans by writing public letters that urged giving up the war. For a time Franklin himself was in danger of being recalled, but he was sufficiently eminent and influential to withstand his attackers. Morris retired from Congress, his prestige injured but not destroyed. Not until the military crisis of 1780 transformed the membership of Congress did the repercussions of the Deane-Lee affair subside. Its effect was to embitter relations among members of Congress and between different sections of the country, to excite public disgust with the party split that frequently animated the decisions of Congress, and, in some degree, to impair the effectiveness of American diplomacy abroad.

The War Economy

A war in which the American, the British, and later the French armies drew all or part of their subsistence from the country stimulated an enormous economic boom. The Continental and state governments alone spent the equivalent of $158 million to $168 million in hard money. Although Britain had to bring over most supplies from the British Isles, it paid hard money to its troops in America and the troops spent their pay locally. Britain also laid out large sums in the course of campaigns—money which found its way into the American economy. Between 1770 and 1781 Britain expended nearly $53 million in America, most of it after the war started and all of it in hard coin or the equivalent. The French after they arrived contributed another $3 million specie. All this money pouring into the economy vastly increased the purchasing power of the American people and created an extraordinary demand for goods of all kinds, not only such provisions as were eagerly sought by the armies but also commodities for the civilian market, particularly imported luxury articles—things that self-sufficient America bought when it had extra income. The result was a real price inflation, multiplied by the depreciation of paper money

Fortunes were quickly made and lost. Business opportunities were such that a loan of ready money in Philadelphia commanded interest as high as 5 percent a month. The profits on imported goods ran up to 600 percent, that is, if the ship that carried the goods was not captured by the enemy, in which case both the ship and cargo had to be written off. Privateer owners made fortunes if they were lucky; if not, they lost everything. Merchants received extravagant prices for provisions sold to the army, if they got paid. Farmers experienced a degree of prosperity they had never known before, unless their crops were confiscated by government officers. The class of the population which stood only to lose, not gain, was urban laborers, whose wages lagged behind the increasing cost of food and housing.

Currency depreciation was a disrupting factor. All classes of the population spent or invested their money as quickly as possible in order to get rid of it before it depreciated in their hands. Ordinary people had no trouble because they seldom hung onto money anyhow. People with fixed incomes in the form of rent received from land or interest from money on loan incurred losses, and old debts paid in depreciated currency returned little to the creditor. Merchants and men of property generally claimed to lose heavily from currency depreciation, and some were, in fact, reduced in fortune. However, most men of property soon learned to protect themselves. They anticipated future depreciation by charging higher prices for goods, entered into contracts stated in hard money rather than paper money values, or, if they were landowners, commuted tenant payments into commodities rather than money. Transactions on a year's or 18 months' credit, normal before the war, now became a rarity: business was on a cash basis.

State and local governments made heroic efforts to stop currency depreciation, keep prices down, and procure supplies for the army. They had at hand a battery of traditional economic controls, dating back to medieval practice, which they had freely employed as colonies. Legal tender laws compelled people to accept paper money at a stipulated value, imposing penalties on those who refused to do so or who charged higher prices in paper money than in silver. The price of goods and labor was fixed by law. Elaborate regulations struck at monopoly and other types of conspiracy to raise prices. A further device was to lay down embargoes preventing the export of commodities needed by the army, thus increasing their availability within the country. All these regulations were enforced at the local level by citizens' committees, who kept merchants and their activities under surveillance and investigated complaints against them.

The result of economic regulation was a nearly universal black market. Except when prices were a matter of public record, such as the pay of soldiers and government functionaries or compensation given to persons whose goods or services were commandeered for public use, transactions moved according to the actual rather than the nominal value of paper money and at going rather than official prices. People would not work at the fixed prices, nor would merchants sell; their goods went into hiding and reappeared only at illegal prices. Similarly, the laws against monopoly accomplished little. American cities and towns were relatively isolated market areas, in which it was easy for a few merchants to corner the supply of a particular commodity and raise the price. Embargoes were in many colonies evaded by merchants who as government procurement officers had special permission to export goods; their cargoes were often private rather than public.

In spite of earnest and sometimes frantic efforts of committees, prices kept moving upward and paper money continued to depreciate. Merchants, who had the most conspicuous opportunities to make gains, bore the brunt of public resentment. It became ever more difficult for the federal and state governments to purchase supplies for the army as the amount of hard money in the hands of private citizens increased from British expenditures and American sales of provisions to the West Indies. The governments had only paper money to offer, whereas merchants could often sell for hard money in the private market; hence they would not offer goods to government except at exorbitant prices, sometimes double or triple what public officers considered a fair price. As General Washington viewed his hungry and destitute army, he raged against the profiteers, considering them a greater danger to America than the enemy. He wanted them hanged. His youthful aide, Alexander Hamilton, who as a new immigrant had taken up America's fight for freedom in a spirit of lofty idealism, sometimes wondered whether the country was so corrupt as not to be worth saving.

Some merchants were unconscionable profit seekers or basically loyalist in their sympathies and unattached to the American cause. But even the most patriotic merchants, who were deeply concerned with the country's welfare, came to believe that reliance upon economic controls was fruitless and destructive. They argued that natural laws governing economic behavior were more effective than legislative decrees. Let all regulations be dropped, they said, and more goods would be produced and come out of hiding. If free competition were allowed, prices would eventually find realistic levels and monopolists would counteract one another. Whatever their patriotism, however, merchants were also deeply offended by what they considered the arrogance of committees, which presumed to regulate their private conduct and judge the morality of their behavior. They felt singled out for persecution.

Committee Rule

Events such as the Fort Wilson riot that took place in Philadelphia in 1779 made men of property feel the menace of popular action. The general background of the Fort Wilson incident was a bitter struggle over the democratic state constitution of 1776, which turned political power over to the popular party and outraged many conservatives and quasi-loyalist Quakers, who refused to take an oath to support it. So deeply was the state divided between "Constitutionalists," or popular party, and the more conservative "Republicans" that the government had difficulty in mobilizing its resources to fight the British. The direct cause of the riot was the failure of price regulations and other economic controls to halt the drastic inflation. For months there had been continuing tumult, committee investigations, and demonstrations against merchants who violated price regulations and who, as government agents, were privileged to export wheat through the embargo. Attempts to enforce legal prices had brought business to a standstill.

A meeting of radical militia was held on October 4 with the idea of seizing and shipping to New York the women and children of loyalists who had gone over to the enemy. The meeting decided instead to rid the city of conspicuous loyalists and "political Quakers." Attracting a large crowd as they moved through the streets, the militiamen seized a few Quakers and, after allowing one of them to eat his lunch, paraded them around town, the drum beating out the rogue's march. The militia and the crowd then went to the house of James Wilson, a prominent politician and Republican leader. Previously warned that he had been named as a target of the day's demonstration, Wilson had gathered a group of friends; they took up arms and barricaded themselves in Wilson's house. During the morning his house was guarded by the City Light Horse, the so-called silk-stocking brigade, an elitist troop of militia that supported the Republican faction; however, the City Light Horse went home to lunch. In its absence the radical militia and the crowd arrived on the scene with two cannons. An exchange of taunts and insults followed, whereupon firing started; as the crowd stormed the house, several militiamen were killed and many of the attackers were wounded. The crowd broke in the door, gained the interior, and would have killed the defenders but for the arrival of Governor Joseph Reed with the Light Horse militia. Order was restored, but the next day, when Germans outside the city learned that several of their countrymen had been killed, their militia advanced upon the city. Governor Reed persuaded them to disband. All parties to this affray were shocked by the unforeseen consequences, and the incident proved to be the high water mark of partisan conflict in the city. Nevertheless, two days later General Benedict Arnold, who had been accused (and rightly) of unprincipled speculation and abuse of his office as commandant of the city after the British evacuation the previous year, was attacked in the streets, and only drove off his assailants by brandishing his pistols.

Such incidents were exceptional in their degree of violence and not typical of Philadelphia or any other city; indeed, during the Fort Wilson riot the popular leaders had tried to restrain the mob. Yet, on a lesser scale similar affrays occurred frequently enough to arouse apprehension and resentment among the better sort of people. In Philadelphia, sailors, striking for higher wages in 1778, boarded ships and dismantled their rigging; they were put down by Continental troops. In Albany, New York, merchants accused of monopolizing were forced to stand on a scaffold in the town center and swear to observe regulations. In Boston, a mechanic who took the name "Joyce, Jr." after one of the executioners of Charles I, raised a mob of 500 men to enforce the antimonopoly laws. Abigail Adams wrote that he was "mounted on horseback, with a red coat, a white wig, and a drawn sword, with drum and fife following." General Horatio Gates wrote from the Virginia backcountry: "We in Virginia live (if it can be call'd living) neither under Monarchy, Aristocracy nor Democracy; if it deserves any name it is a Mac-ocracy— that is, that a Banditte of Scotch Irish Servants or their immediate Descendants (whose names generally begin with Mac) are our Lords and Rulers." A loyalist who was driven out when he attempted to return to his home in New York in 1783 wrote: "The country in general is under the dominion of committees. . . . The language of the committees is that none shall rule but the majority of the people, and that the committees represent the majority—that the acts and agreements of the Congress, the legislatures, governors and rulers, are all to be subject to the will of the people expressed by the committees."

Mass Expropriation

As paper money depreciated to the point where it would buy little, no matter how much was spent, Congress and the states began to rely upon impressments, a kind of official violence that most Americans would have denounced in any government but their own. Washington and other commanders occasionally authorized seizures of produce and wagons in the early stages of the war, preferably from loyalists and others who refused to sell goods to the army. In recognition of state sovereignty, Congress requested the states to establish procedures for carrying out impressments under state authorities. By 1779 impressments were one of the ways that the army was kept in the field; within another year they were the only way.

Continental and state officers took whatever the army needed from the inhabitants without regard to their political loyalties. When military forces camped nearby or when procurement agents operated in the neighborhood, farmers lost their grain, their livestock, and sometimes the horses and wagons they needed for their harvests. When procurement agents got wind of commodities stored in a merchant's warehouse, they took them. Wagon drivers frequently found themselves and their teams working for the Continental army. As long as government agents had money, their victims had a choice of accepting payment in the absurdly low prices set by price control laws. But increasingly they received only certificates, which neither the federal nor the state governments had money to redeem.

From 1778 on, impressments were implemented wherever the war moved by drastic state legislation that gave authorities unlimited power of seizure on the principle that "those who are nearest to where the scene of action is to be, must expect to give up everything they have which is wanted for the enterprise." Frequently all goods above family need were declared subject to confiscation. In the circumstances, farmers in some areas began raising nothing more than their families consumed. They hid their horses and took the wheels off their wagons. In some cases impressments were conducted at the point of a bayonet; occasionally they caused bloodshed. Nevertheless, given the magnitude of this general levy upon the people, there was surprisingly little resistance.

The Unity of Patriots

The willingness of the people at large to submit to the arbitrary actions of their own governments testified to the underlying unity of patriots, which was never broken by the vicissitudes of war. Loyalists were the divisive element, and they revealed themselves wherever the country was occupied by British troops. Also, for many Americans the war lasted too long; they became disenchanted and lost their zeal in the cause. Yet the effective patriotism of the country never wavered. From the time Massachusetts stood alone as the object of British reprisals, Britain was never able to disrupt the line of American states nor deal with any one of them singly. Except in Georgia, which had been settled only recently, the British could not establish a civil government in any area that they invaded. Their authority extended only to the limits of their military power. At no stage of the war was there the slightest indication that the patriots in any state or section of the country could be induced to desert the cause. There were, in fact, almost no outstanding traitors; Benedict Arnold gained immortality because he was an exception.

This unity, moreover, was voluntary and not coerced by overwhelming power at the center. Congress would have had the greatest difficulty in repressing defections if they had been supported by state governments. Without even the constitutional authority to compel obedience among the states, Congress relied upon their free acceptance of its decisions. The response of 13 sovereign governments, each with its own interests and urgent problems, was, in the circumstances, remarkable. Congressional decisions were variously interpreted by the states as they consulted their own necessities, but in all that related to the war effort they never denied Congress's right to act for the Union or their obligation to support the central government, and they tried, often at great cost, to fulfill the requests of Congress.

One source of unity was the person and legend of George Washington, who was already an international hero. For the educated and liberal intelligentsia of Europe and America brought up on the literary classics of antiquity, Washington appeared as the incarnation of Cincinnatus, the old Roman patriot who, called to his country's defense, threw aside his plow and took up his sword to repel the enemy and then, disdaining all rewards of wealth and position held out to him by a grateful nation, returned to the life of a simple farmer. Washington was the archetype of republican virtue, and his conduct put not a single taint upon that image. He was not a great general, and yet in his hands the war succeeded. He persevered under the most distressing and infuriating difficulties, with untrained, undisciplined troops and raw militia levies which could not stand the enemy's advance. He kept going with pitifully small forces when even those forces were virtually incapacitated for lack of supplies. In defeat, he remained imperturbable, sustaining the confidence of those around him. He withstood with dignity the conspiracies of rival military officers and their friends in Congress to oust him from his command. Always, he scrupulously observed the subordination of military to civilian authority, even when, in his opinion, the decisions of Congress were irresponsible and destructive. Above all, he was incorruptible, particularly where it was important—in resisting the lure of power. During the darkest days of the war in 1780, there was much talk of making him a "dictator," and some of his officers urged him to assume such authority. Washington carefully observed the limits of his military duty. At the time of the British evacuation, one Englishman wondered why he did not become king of the United States. The Englishman misconceived the views of Americans; one thing they would never have accepted was a king. However, if a king had been thrust upon them, they would have chosen Washington. No other man was so highly respected or trusted. His honor helped to sustain the nation's morale.

CHAPTER VIII

Social, Economic, and Political Change

Interpretations

In 1835 the great French social theorist Alexis de Tocqueville remarked that, in the last 700 years of European development, every historical incident, every social and economic change, had so consistently fostered the growth of democracy as to lead one to the belief that it was God's will. Tocqueville made this observation in reflecting upon the nature of American society, which he considered the world's most fully realized example of democracy. In explaining democracy in America, Tocqueville credited the Revolution with breaking the country's ties with Europe and setting it on the path of its separate evolution, and yet he also took note of the conditions of settlement and the frontier environment which at an earlier time had set a pattern of growth different from that of the Old World.

Historians are still debating the relative importance of the factors that Tocqueville mentioned. One school of interpretation emphasizes the effect of the American Revolution in bringing about democratic change. The Revolution was not only a struggle for home rule, but over "who should rule at home." Patriots, it is said, were divided by class and sectional differences and not wholly in agreement as to their ultimate goals. Those who had wealth or status under the existing order wished in the main to preserve that order. From this group came the aristocratic "Whigs" who provided the higher leadership of the Revolutionary movement. Many of them at first opposed independence, fearful of unchecked majority rule if the colonies should cast off British authority. When their opposition proved unsuccessful, they struggled to maintain, as far as possible, the rule of the elite and a social order based on deference to higher rank. But the Revolution drew in the common people. Tradesmen and mechanics of the towns and the small farmers of the countryside supported and implemented the actions that led to war and independence. To them Britain represented not only the oppressor but an Old World system of aristocracy and privilege. Implicit in the struggle against Britain and her loyalist adherents was an attack upon aristocracy and privilege at home. Irresistibly, the Revolution moved in democratic channels. The departure of loyalists weakened the aristocratic segment of American society. The confiscation and sale of their property broke up large estates and widened the distribution of land. The disestablishment of the Anglican church removed one of the props of elite dominance and fostered religious freedom. Finally, new revolutionary governments were constructed on the principle that government derives its authority from the people, and in their structure and function these governments were more democratic than in colonial times.

This view of the Revolution is sharply challenged by another school of historical interpretation which either denies that significant social change took place or minimizes the importance of changes that did occur. Historians of this school deprecate the emphasis on class and sectional conflict, stressing instead the degree of consensus that prevailed among the American people, who, they say, were in general committed to the existing forms of government and society. They argue that the Revolution was not associated with any crusade for internal reform, that its object was merely to preserve a status quo satisfactory to the colonists but threatened after 1760 by British measures. There was no lower-class uprising, and because so many of the upper class embraced the patriot cause, the elite that governed the country in colonial times held control of the revolutionary movement and never lost its prestige among the people or its leadership. Finally, so it is said, there was no great change in class relationships based upon ownership of property. An attribute of the French and later the Russian revolutions was a sweeping redistribution of property which depressed some groups and elevated others. This, it is said, did not occur to any extent during the American Revolution. Although a vast amount of loyalist property was confiscated and sold, it frequently ended in possession of the same class of men as its former owners. In short, the Revolution did not materially alter the existing distribution of property.

The conflicting interpretations expressed by these arguments are sometimes rooted in the different appraisals that historians make of colonial society. One historian will portray colonial society as the virtual image of English society, emphasizing the similarity in institutions. In terms of this perspective, the Revolution brought pronounced changes. Another historian will stress the differences between colonies and mother country, the degree to which democratic modes and fluidity of social classes already existed in America. Against this background the Revolution will scarcely exhibit any democratic content not already attributed to colonial society.

Interpretations of the American Revolution, then, are in flux. Yet differences of emphasis do not necessarily indicate a contradiction. Historians dispute the *degree* of change. Most would agree that the Revolution did not overturn the existing order as did the later French Revolution or the Russian Revolution of the 20th century. Yet few would deny that it brought about changes in government and society, and that these changes led to greater democracy.

The extent of change must be measured by what was possible at the time. Unlike 18th century French Revolutionists, Americans were not living under the old regime, and they had no need to stage a social revolution away from *that,* except, perhaps, to get rid of the king, which they did, and to cope with what was left of aristocratic privilege, which was a task before them. Modern collectivism had not yet been born, nor did Americans conceive of it. They were thoroughly committed to Enlightenment principles, which prescribed the *form* of their institutions; they nearly all agreed, rich and poor, on the value of republican government, private property, legal equality, and a capitalist, free-market economy, the essentials of which they largely possessed before independence. The Revolution formally established these institutions. Internal struggles were not about these things. They were about democracy, not only in institutions left over from the feudal past but in arrangements being laid down in the present. The tendency of the popular movement was to drive democracy as far as it would go within the existing framework of institutions.

The Loyalists

It was said at the time that a third of the American people were patriots, a third indifferent, and a third loyal to Britain. The estimate no doubt understates the number of sincere patriots, but it gives some idea of the magnitude of the divisions among Americans. It is certainly true that a considerable part of the population was openly or secretly attached to the British cause. Loyalism had many sources. The hard choices that revolution thrusts upon people are more often determined by emotional attachments than by rational judgment. Loyalty to Britain sprang from residual love of the mother country and an inbred sense of British nationalism. It was sharpened by resentment against rabble-rousing patriots and the mobs that abused British supporters and destroyed their property. It was mixed in varying proportions with self-interest. Men of large property or those attached to British official society in America were reluctant to consign their fortunes and their prospects in life to the dubious issue of rebellion. This kind of loyalism, in fact, preceded the Revolution. In colonial times a segment of the upper class had always identified itself with British culture and often with the Anglican church, in opposition to the homespun, fundamentalist mass of the common people. As a result of this British attachment, such persons frequently held lucrative offices and high status in society. Typically, they supported the American cause during the 1760s but, as the disputes deepened into rebellion, their basic identification with Britain pushed them into loyalism. In spite of wealth and social position, they were unable to organize much support for their side. Indeed, they were handicapped in trying to do this by fear of the people and of popular movements. Aware of being a privileged minority, they felt that their main hope lay in the continuation of British rule.

There were loyalists in all colonies. Possibly a majority of the leading families of eastern Massachusetts and of Connecticut, and many if not most of the prominent merchants of New York City and Philadelphia, were loyalists. The Virginia aristocracy was overwhelmingly patriot, but Britain had a more numerous following in South Carolina and Georgia. A large proportion of loyalists in the south were English and Scotch merchants who had lived in the colonies only a short time. Everywhere the Anglican clergy was predominantly loyalist. Loyalists, however, were to be found in all ranks of the population, especially among minority groups threatened by majority domination. The Quakers and German sects of Pennsylvania were neutral by faith; in fact, many were loyalists. Farmers in the upper Hudson River Valley, who a decade earlier had rioted against their landlords, sided with Britain, as we have seen, because their landlords were patriots; for similar reasons loyalism was prevalent among ex-Regulators of the Carolina backcountry whose eastern foes were now patriot leaders. A different set of circumstances attached merchants and tradesmen in northern New Jersey and Long Island to the British interest; loyalism enabled them to conduct profitable trade with British-held New York City.

Persons stigmatized as loyalists suffered varying degrees of persecution, and by 1778 all the states had enacted laws confiscating the property of those who actively aided the enemy or took refuge within the British lines. Of the more than 100,000 who left the country, most went to Canada, where they formed the first considerable body of English inhabitants. The loyalists migration deprived the United States of many of its first families. Gentlemen of wealth, education, and position were conspicuous among the émigrés: De Lanceys, Van Cortlandts, Morrises, De Peysters, Jessups, and Philipses of New York; Higginsons, Chandlers, Pepperells, and Hutchinsons of Massachusetts; Wentworths of New Hampshire; Whartons, Penningtons, Galloways, and Pembertons of Pennsylvania; McCullochs of North Carolina; Fenwicks of South Carolina. The fact that at least as many other gentlemen espoused the patriot cause ensured that the Revolution would not develop into a class conflict. Nevertheless, the defection of so many outstanding citizens damaged the prestige of the American elite, and it seems clear that the departure of the loyalists altered in some degree the social composition of the nation and strengthened its democratic propensities. The emigration was substantial in numbers. Relative to the population, five times as many émigrés left America as fled France during the French Revolution, and unlike the French émigrés, most of them did not return. The behavior of those who remained and of the few who came back after the war strongly suggests that the exodus of loyalists divested American society of elements which would have exerted a conservative influence upon the nation's development.

The Distribution of Land

The confiscation of loyalist property resulted in a major shift of land ownership. After the war about 5,000 loyalists entered claims against the British government for £10 million as compensation for their losses. Eventually they received £3,292,000, a sum considerably less than the actual value of property seized by Revolutionary state governments. Several large proprietary holdings were wiped out by the confiscations: the land held by the Penn family, valued at $1 million, the Baltimore estates in Maryland, and the holdings of Lord Fairfax in the northern neck of Virginia.* Lesser proprietary estates from Maine to Georgia also went on the block. In some cases tenants on the land were

---

* The Penn and Baltimore families received partial compensation from Pennsylvania and Maryland respectively after the war.

given the right to purchase it, but there is little to indicate that state governments aimed to widen the distribution of land or accomplish any other social purpose. Apart from punishing loyalists, their object was to raise money to wage war and discharge public debts.

Confiscated estates were divided up and sold, often to speculators or to people who were already substantial landowners. There is evidence, on the other hand, that estates were purchased by former owners, by tenants, or by small and middle-sized farmers. In either case, the end result was the destruction of many large estates and a wider distribution of land. However, the evidence scarcely suggests an agrarian revolution. The dispossession of loyalists may have weakened the economic base of the gentry, but transfer to small holders was not on a sufficient scale to affect the social structure.

Elimination of feudal survivals in land tenure also had no far-reaching results. Quitrents, formerly due in most colonies to king or proprietor, were abolished during the Revolution. Except in Maryland, however, they had never been regularly collected in colonial times. Another reform more symbolic than real was the abolition of primogeniture and entail. These institutions were designed to buttress a landed gentry and to keep large estates intact, but studies of Virginia indicate that they were not very effective in late colonial times. Primogeniture, by which an estate passed entire to the eldest son, operated only when the possessor died intestate; but most Virginia gentlemen made wills, parceling their estates among their descendants. Entail, a legal device by which one could prevent the alienation of any part of his estate by a descendant, was regularly broken by recourse to law.

Expansion of Small Farmer Society

Of far greater significance than any changes in the distribution of existing land ownership was the opening of a new agricultural empire. In the late colonial period, as we have seen, economic opportunity declined with the increasing shortage of cheap land. Older lands of the east wore out and in some areas were not sufficient to support the population. Expansion into fresh western land was retarded in some of the colonies by the existence of large land grants and proprietary estates, notably those of the Penns and the Baltimores, which were held for sale at high prices. Migration beyond the Appalachians, blocked by the French before the French and Indian War, was prohibited afterward by the Proclamation of 1763. Confined in geographical area, American society grew more stratified.

With the Revolution, a vast area stretching from the occupied areas of the existing states westward to the Appalachians and beyond them to the Mississippi River fell into possession of state and federal governments. This land was immediately put into the course of settlement, given as bonuses to Continental and state troops, paid to federal and state creditors, and sold to speculators who undertook colonization schemes. The Indians had to be beaten back before the land could be occupied and the immediate profits often went to speculators and wealthy men; yet a multitude of farmers gained a homestead. The economic base of a small farmer society was preserved.

The Revolution was hardly over before a massive wave of migration entered the mountain valleys of the southern backcountry and pushed over the Appalachians into Virginia and Kentucky. In 1779 the population of Kentucky was less than 300; by 1785 it was 30,000, and by 1790, over 73,000, including 12,430 slaves. Tennessee's population was 7,700 in 1776; by 1790 it was 35,700. New Englanders went mainly to the northern frontiers of Maine and Vermont; an estimated 100,000 emigrated before 1790. Many regions of the east were virtually unpeopled as farmers deserted the rocks of New England and the exhausted clay of the Tidewater. The migration was continuous, unorganized, spontaneous, and irresistible, a swarming of people that many easterners were afraid would soon make the west the most populous area of the country.

Political Ideas and the State Constitutions

Americans of the Revolutionary generation inherited the same political traditions, read the same books on political theory, and as colonists shared a common experience in matters of government. Their political ideas were therefore singularly uniform, well defined, and held with certitude, for it was characteristic of the Enlightenment for men to think that the principles underlying government had the same scientific validity, once discovered, as those revealed by the study of nature.

Americans distinguished between liberty, which concerned private rights, and democracy, which involved the location of power in government and the community. The Lockean tradition with its distrust of government and its emphasis upon natural rights had to do with liberty, which it defined mainly in terms of the protection of individual rights against government. There was nevertheless a fundamentally democratic implication in the natural rights philosophy because it asserted the principle of majority rule. Conflicts of interest within society itself were dismissed with the simple argument that so far as men's interests related to government, they were harmonious; everyone had a common stake in his natural rights, which it was the function of government to serve. As men were rational creatures, with compatible interests, there was no danger that a political majority would oppress the minority. "Property," Thomas Paine once said, "has nothing to fear from the people."

There was, however, a countervailing political tradition, more ancient than Lockeanism, which was based on the premise that property has everything to fear from the people. This body of theory defined liberty mainly in terms of preserving minority rights against the majority. Unlike Lockeanism, which anticipated the invasion of private rights chiefly from government, its main concern was the tyranny to be expected from an unchecked majority. As formulated by Plato and Polybius, the classical theory envisaged government not as standing above society, but as reflecting the nature of the society and the relative power of different social groups. Government was therefore the arena of class conflict. There were three ideal forms: rule by one, by the few, and by the many. But monarchy, aristocracy, and democracy were each liable to corruption, and as one form of government degenerated, it lapsed into another; thus a corrupt monarchy was superceded by aristocracy, and a corrupt aristocracy by democracy. Each form had its characteristic virtues and vices, but a degenerate democracy was the worst government of all. As the history of Greece and Rome as well as more modern states abundantly proved, unchecked democracy always ended in expropriation of the propertied classes and a regime of lawlessness and violence from which the state had eventually to be saved by the restoration of a monarch. To arrest this cyclical progress, the ancients conceived that a government must incorporate elements of the three basic forms—monarchy, aristocracy, and democracy. The balance thus attained allowed scope for the pursuit of class interests in a legal way, and, because social classes checked one another, such a government could be stable.

From the viewpoint of the classical theory, the ability of any government to maintain a balance of classes and prevent the spoilation of one class by another was its primary virtue. In colonial times Britain was regarded as presenting the model of a balanced government. It had a limited monarchy in the king, an aristocracy seated in the House of Lords, and a Commons in which the people were represented. To this symmetrical arrangement, it was believed Britain owed its relative stability and the security of rights and property which all classes of citizens presumably enjoyed. It was the corruption of this government by monarchical usurpation of power which Americans said they were revolting against.

At the outset of the Revolution, Lockeanism rather than the classical theory was uppermost in the minds of patriots who were seeking intellectual justification for rebellion. Conscious of patriot unity, they scorned any idea of a division of interest, except as between the foes and the hirelings of British power. It was the loyalists who were most inclined to recite the danger of power in the hands of the multitude, to which they attributed the breakdown of order and the drift toward revolution. Nevertheless, even among patriots, there were some who because of principle, position, or wealth could not forget the well-known dangers of democracy. As resolute as anybody else in the fight against Britain, they were apprehensive of danger to liberty not alone from the king but from the people.

The state constitutions adopted during the Revolution exhibit an unresolved clash between the democratic thrust of the patriot movement and the defense of elite privilege. With respect to the form of government they present no radical innovations. The new governments were similar to those of the past, adapted to republicanism by the substitution of electoral processes for the appointive powers formerly exercised by the king. With respect to everything connected with protection of individual rights against abuse of power by government, Americans were in agreement. The constitutions were, first of all, written documents, which defined the structure and powers of government—a higher law beyond the reach of transient bodies of legislators. The purpose was to ensure the rule of laws, not of men. Seven of the constitutions were prefaced by bills of rights, which spelled out the rights and immunities of citizens. Americans also agreed in principle on the separation of powers, although this concept had a different meaning to different people. To most Americans, the creation of separate executive, legislative, and judicial branches, each able to function independently, was a Lockean device to prevent a single individual or faction from gaining control of the entire government, a way of protecting liberty against government. To conservatives, however, who were primarily concerned with the dangers of majority rule, the establishment of independent branches of government, with one or more reserved for the elite, was a way of protecting liberty against the majority.

In all the states controversies arose over democratic reforms, and many shades of opinion appeared. Popular leaders showed a disposition to reduce property qualifications for the suffrage, correct inequalities in representation, and give the legislature, particularly the lower house, which was most directly responsive to popular will, supremacy over the other branches of government.

Their conservative opponents generally tried to maintain property qualifications, deny equal representation to western and poor farmer districts, establish an upper legislative house or senate which would represent property rather than persons, and strengthen the executive and judicial branches against the legislature.

The results of this struggle varied in different states. In many cases suffrage was extended beyond the liberal standards that already prevailed. Any adult male who paid taxes had the right to vote in Pennsylvania, Delaware, North Carolina, and Georgia. In most states, the legislature overshadowed the executive and the judiciary. The powers of the governor, formerly the agent of king or proprietor, were drastically reduced. In seven states he was elected by the legislature, and in nine states for a one-year term. Most states had a plural executive, in which the governor was merely the chief officer. His powers of appointment were typically assumed by the legislature, and in only one state did he have a veto over legislation. These arrangements were democratic in the sense that they enhanced the power of the legislature.

Democratic tendencies were checked by restraints upon majority rule. With one or two exceptions, the inequalities of representation prevailing in colonial times were perpetuated. In South Carolina, for example, the populous upcountry, which contained three-fourths of the population, had (in 1778) only 58 seats in the assembly, the low country 144. In Virginia, where counties still had equal representation under the state constitution, the sparsely inhabited Tidewater continued to outweigh the populous interior. In these and other states the provisions made for the upper house of the legislature, or senate, threw additional obstacles in the way of direct popular rule. Suffrage requirements were generally higher than for the lower house, and membership was restricted to persons of substantial property. In Maryland and New Jersey, senators had to own a landed estate of £1,000. In South Carolina, they had to have an estate of £2,000 and the governor an estate of £10,000. Such provisions were designed to give men of property a separate and weighty influence in public affairs.

The Revolutionary constitution of Pennsylvania was outstanding in its democratic features. Because the old colonial leadership resisted independence, the popular party was able to seize power and to write a constitution which was a model of its views. The constitution provided for a single-house legislature. The governor was merely president of an elected executive council, which had no veto over legislation. There were no property qualifications for holding office, and the legislature was elected by all taxpaying adult males. Representation, hitherto weighted heavily in favor of the east, now favored the backcountry. There were no checks against simple majority rule, and for this reason conservatives despised the constitution and for years refused to take an oath to uphold it, even though, because they refused, they were excluded from voting or holding office.

Massachusetts was the one state which went through the whole procedure implicit in the idea that government derives its authority from the people. Elsewhere, the constitutions were drafted by legislative bodies and not submitted for popular approval. Massachusetts called a special convention to write a constitution, and this was subsequently put to a popular vote. The people rejected it, but they approved a second draft. The result, achieved by political manipulation, was a victory for the conservatives. The constitution set up a strong governor with appointive powers and a veto over legislation. The bicameral legislature included a senate in which representation was based upon the amount of taxes paid rather than population. Voting was restricted to persons who owned property valued at £60, a figure higher than in colonial times. Members of the legislature had to own substantial property: a £100 freehold or other property worth £200 in the lower house, and a freehold of £300 or other property worth £600 in the upper house. The governor had to own a freehold of £1,000.

Government by the People

The democratic impulses of the Revolution were not fully expressed in the organization of new state governments; nevertheless certain fundamental changes took place. No longer did the apparatus of British rule interfere with self-determination. Laws were not subject to review and disallowance by the Privy Council, and Americans did not have to contend with governors who were under instructions of the Board of Trade. More important, all branches of government, including the executive as well as both houses of the legislature, were now elected, and the lower house, which was the most popular branch, had most of the power. Notwithstanding property qualifications and other restrictive devices, events proved that the new governments were extremely susceptible to popular influence.

Most important was a change of the spirit in which the government was carried on in the United States. A republic had been founded in a world of kings. Its official creed, still debatable elsewhere, was that government derives its authority not from divine mandate, ancient right, or irrevocable contract, but from the continuing will of the people. The popular movement of the Revolution ensured that the will of the people would mean the will of the majority. In colonial times public office had been almost entirely the prerogative of men of wealth, family, and culture. Legislators looked upon themselves and men like themselves as persons to whom governing had been entrusted, not as mere deputies of the people. Although ultimately responsible to the electorate, they prided themselves upon their independence, conceiving it their duty to act in terms of the public interest as they interpreted it rather than according to the views of their constituents. They were an elite body vested with the conduct of government as a function of their status.

From the outset of the Revolution the politicization of the people invaded the elite monopoly of government. The top leadership changed in some degree as many prominent men became loyalists and their places were taken by patriots, in some cases by men who had risen to eminence by appealing to the crowd. The composition of legislatures changed markedly. After the Revolution men of inconspicuous family and little wealth were frequently elected, and the balance of power in legislatures shifted westward as newly settled districts gained representation. By the mid-1780s members of state legislatures on the average owned half as much property as in colonial times; corresponding changes in their occupations took place as the proportion of merchants and lawyers elected to legislatures sank by half and that of farmers more than doubled.

These differences in part reflected more liberal qualifications for voting and holding office, but their primary cause was a shift in voter attitudes. Political office was not so generally considered as belonging by right to the upper class. In fact, it became increasingly possible to win elections by playing upon popular distrust of the great and the powerful. Similarly, government over the whole range of its activities was conducted more openly and with more regard for public opinion. Legislators had to stand for election every year. Debates were reported in newspapers, along with the more frequent roll call votes now taken in legislative proceedings. Town meetings and other political bodies instructed delegates how to vote and what to stand for, and even insisted that these instructions were binding.

Alarming to conservatives was a propensity toward mass political initiative that had begun with the committees and conventions of the Revolution. Popular meetings were now held in times of stress to discuss and pass resolutions on public issues. Conservatives regarded such bodies as anarchic and disruptive of all order in society because they usurped the right of the duly constituted legislature to decide upon public issues. In fact, that right was challenged by some radical populists who, mulling over the implications of the sovereignty of the people, refused to acknowledge the legitimacy even of their own legislatures if their actions ran counter to popular will.

The Articles of Confederation

The conception that Americans had of central government was shaped by their attitude toward Britain. Since British authority had limited their self-rule in colonial times, they regarded a central government as by its nature restrictive of local freedom. In throwing off British rule, the patriots in each colony aimed at governing themselves. Although Congress emerged as a central authority after the war started, Americans did not propose to bind themselves anew in fetters similar to those they had cast off.

Their negative attitude toward central government was sharpened by widespread criticism in both Britain and America of the corruptness of the British system. With the example of Britain and the European monarchies in mind, Americans thought of central government as given to excessive bureaucracy, standing armies, large and permanent public debts, and heavy taxes. It was a distant force, inaccessible to the common people, and too often guided by sinister private influence. Americans, as we have seen, glorified local government, which they thought of as minimal in its functions, cheap, simple, and unburdened by debt. The ideal local government was visible, conducted by the people's representatives, weak enough to be checked and in the last resort withstood—in a word, consonant with liberty. This concept was supported by a body of political theory which held that a republic could exist only on a small scale and in a simple, agricultural society. This idea, in turn, was coupled with romantic notions, much in vogue during the 18th century, which eulogized the honest husbandman and the agricultural way of life. In terms of the pastoral ideal of a simple, virtuous, agricultural, self-governing, and free society which most Americans cherished, central government was at best a necessary evil.

Local government was in common opinion associated with liberty; it was also, at least among conservatives, linked with democracy. Even before the Revolution there were some Americans who wanted to strengthen British authority and reduce the powers of colonial legislatures in order to restrict popular influence upon government. This idea was often held by men who became loyalists, but was expressed by many patriots. Such men, particularly in the middle colonies, dreaded breaking ties with Britain, but when the movement for independence became irresistible they attempted to create a substitute. At the time that Congress appointed a committee to draft the Declaration of Independence, it instructed another committee to draw up plans for a confederation. This committee, headed by a Pennsylvania conservative, John Dickinson, reported a plan which represented an effort to establish a relatively strong government. The Dickinson draft was eventually revised, however, and the Articles of Confederation that Congress submitted to the states in November 1777 reduced the central authority to the minimum. The Articles were finally ratified by all the states in 1781.

Under the Articles of Confederation, the Union was a league of states, each of which retained its sovereignty and every power not expressly granted to the federal government To promote amity and friendship among the states, their citizens were guaranteed equal rights and freedom of movement. Congress was the legislative and executive authority of the Union. It consisted of delegates representing the states rather than the people. In the determination of questions each state had one vote, regardless of population, and important questions had to be decided by a two-thirds vote. Congress had sole power to conduct foreign relations and to declare war. It had concurrent power with the states to borrow money, issue paper money, and maintain an army and navy. It had authority to judge disputes between states. Its revenues were to be raised by laying requisitions on the states in proportion to the value of their lands. The states were to supply soldiers for the Continental army in proportion to the number of their white inhabitants.

The Confederation was considerably more than an alliance Congress had important functions, and although the states retained their sovereignty they were legally and morally bound to comply with its decisions. On the other hand, Congress had no way of compelling a state to observe its rulings. The basic limitation upon its authority, however, was its inability to levy taxes. No matter what powers Congress might have or attempt to exercise, it had to have money, and for money it had to depend on the voluntary contributions of the states. So fundamental in the political thought of the times was the relationship between sovereignty and the taxing power that even the Dickinson draft of the Articles of Confederation reserved taxation to the states.

Finally, the Articles of Confederation required unanimous consent for amendments, thus ensuring to each state that the terms of the compact could not be altered without its consent.

The Articles of Confederation were in a sense what one supporter said of them: "a work of time and great wisdom." They expressed hatred of authoritarian governments, with all their abuses, which existed under European monarchies. Americans had done away with a king and formed a republic, and yet they were moved by an impulse to fortify private rights even further by making local government supreme over central government. Before the Articles of Confederation were submitted to the states for ratification, the weakness of Congress was already recognized as a handicap in prosecuting the war. For most people, this was a calculated risk. The Revolution was "a struggle for liberty, not for power." Americans took care to avoid laying the foundations of despotic centralism.

Business Enterprise

In terms of the development that characterizes modern economically advanced nations, the colonies, as we have seen, were in some ways backward. The Revolution, however, was a powerful stimulant to economic progress. Wartime prosperity resulted in an accumulation of native capital. The scale on which this occurred is suggested by the size of private fortunes. In the late colonial period Thomas Hancock, reputedly one of the richest merchants in the country, left at his death an estate of $333,000. During the Revolution it was said that Robert Morris, the country's leading merchant-capitalist, had a fortune of $8 million. Allowing for exaggeration, the fact that such a figure could be suggested is indicative of the new wealth that was flowing into commerce and land speculation on a scale unknown in colonial times. New wealth was also represented by massive investment in federal and state debts. Additional funds were still at hand to found the country's first banking institutions in Philadelphia, New York, and Boston during and after the war.

Inevitably, as some men rose to fortune, others fell, and in the process the membership of the affluent classes was in some degree reshuffled. As older channels of trade and established business relationships changed or were closed off, some men of conspicuous wealth and position could not make the necessary adjustments and were displaced by new men who found ways to grasp the opportunities.

The Revolution contributed to the integration of the economy. The procurement of army supplies overrode state boundaries, drawing different parts of the country into trading relations with one another. War contracts which required large outlays of capital promoted interstate combination of merchants. Speculation in land and securities drew investors together from all parts of the country in search of local opportunities. The interests, relationships, and general outlook of busines became less provincial and more national in scope.

Although capital gains and the growth of credit institutions established a platform for economic advance, the general shape of the economy remained relatively unchanged. Farmers still practiced subsistence agriculture, most manufactures were still performed in the home, and the market economy depended upon extractive industries—the production, simple preparation, and exportation of commodities yielded by fields, forests, and mines. During the Revolution, manufactures were stimulated by the reduction of British imports and the demand for articles needed by the army. When normal patterns of trade were resumed after the war, domestic manufactures receded in the face of renewed British competition. Yet some gains were held.

Religion: Definitions of Freedom

In religious matters the Revolution fostered a spirit of amity and toleration. The dominant Anglican establishment in the south suffered a decline of prestige, relative to other sects, as a result of the loyalism of many of its clergy. In New England, by contrast, the ardor of the Congregational church in the Revolutionary cause confirmed its hold upon the mind and hearts of its adherents, but the relative position of other sects was strengthened by the general criticism of all religious establishments. The war itself was a force for unity. Conciliation was necessary in order to get the support of all denominations; they all joined in the struggle, and they gained mutual acceptance by fighting against the common enemy. In Massachusetts, Connecticut, and New Hampshire, as we have seen, the established Congregational church had already conceded to Quakers, Anglicans, and Baptists the right to have the religious taxes imposed on them paid to their own churches. In all parts of the country, the bills of rights being written into new state constitutions proclaimed the dedication of Americans to religious freedom. Typical was the clause inserted into the Virginia Bill of Rights of 1776 by James Madison, which said that

> religion, or the duty which we owe to our Creator, and the manner of discharging it, can be directed only by reason and conviction, not by force or violence; and therefore all men are equally entitled to the free exercise of religion, according to the dictates of conscience. . . .

In Maryland, North Carolina, South Carolina, and Georgia, as well as New York, the Anglican church was disestablished in 1777 and 1778. In the middle states and Rhode Island, there were no established churches.

Having enunciated the principle of religious liberty, it remained for Americans to determine what it meant. It quite evidently did not mean unqualified liberty for Catholics, who, although permitted to worship, were generally excluded from public office. People of other beliefs were sometimes excluded. South Carolina and New Jersey allowed only Protestants to hold public office; North Carolina excluded Catholics, agnostics, and atheists; and to hold public office in Delaware one had to profess a belief in the Holy Trinity. In New England, Catholic disabilities were retained into the 19th century and not entirely dropped until after the Civil War. Obviously, Americans defined religious liberty as subordinate to general Protestant ascendancy in society and government.

Religious liberty did not at first always mean religious equality, even of Protestant faiths. Although the Massachusetts constitution of 1780 declared that religions were equal, nothing changed: the established Congregational church continued as before, supported by public taxation, although specific dissenting groups were allowed to contribute toward their own churches. In Connecticut, where similar privileges were given dissenters, Congregationalists carried on a vendetta against other Protestant denominations, ignoring the law, and preventing their building churches. In Virginia, the declaration of religious freedom of 1776 did not put an end to the establishment. Jefferson, James Madison, and George Mason had to carry on a long struggle to get a law passed exempting dissenters from taxes laid to support the Anglican church, and not until 1779 were they able to bring about a formal disestablishment in Virginia.

Religious liberty, as most Americans understood it, did not mean separation of church and state, a complicating factor in the opposition to established churches. Americans thought that Protestant religion was a good thing, that it contributed to general morality and upheld law and order. The notion was widespread that religion of every kind had gone downhill since the beginning of the Revolution for lack of public financial support, and that the country was the worse for it. Americans tended to view churches as public institutions, like the government, which were rightly maintained by general taxation. The objection to established churches was not their connection with the government but that they were favored over other churches.

A movement rose after the Revolution to bring about the establishment of *all* Protestant churches by a "general assessment," that is, a tax levy which allowed an individual to direct payment of his contribution to the church of his choice. The system was already institutionalized in New England, where it was to continue well into the 19th century, and it had strong backing in the southern states. General assessment bills were introduced into southern state legislatures during the early 1780s; despite strong advocacy by their promoters, they all failed. The reason was that although many dissenters wanted their churches to be funded by public taxation, they were afraid that the politically dominant Anglicans would find in general assessment a way of restoring the established church.

In the early years of the nation, the meaning of religious liberty was being defined in practice and tested in controversy. The idealism of the Revolution had set a course toward religious equality and the separation of church and state, goals which were not completely realized then or now. Although some religious groups like the Quakers endorsed these goals for reasons of faith, the clearest affirmation of religious liberty on grounds of principle came from Deists like Jefferson who thought that one religion was no truer than another but were willing to believe that there was some good in all of them. Far more important than any question of doctrine to Jefferson and men like him was the desire to take religion out of politics, where it had historically played a disastrous role, and to banish forever the censorship and the suppression of intellectual freedom that had always gone along with official religion. After a ten-year struggle, culminating in the disestablishment of the Anglican church in Virginia and the defeat, by a perilously narrow margin, of a general assessment bill, Jefferson in 1786 secured adoption of Virginia's statute of religious liberty, a landmark of the times and a testimony to Jefferson's idealism, one that he wanted posterity to remember him for. It reads:

> No man shall be compelled to frequent or support any religious worship, place, or ministry whatsoever, nor shall be enforced, restrained, molested, or burthened in his body or goods, nor shall otherwise suffer, on account of his religious opinions or belief; but that all men shall be free to profess, and by argument to maintain, their opinions in matters of religion, and that the same shall in no wise diminish, enlarge, or affect their civil capacities.

Blacks and Slavery

In the provisional articles of peace the British promised not to take American-owned slaves with them when they left the country. After considerable soul-searching, the British commander, Sir Guy Carleton, decided that the pledge did not apply to slaves who had fled to the British on the promise of being given their freedom. To return them to slavery and punishment by their masters he considered "a dishonorable Violation of the public Faith," whereupon, in spite of Washington's resounding protests, he exempted from return all blacks who had joined the British before November 30, 1782, the date of the preliminary articles of peace. These blacks, who were currently attached as servants to British officers or otherwise employed in jobs behind British lines, were evacuated when the British forces left Savannah, Charleston, and New York, perhaps 20,000 to 25,000 of them, in addition to numerous slaves of loyalist refugees who were also on the ships. A certain number of slaves mingled with the French army, which also took them away. The total number of slaves lost to the south is highly uncertain; it was said at the time to approximate 25,000 for South Carolina and 20,000 for Virginia, an exaggeration, probably, but indicative of how seriously the loss was regarded and how damaging it was to the economy. The departing blacks ended up in all sorts of places, a few in Britain, Europe, and on the west coast of Africa; a few in Canada, where they were promised land but seldom received it; many, at first, in West Florida, from which most migrated when Britain, which had held the province since 1763, restored it to Spain. The greatest number, however, sailed to British islands in the Bahamas and the West Indies, especially Jamaica. They seldom prospered, and many were re-enslaved.

Revolutionary idealism and natural rights ideology fostered moral opposition to slavery, and, as we have seen, the movement against it began before the Revolution, gathering momentum during the war. "Can we expect to triumph over Britain to get ourselves free," ran the argument, "until we let those go free under us?" This kind of reasoning was most effective in places where slavery was weak and inessential to the workings of the economy, as in the northern states. In those states, too, the politically activated workers competed with slaves and were quite hostile to slavery. John Adams wrote years later that if slavery had not been abolished, white workers would have removed slaves by force. In any case, all the northern states began, in the years during and immediately after the Revolution, to prepare for the abolition of slavery. Religious groups such as Quakers, Methodists, and Baptists denounced it as against God's will and directed their members to free their slaves, sometimes on pain of expulsion. Quakers set up schools for blacks; Baptists, even in Virginia, admitted them to full membership on terms more egalitarian than ever afterward, and allowed blacks, both free and slave, to act as ministers. Antislavery societies were founded in state after state during the 1780s. They preached the abolition of the slave trade and of slavery, tried to persuade masters to liberate slaves, sometimes pledging compensation to masters and underwriting the support of the freed slave; they maintained schools, got jobs for blacks, and protected them against re-enslavement. The first national convention of antislavery societies met in 1794; ten states were represented, including Virginia and Maryland. The consensus against slavery was so pervasive that the number of manumissions rose in the southern states, 10,000 in Virginia alone during the 1780s, giving rise to a much larger class of free mulattoes. Tobacco planting in the Chesapeake states was at an ebb in prosperity, and cotton had not yet taken hold.

The slave trade was the first and easiest object of attack. New Jersey in 1774, and the next year Pennsylvania, Delaware, and Rhode Island, prohibited slave imports. Pennsylvania was the first to adopt gradual abolition. In 1780 all slave children born after that date were declared free upon reaching age 28, their servitude until that age being regarded as compensation to their masters for the expense of rearing them—a provision which became a feature of gradual emancipation schemes in several other states. Outright abolition was first achieved in 1783 by

Massachusetts (Vermont abolished slavery in its 1777 constitution but was not in the Union), when, in the celebrated Quock Walker case, the Massachusetts supreme court said that slavery violated the clause in the state constitution which declared all citizens born "free and equal." The decision soon put an end to slavery in Massachusetts. By 1787 every state except Georgia had barred slave importations (Georgia did so permanently in 1798), and by 1800 every state from Pennsylvania north had either abolished slavery or provided for gradual emancipation.

It was harder to strike at slavery on the federal level because Congress had to straddle a greater diversity of interests than state governments. Thomas Jefferson, drafting the Ordinance of 1784 for the organization of Congress's western territories, proposed to abolish slavery in the northwest after 1800. His motion lost by one vote. A northerner commented bitterly: "To suffer the continuance of slaves until they can gradually be emancipated in States already overrun by them may be pardonable, because unavoidable without hazarding greater evils; but to introduce them into countries where none exist, countries which have been talked of—which have even boasted of—as an asylum to the oppressed of the Earth—can never be forgiven." Later, however, when Congress passed the Northwest Ordinance of 1787, the abolition of slavery in the territory was carried without dissent. Why southerners in Congress consented to it has been debated by historians, and the suggestion has been made that they wanted to discourage the production of staple crops in the northwest competitive with those in the south; other historians have suggested that the prohibition may have been a tacit trade-off for later extension of slavery to the southwest territory. In any case, a part of the country was closed to the institution.

When the Constitutional Convention met in 1787, most delegates thought, and some feared, that action on slavery was within the scope of the new government's powers. It was, in fact, generally agreed that the power to regulate trade included the slave trade, and from the first debates on the subject, as we shall see, a majority favored stopping the slave trade in ten years. The date was eventually set back to 20 years, but it is clear that the

Founders expected the new government to eliminate the slave trade in the near future.

The climate of opinion in America was clearly opposed to slavery, and it was on its way out in the northern states by the time the Revolution was over. It was even beginning to crumble in Maryland and Virginia before cotton planting revitalized it. The country's elite leaders nearly all viewed it as a tragic evil and, when they could, took steps to limit or eradicate it. Their success in abolishing the slave trade was in itself a fundamental stroke: limits were set to it at the very time that the Industrial Revolution and the demand for cotton would otherwise have blown it sky high. The founders were restrained, however, by the fact that in some places slavery was entrenched, economically and socially, and vested interests created which could not be overridden without seriously dividing the nation. The Founders were never willing to sacrifice national unity to destroy slavery. It was always regarded as the lesser evil.

The legal institution of slavery, the ownership of one man by another, was only a single aspect of the broader problem of race relations. Enlightenment thought, with its emphasis upon natural virtue and the formative influence of environment, had led a few people to question whether the apparent inferiority of blacks was the result of nurture rather than nature. Nevertheless, the overwhelming majority of Americans believed that blacks were basically inferior. Even Thomas Jefferson, sensitive though he was of the need to rise above prejudice, could never shed this conviction. Such attitudes were almost universal among whites, not only in the south, but in northern areas where blacks resided in sufficient numbers for their folkways to affect the white community. Whatever the issues involved in slavery or abolition, the integration of blacks into white society on equal terms was not contemplated.

The Nationalist Movement, 1781–1783

In the years between Saratoga and Yorktown the patriot cause, as we have seen, often seemed in danger of failure. State and federal currency sank to the point of worthlessness. The Continental administration was generally believed to be honeycombed with fraud. The army was so weak and ill-supplied that at times it could scarcely fight. Government was feeble and also oppressive, creating disaffection by widespread impressments and the futile attempt to enforce economic controls. Merchants and propertied men were embittered by what they termed the "imbecility" of popular governments, while the people at large ranted against speculators and monopolists whom they accused of driving up prices.

In the shadow of defeat a movement arose to reinvigorate the war effort by strengthening government, particularly by giving greater powers to Congress. As this movement became more influential, less was heard about liberty and more about the need for authority. Coupled with proposals for stronger government was a conservative program of economic reform: the discontinuance of paper money, heavy taxation, and the abandonment of tender laws, price controls, and other economic legislation. The overwhelming fact was that by 1780 the popular movement which initiated the Revolution had exhausted its resources. Conservatives brought forward a formula of strong government and laissez-faire as the only means of saving the country.

The nationalists registered their first gains in Congress during 1780 and 1781 in a number of significant policy reversals. Discarding militia concepts of war, Congress adopted long-term enlistments and promised life pensions to officers who served to the war's end. Paper money was abandoned. Congress recommended the repeal of all tender laws and began levying requisitions upon the states in specie. Old maxims about the danger of delegating authority were set aside as Congress placed its departments of war, foreign affairs, and finance under single executives. Most significant of all, Congress undertook a revision of the Articles of Confederation. Early in 1781 it submitted the impost amendment to the states for ratification. This amendment provided for a 5 percent duty on imports, to be collected by federal officers and reserved solely for the use of Congress. Since it conferred the power of taxation upon the central government, it struck directly at the main source of Congress's weakness and involved a basic change in the nature of the Union.

Such outstanding men as George Washington, Alexander Hamilton, and James Madison were prominent nationalists, but the foremost leader at this time was Robert Morris. A wealthy merchant, who as a member of Congress had held positions of the highest responsibility, Morris had the confidence of the mercantile community and possessed an unrivalled grasp of Congress's administrative affairs both at home and abroad. In a last effort to solve its problems and inject vitality into the war effort, Congress in 1781 appointed him Superintendent of Finance. Given sweeping grants of authority, he became a virtual prime minister, some said a dictator. Until the disbandment of the army in 1783, he was the effective head of the federal government and, except for George Washington, the nation's most influential leader.

Under Morris's direction, the federal administration recovered its vigor and for the first time became economical. But Morris was also a statesman who aimed at long-range political and economic reforms. As a result chiefly of his leadership, the component elements of the nationalist movement were united behind a coherent program which combined constitutional change with economic reform. It appealed primarily to the classes of the population that had wealth and status.

The foundation of the nationalist program, upon which its other objectives depended, was the adoption of the impost amendment. Once it was ratified and a precedent established for federal taxation, Morris and his supporters intended to secure other taxes—excise, poll, and property taxes—which would give Congress adequate revenues independent of the states. Having surmounted the basic constitutional checks of the Articles of Confederation, Congress could be expected to evolve by the assumption of new powers and responsibilities into a truly sovereign government.

A vital element in this process was the existence of the Revolutionary debt. As the war ended and military necessity could no longer be pleaded, payment of the debt became the main justification for giving Congress the power of taxation. Since the debt was a valuable property for the nationalist cause, Morris took steps to increase it. In 1782 he initiated a procedure under which Congress, rather than the states, assumed the mass of unsettled debts left over from the war. Commissioners were sent into all parts of the country to settle accounts with soldiers and civilians, who received federal securities in recognition of unpaid claims. As a result, the federal debt increased from 11 million at the close of the war to about $28 million.

The debt was a potential "bond of union." Its payment out of federal taxes entailed amending the Articles of Confederation to give Congress the taxing power. If this could be managed, moreover, the debt would create an economic interest that would weld the nation together. Most of the securities issued during and immediately after the Revolution were in the hands of propertied men who, if they received payment from Congress, could be expected to support central government. Federal taxation, debt payment, and an economic interest attached to the Union—this mixture of political and economic aims constituted the nationalist formula.

To this formula was added a program of economic reforms connected with the payment of the debt. Whenever Congress should be in a position to "fund" the debt, that is, appropriate solid revenues such as the impost to the payment of interest, the market value of securities was certain to rise. At the close of the war, the market value was only 10 or 15 cents on the dollar. Regular payment of interest by Congress could be expected to raise the value of securities toward par, creating millions in new capital in the hands of the people who held them. More capital would thus become available to promote the economic development of the country.

Funding the debt also afforded means for reorganizing the currency and credit system of the country. Disgusted by the general depreciation of paper money during the Revolution, merchants and creditors had lost all confidence in the monetary practices of state governments, which they linked with democracy and mob rule. But the same economic necessities that had compelled first the colonial governments, and then the state governments, to issue paper money and establish land banks still remained. The shortage of hard money and the need for ample sources of credit created a void in the American economy which had to be filled. Funding the debt promised a solution to the problem that was satisfactory to creditors and merchants. Well-funded federal securities would be negotiable, that is, readily acceptable in all kinds of transactions and convertible into hard money. They would themselves constitute a currency. More important, however, they could be used as capital for banks. With relatively small amounts of negotiable securities held as a reserve, banks could issue far greater sums in bank notes, which would enter into circulation and serve as currency. Not only would the capital represented by the securities be multiplied, but the bank notes would give the nation a sound currency beyond reach of popularly controlled state legislatures.

Preparing the ground for this development, Morris in 1781 induced Congress to charter the Bank of North America, the first bank of any kind established in the United States. It was a national bank in the sense that it held the funds of the Continental government and its main business was to lend money to the government. Although its shares were in part privately owned, it operated under the supervision of the Superintendent of Finance. Morris hoped eventually to increase its capital to the point where its shares would be held by numerous investors in every state. It would then be additional "cement to the union," for its shareholders would have an economic interest in the central government. Morris also hoped that its notes would supplant state paper money and afford a circulating medium for the entire country.

As the nationalist movement grew, it gained the support of public creditors—holders of federal securities who would receive payment if Congress gained the power to levy taxes. It also appealed to political conservatives, especially in the middle states, who felt the need for a stronger central government to protect minority rights against popular majorities in state legislatures. It was attractive in varying degree to merchants and men of property everywhere because it promised to liberate them from state paper money. Merchants also took cognizance of the positive aid which an effective central government could furnish in promoting the country's economic development.

The scenery was altogether familiar: funded debt, national bank, the promotion of business enterprise, and strengthening government by creating an economic interest in it. Britain had walked along this path from the beginning of the century, and it had led to national greatness, to being the first nation of Europe in terms of economic strength and military power. Morris, and such close associates of his as Alexander Hamilton and Gouverneur Morris, were open admirers of the British system. They hoped to institute it in the United States, which they foresaw as rising to "power, consequence, and grandeur." The British system had other commendable qualities. Morris and his associates were statists, who tended to hold popular government in contempt, impatient of what they considered its stupidity and its anarchic qualities. "There is no *order* that has a will of its own," wrote Hamilton. "The inquiry constantly is what will *please*, not what will *benefit* the people." The people they regarded as incompetent, ignorant, guided by mean and shortsighted motives, given to "licentiousness," "vulgar souls whose narrow optics can see but the little circle of selfish concerns," and oblivious to those general principles of natural law which should properly govern society. Their version of Enlightenment principles centered on powerful government, general and uniform laws, social discipline and subordination, and economic institutions oriented toward commerce and financial capitalism. It was opposed on a broad front to the existing attachment of Americans to local rights and privileges, particularism, economic institutions oriented toward agriculture and pre-industrial modes of production, "country party" political attitudes, and a popular movement always pushing toward political and social democracy. From the Nationalist standpoint, the solution lay at hand: Morris and the Nationalists desired to import the British system, with its proven results, into the United States.

The future of the Nationalist program rested upon the adoption of the impost amendment. It was the first step, for without federal taxes there could be no augmentation of Congress's powers, no creditor interest to cement the union, no stable national currency. Morris possessed great influence, and he used it to the full. Urging Congress to be aggressive in its demands, he lashed out at states which were dilatory in ratifying the impost. He conspired with public creditors to put pressure upon state legislatures. He pronounced the impost amendment as necessary to the preservation of the Union. His arguments, and those of Congress, had considerable effect, besides which there was a growing recognition of the need to "patch" the Union together. During 1781 and 1782 all the states except Rhode Island ratified the impost.

On the threshold of victory, however, the Nationalist effort faltered. When in October 1782 Congress delivered a peremptory request to the Rhode Island legislature that it approve the impost, the legislature rejected it by unanimous vote, and before Congress could take further action, Virginia rescinded its previous grant. With peace in sight, the Nationalist program lay in shambles, broken upon the rule that required unanimous consent to amend the Articles of Confederation.

Having lost "that great friend to sovereignty, a foreign war," the leading Nationalists were apprehensive of the approach of peace. The common struggle had held the states together, and they were afraid that with peace the nation would disintegrate into a collection of feeble and disunited states. Washington confided to a friend his opinion that "if the Powers of Congress are not enlarged, and made completer to all general purposes, . . . the blood that has been spilt—the Expenses which have been incurred—and the distresses which we have undergone will avail us nothing—and . . . the band which at present holds us together, by a very feeble thread, will soon be broken, when anarchy and confusion must ensue." The French minister to the United States, La Luzerne, was more specific in reporting to his superior early in 1783:

The appearances of an approaching peace have given occasion to examine questions of a great importance for the United

States; and so many persons of weight and experience have spoken to me about them that I cannot doubt that they are actually at this moment one of the principal objects of the attention of men charged in this continent with the management of affairs. Can the federal assembly subsist when it shall cease to rest on a common peril and common interest? And what would be the consequences of a dissolution of Congress? The United States, they have said to me, represent a vast country divided into thirteen republics, and susceptible of being divided into still more states, in proportion as population and culture make progress. These states, if their union is close and permanent, will be of consideration and respect; if division is introduced among them, they will be contemptible abroad and miserable at home. Congress up to this day has been the common centre of union; it has maintained itself by extraordinary means, by the general danger, by the assistance in men and money received from France, by the prestige of a money which cost nothing for its creation but an act of sovereign will. If all these means were to fail at once, nothing would be more easy than to break the bonds of union.

The Newburgh Conspiracy

Driven to desperate expedients, some of the leading Nationalists, including Morris, Hamilton, who was in Congress, and men in their confidence, attempted to make use of the army—the first recorded instance of military conspiracy in American history. The conspiracy was rooted in the discontent of Washington's army encamped at Newburgh on the Hudson River. Officers and men had long considered themselves betrayed by their country. They were as aware as anybody of the approach of peace and were afraid that, when the country no longer needed them, their claims would be disregarded. These included pay they had not received, bounties, and the life pensions promised to the officers. Washington considered the situation at camp so threatening that, instead of going home to Mount Vernon for the winter, he had stayed with the army, and it was largely through his efforts that its discontents were channeled into a petition to Congress. The petition was carried to Philadelphia late in December 1782 by a delegation of high military officers.

Upon their arrival, the officers were immediately drawn into conference with Nationalists in Congress and persuaded to join with them and the public creditors in forcing revision of the Articles of Confederation upon the states. The Newburgh conspiracy, as it unfolded, had many layers, but the basic intent was to align Congress, the army, and the public creditors behind an ultimatum to the states, with a threat that if the powers of Congress were not strengthened the army would rebel. The scheme required first the organization of forces and then a public declaration by the army.

The delegates from the army had several demands. First of all, they wanted some immediate pay given to officers and soldiers, who had received little pay for over two years; otherwise, they said, the army would be hard to control. They asked that accounts be settled and the sums due to the army be acknowledged before it was disbanded. They were afraid that if the settlement was postponed, the nation would ignore these claims. Finally, and this was from Congress's standpoint the most critical request, they wanted Congress to commute the life pensions promised to officers into a lump-sum bonus. After long discussion at camp, the officers had decided that, because opposition among the states to life pensions was so great, they were more likely to get a simple money payment. Originally, the delegates to Philadelphia had been instructed by the officers' council at camp merely to ask Congress to determine the amount of the payment and then request the states to discharge it. After they talked with the Nationalists, however, the delegates shifted their position. They now insisted that Congress pay the commuted pensions out of federal taxes to be granted by the states to the central government.

Having won over the army to their cause, Nationalists in Congress began to organize pressure upon Congress and the country. Rumors were propagated that the army had secretly made a decision not to lay down its arms until its demands were met and that a public declaration would soon be made. Washington's prestige was indispensable to the scheme, and in several letters Hamilton tried to tutor him in the part which had been assigned to him. Washington's role, Hamilton told him, was to remain in the background, not espousing the army's cause so openly as to lose the confidence of the civilian population nor opposing it to the extent that he alienated the army, until the moment of crisis, when he was to emerge as the charismatic leader and place his enormous reputation on the side of the Nationalists. Morris contributed to the tension by announcing to Congress in a letter which he also published in the newspapers that the course which the nation had taken in not paying its just debts affronted his sense of honor, that he would never be the "minister of injustice," and that unless Congress immediately demanded and the states granted sufficient federal taxes to meet all its obligations, he would resign. An additional part of the scheme, it appears, was to persuade Congress to declare that it could not go on without federal taxes and for the members to go home and address their state legislatures on the subject.

At camp the anticipated crisis was soon contrived. A friend of General Gates, John Armstrong, Jr., sitting in Gates's tent, drew up an anonymous address which was circulated among the officers. Eloquently written, it played expertly and passionately upon their emotions, reciting the wrongs done to them.

> If this then, be your treatment, while the swords you wear are necessary for the defense of America, what have you to expect from peace . . . when those very swords; the instruments and companions of your glory, shall be taken from your sides, and no remaining mark of military distinction left but your wants, infirmities and scars? Can you then consent to be the only sufferers by this revolution, and retiring from the field, grow old in poverty, wretchedness and contempt? . . . But if your spirit should revolt at this; if you have spirit enough to oppose tyranny under whatever garb it may assume . . . attend to your situation and redress yourself.

The officers were urged to give up the "milk and water" style of previous petitions to Congress and to unite in a manly declaration that they would not allow themselves to be disbanded until they had obtained justice. Significantly, the Newburgh address called upon the officers to hold a meeting unauthorized by Washington, and therefore by implication designed to throw off his leadership.

Washington had not been a party to the plotting in Philadelphia, and his behavior in this crisis proved that America's confidence in him was not misplaced. Although deeply convinced that the nation's welfare depended upon strengthening the Union, he would have nothing to do with conspiracies, especially anything that involved pitting the military against civilian authority. As commanding officer, his basic commitment was to the army, and he knew enough of his countrymen to realize that any threat of military force would discredit the army and its legitimate demands in the eyes of the nation. He suspected the Nationalists in Philadelphia of merely using the army to secure their purposes without regard for its welfare.

To forestall the unauthorized meeting called for by the Newburgh address, Washington convened a regular meeting of the officers' council, held under his auspices. In a poignant and moving speech, he reminded the officers of their honor. The world would always marvel, he said, at the heroism and dedication of a true republican army, which had endured extremes of suffering and neglect without complaint and had carried the long struggle against a superior enemy to victory. Let not that reputation be stained by an ignoble deed. He told the officers that he would stand behind any decision they should take, but he warned them of the impossibility of opposing the country, and urged them to repudiate the sentiments contained in the anonymous address and to place their confidence in Congress. The meeting was, as one officer later recalled, "exquisitely critical," and many of the officers were so outraged by their sense of wrong that they thirsted for drastic action, but Washington carried the day. His prestige was so great that nobody dared to speak against him. The upshot was merely another petition, which Washington hurried to Congress with the warning that the temper of the army was dangerous and that immediate steps must be taken to comply with its demands.

Washington had blunted the conspiracy. It was broken by the arrival of news that the preliminary articles of peace had been signed. After this news was published, the army soon lost any political usefulness that it might have possessed. The military forces in the south disintegrated. At Newburgh the soldiers who had enlisted for the duration of the war clamored to go home and insulted their officers. An army without soldiers was no threat; Congress therefore took time to debate the army petition. The Nationalists scored a major point when Congress commuted officers' pensions to five years' full pay and assumed them as a federal rather than a state obligation, thus increasing the federal debt. As to the other demands, Congress was in a dilemma. There were not funds to permit any immediate pay to the army. The settlement of its accounts was a complicated business, which could not be completed in any reasonable period. At last Morris agreed to give the army three months' pay in his personal notes, remaining in office until he could redeem them. The army, however, could not be held together any longer and, finally, at Washington's request, Congress, which was not entirely certain that the war was over, authorized him to send the troops home on furlough. The men walked away with their accounts unsettled and with either no pay or with Morris's notes which, in order to reap some benefit, they had to sell to speculators at discount. The soldiers were never recalled. The virtuous army of the Revolution thus fulfilled the republican ideal. It withstood the enemy, submitted to privation and neglect, and, with victory won, quietly disappeared into the population, no menace to the nation's liberties.

The Nationalists rapidly lost ground in Congress. Most members did not have to be convinced of the need to strengthen the central government, but they were restrained by their knowledge of the states' rights views of their constituents and their realization of what the states would accept. The result of their deliberations after the Newburgh affair was merely another request for the impost, modified this time to meet objections raised by Rhode Island and other states. Hamilton quit Congress in disgust. Madison chose not to serve out his full term. Morris stayed in office for a time, but refused any part in the determination of policy. Congress itself almost ceased to exist in 1784, when it was replaced by a Committee of the States.

Though the Nationalists failed in the closing years of the war, they had laid the foundations for ultimate victory. They had vested the Revolutionary debt in Congress and had committed the country to paying it out of federal taxes, a policy which entailed strengthening the Union. By uniting economic interest with social conservatism, they had formed the core of a party which in 1787 was able to write the Constitution and endow the central government with permanence as well as power.

CHAPTER IX

The Confederation

The Postwar Economy

The most important single factor in shaping the course of public events during the Confederation was the postwar economic depression. It was caused in part by the war itself and partly by the dislocations consequent upon separation from the British empire. The nation's economy had been molded by British regulations and the integration of American trade with that of the empire. Separation entailed a period of readjustment while new paths of enterprise were being explored. Historians are not certain when the depression started or ended, or how severe it was. It is clear that the immediate cause was an overexpansion of credit by European merchants trading with the United States. With an exaggerated notion of the ability of the American people to pay for imported goods, British merchants in particular extended large credits. During the first three years after the war, imports from Britain were valued at £7,592,000, over three fourths of which were bought on credit.

Imports had to be paid for by exports of American commodities, but circumstances operated to reduce overseas shipments. The production of southern staples was curtailed immediately after the war by a shortage of slave labor resulting from British evacuation of slaves. Tobacco production was below prewar levels. Rice and indigo production, already hard hit by the loss of slave labor, suffered from successive crop failures in 1784 and 1785. Other sections of the country had difficulties of another kind. New England shipbuilding no longer enjoyed the benefits of the Navigation Acts, which had required all British ships to be built within the empire; the loss to New England was estimated as high as £100,000 a year. The whaling industry felt the effects of the exclusion of American oil from the British market. Returns from naval stores fell off as a result of the withdrawal of British bounties. Although the domestic market for iron products expanded, exports of iron to Britain sank to a fraction of prewar levels.

In colonial times debts, piled up in direct trade with Britain, had been in part offset by colonial earnings in the West Indies trade. Britain now excluded American vessels from its West Indies islands. American products still went there in British bottoms, and Yankee captains found ways to conduct trade by smuggling and other well-known dodges; nevertheless this important branch of commerce was obstructed. Trade with non-British areas increased, as we shall see, but not enough to compensate for the exclusion of American shipping from the British West Indies and for small crops in the southern states, whose exports ordinarily loomed large among American exports. Specie flowed out of the country at a time when the states were withdrawing their wartime currencies. There was a general shortage of money, and people could not pay their debts. The depression was most severe in New England, but it was felt in varying degrees throughout the nation.

During the remainder of the decade, foreign trade struggled slowly and incompletely back toward the levels of late colonial times. Britain retained its dominant position, supplying the bulk of imported manufactured articles Americans consumed, but in terms of population, those imports were a fraction of what they had been before the Revolution. Still trying to adapt their economy to expulsion from the empire, Americans were not selling as much abroad, and therefore had less money to buy foreign goods. Prospects, even in foreign trade, were not entirely discouraging. Released from the Navigation Acts, American merchants were trading directly with European nations. France, which was eager to increase its commercial ties with the United States, extended privileges to American merchants in her home ports and, as in colonial times, admitted American ships into its West Indies islands. But France never became, as the government hoped, the replacement of Britain as supplier of manufactures to Americans. They were too used to British commodities which were also good and cheap; French products tended to be high-priced luxury items; and British merchants who had ties in the United States gave longer credit. But, if American imports from France were minimal, exports to France and its possessions increased and yielded a favorable balance. Trade also grew with Holland and its West Indies possessions. Spain, which had opened its colonies to American vessels during the war, returned to an exclusionist policy in 1784. However, in distant parts of the world, new lines of American enterprise were charted. American vessels went on peddling voyages to the French and Dutch East Indies, as well as to British possessions in India, which were opened to them. In 1784 Americans began the China trade, a source of fabulous profits. Some segments of the economy were permanently injured by separation from the British empire, but the economy as a whole was recovering and adjusting to independence.

One aspect of economic recovery was the significant progress made in domestic manufactures, which had increased during the Revolution. Although still backward by British standards, American manufactures produced a fairly wide range of goods, particularly iron, glass, and paper products, wool and cotton thread, coarse fabrics, and simple tools and machinery. British imports continued to dominate the market, and yet there was an exuberant growth of small-ship industry in the middle states and New England. A few mills and factories were trying to produce on a larger scale for an interstate market. Actual progress, however, was nothing compared with expectations of the future. Outside the south, which was wedded to agriculture, the state governments actively promoted manufactures by giving loans, bounties, and land grants to favored industries, exempting them from taxes, and enacting protective tariffs in their interest. Societies were formed to investigate new methods of production and ways of raising capital. Intense interest was shown in the use of machinery and in factory organization. Industrial growth was preached in the name of patriotism, as a way of stopping the drain of money to Britain and freeing the country from economic dependence upon its former enemy. General war broke out in Europe in 1792, and as in all the preceding wars of the 18th century, Americans were able to take advantage of it, entering upon nearly 20 years of unprecedented prosperity. Profits were high in commerce; investment flowed into it and into land, whose value having sunk by half during the 1780s now escalated. If war had not occurred and enterprise not been channelled into agriculture and commerce, it is possible that Americans, driven in upon the resources of their own country by the separation from Britain, would have entered upon the Industrial Revolution sooner than they did.

Federal Regulation of Trade

Merchants, who of all classes were hardest hit by the depression, attributed their distress to political causes, especially the exclusion of American vessels from the British West Indies. During the peace negotiation in 1782 the American commissioners had tried to make a commercial treaty with Britain which would give equal privileges to merchants of both countries and preserve the basic relationship existing in colonial times. Prospects at first seemed good, for the ministry was dominated by Whigs who were friendly to the United States. Such statesmen as Lord Shelburne and William Pitt were responsive to free-trade ideas, and there was much to be said for maximizing trade between the two countries by leaving it free of restrictions. Nevertheless, when the issue was thrown into Parliament, conservatism triumphed. Traditionally, the Navigation Acts were the foundation of British sea power and of her commercial greatness. It was argued that the United States was so dependent upon British manufactures, shipping, and credit, that Britain could shut Americans out of its West Indies and still hold its position in the American market.

Accordingly, the peace treaty gave the United States only the status usually accorded foreign nations under the Navigation Acts. American ships were allowed to carry goods of American origin to Britain and take back cargoes, but were barred from the British West Indies islands, whose trade was to be a monopoly of the mother country.

This restriction cut across established avenues of American commerce. As already noted, considerable trade was pursued illegally after 1783. Eighteenth-century merchants were skillful in circumventing governmental regulations. Ships carried different sets of registration papers to show to the appropriate authorities. The ownership of vessels was shifted back and forth between American and British partners. Customs officers were bribed. The people and governing officials of the British islands connived at illegal trade because they wanted cheap American provisions. Nevertheless, the restrictions were a serious impediment to normal commerce.

American merchants demanded that retaliatory duties be placed on British ships entering American ports. Apart from giving native carriers an advantage, the object was to force Britain to relax its restrictions. State governments responded by laying special tonnage duties on British vessels and special taxes on the goods imported in them. New Hampshire, Massachusetts, and Rhode Island even prohibited British vessels from loading American products. But action by individual states was no solution to the problem. The states did not, as is sometimes said, engage in commercial war with one another; but different interests prevented the enactment of uniform laws. States that had the most vital interest in wringing concessions from Britain by retaliatory legislation could not maintain their stand when adjacent or nearby states failed to enact laws of equal severity. British commerce flowed into the states whose duties were lower, and the others had to relax their laws. Uniform legislation at the federal level was needed; hence a demand arose for giving Congress the power to regulate trade.

A sectional division existed on the issue. Southerners were reluctant to limit or exclude British ships and thereby give the north a monopoly on their carrying trade. Even in the south, however, patriots were roused to anger at what they considered Britain's implacable hostility to the United States and were therefore willing to support commercial retaliation. In 1784 Congress proposed an amendment to the Articles of Confederation giving the central government power to pass navigation acts. Accompanying the amendment was a draft of a specific law. Nearly every state endorsed federal regulation of trade in principle, but Rhode Island and North Carolina objected to the specific legislation proposed. As a result, the amendment was not ratified.

Manufacturers as well as merchants desired federal trade regulation, although their interest was different. Whereas merchants wanted navigation acts that would favor native as opposed to foreign shippers, manufacturers wanted tariffs that would protect American-made products against the competition of foreign goods. "Mechanics" of the northern towns, who constituted the majority of the population in urban centers and who had become a political force, at first appealed to their state governments. New Hampshire, Massachusetts, Rhode Island, New York, and Pennsylvania enacted protective tariffs, and nearly all the other states gave preference in varying degree to goods of American origin. But individual state action again proved to be ineffectual. The most successful manufacturers in the north looked forward to capturing southern markets from the British, but the tariffs enacted by southern states were not high enough to give northern products a competitive advantage over British imports. A federal tariff was the answer. The enlistment of urban mechanics in the movement for constitutional revision gave it an important popular base.

Western Lands and the Ordinances

The acquisition of the trans-Appalachian west represented many things to many people: to prospective settlers a chance to rise in a new society, to rural gentlemen an opportunity to own broad acres and lead the life of a country squire surrounded by

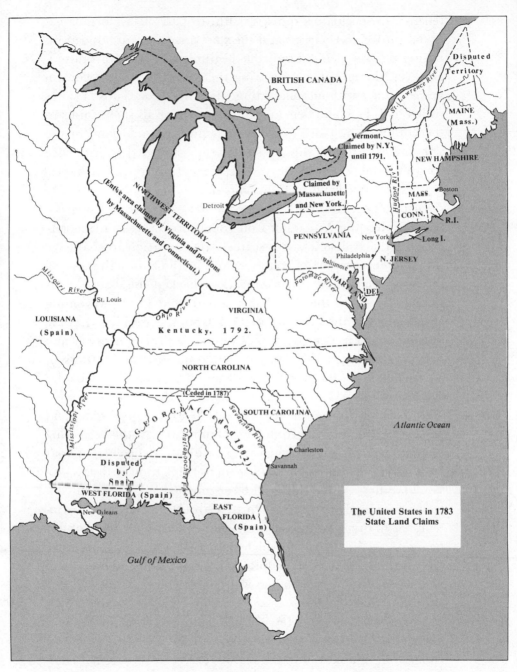

BRITISH CANADA

St. Lawrence River

Disputed Territory

MAINE (Mass.)

Vermont, Claimed by N.Y. until 1791.

NEW HAMPSHIRE

Claimed by Massachusetts and New York.

Hudson River

MASS. • Boston

CONN.

R.I.

NORTHWEST TERRITORY

(Entire area claimed by Virginia and portions by Massachusetts and Connecticut.)

Detroit

PENNSYLVANIA

New York

Long I.

Philadelphia

N. JERSEY

Baltimore

Potomac River

MARYLAND

DEL.

Missouri River

St. Louis

Ohio River

VIRGINIA

LOUISIANA (Spain)

Kentucky, 1792.

NORTH CAROLINA

(Ceded in 1787)

GEORGIA (Ceded in 1802)

SOUTH CAROLINA

Savannah River

Mississippi River

Chattahoochee River

Charleston

Savannah

Disputed by Spain

WEST FLORIDA (Spain)

New Orleans

EAST FLORIDA (Spain)

Atlantic Ocean

Gulf of Mexico

The United States in 1783
State Land Claims

tenants, to speculators quick wealth, to patriots a glorious national future, to Congress and the state governments a means of paying off war debts. From the beginning of the Revolution, however, the prospect of securing the west had aroused controversies. States without land claims challenged the rights of states which had them and demanded a cessation of all such claims to the Union. States with overlapping claims granted land in the same areas. Rival groups of speculators struggled to influence congressional policy. In the west itself squatters fought with speculators over the validity of land titles.

Disputes between the states frequently came before Congress, which under the Articles of Confederation was cast in the role of arbiter. Rival states were scarcely in a position to challenge Virginia's occupation of Kentucky or North Carolina's incorporation of Tennessee. But Connecticut backed the claims of its citizens to whom the state had granted land in the Wyoming Valley, despite the fact that in 1782 Congress decided that the area belonged to Pennsylvania. Congress was also involved in a dispute coming down from colonial times between settlers in Vermont and the states of New York and New Hampshire. Under the leadership of Ethan and Ira Allen, the Vermonters denied New York's claim to the area because it would invalidate land titles they had obtained from New Hampshire. At the beginning of the Revolution they formed a separate state, defied New York's authority, and applied for admission to the Union with the proviso that their right to the land be acknowledged. A similar controversy existed in western North Carolina, where settlers attempted to organize the separate state of Franklin, their object being to invalidate grants which the North Carolina legislature had given to speculators. Despite much confusion and occasional violence, most of these conflicts were resolved during the Confederation period.

The most important territorial dispute was about the land north of the Ohio River, destined to become the Northwest Territory. Virginia's claim to the region, based on its original charter, was opposed by other states on the ground that the war had been a common effort and therefore the territory should be the property of the Union. The state was in a strong bargaining position as a result of George Rogers Clark's campaigns during the Revolution; nevertheless, by 1781 Virginia was willing to yield. It had ample lands in Kentucky and lacked the military resources to control the northwest. Hence, it offered cession to Congress with the stipulation that the state be reimbursed for Clark's expenses, that a large tract be reserved for its own war veterans, and that all previous grants and private land purchases from the Indians be annulled. These terms were at first refused, but Congress finally accepted them in 1784. Other states, meanwhile, had ceded their claims to the region on one condition or another, and the way was clear for federal possession of the Northwest Territory.

The policy that Congress would adopt with respect to its western domain was certain to create momentous precedents. Congress's most immediate concern was to sell the land in order to reduce the Revolutionary debt, but the provision made for establishing government in the territory would in some measure determine the procedure to be followed in dealing with future territorial annexations. Congress's first plan, the Ordinance of 1784, was drafted by Thomas Jefferson and based upon democratic principles. It envisaged an early stage of local self-government in which the settlers would meet and elect their own officials. When the population reached 10,000, the settlers were to hold a convention, frame a constitution, and send a delegation to Congress. When the population equalled that of the smallest existing state, the territory was to enter the Union on the basis of full equality with other states. The Ordinance of 1784 showed Jefferson's regard for the small farmer and his trust in popular government. Conservative easterners, on the other hand, looked down on frontier settlers as an ignorant lot and were reluctant to admit them into the Union on equal terms. With its emphasis upon local self-government and its concession of equal status to the west, Jefferson's ordinance was in accord with the democratic impulse of the times. Although it was superseded by the Ordinance of 1787, it helped to lay the foundations of national policy.

In 1785 Congress considered ways of selling land in the Northwest Territory. One question that had to be decided was whether to foster the acquisition of large tracts by speculators and pro-

moters who would sponsor settlement, or to sell land directly to
settlers. A second question was whether, as under the New England township system, to promote compact settlement by requiring presurvey and the sale of limited areas one by one or
whether, as was customary in the south, to encourage rapid but
more dispersed settlement by allowing people to stake out and
then register their own plots. Congress wanted to sell the land
quickly, a purpose best served by large grants to speculators, but
the Ordinance of 1785, as finally drafted, sustained both the idea
of compact settlement and that of selling directly to settlers.
The land was to be divided into townships each containing 36
square miles, and the towns in turn were to be divided into 640-
acre sections. Four sections in each township were to be reserved
for the United States, with one section set aside for the support
of public schools. Certain townships were to be devoted to the
discharge of land bounties given federal troops during the war.
The remaining townships were to be offered for sale by auction
in the various states at a minimum price of one dollar an acre,
payable in public securities. Since the market value of public
securities at this time was 12 or 15 cents on the dollar, the
actual minimum price was very low.

The Ordinance of 1785 was not operative at the time. Although surveys began at once, they went slowly, partly as a result
of inherent difficulties, partly because the surveyors were driven
from their work by hostile Indians. Sales were negligible. Congress therefore became receptive to proposals from land-specu-
lating companies which offered to buy large tracts. Shelving the
Ordinance of 1785, Congress in 1787 granted 1.5 million acres to
a group of ex-army officers organized as the Ohio Company. The
price was 66.6 cents an acre, payable in depreciated securities and
soldiers' land bonus certificates. With the dam broken, other
groups of speculators moved in. To get congressional approval
of their proposal the Ohio associates had been forced to couple
it with a project advanced by the Scioto Company of New York,
which included members and officers of Congress as well as
"many of the principal characters of America." The Scioto Company received an option, never exercised, of buying 3.5 million

acres. A more successful company, headed by John Cleves Symmes, contracted for 1 million acres on the same terms as the Ohio Company.

The companies now sponsoring western settlement were not willing to leave government in the territory to self-constituted bodies as was provided by the Ordinance of 1784. Moreover, they wanted the federal government to provide protection against Indian attack. Congress therefore revised the Ordinance of 1784. Although its more democratic elements were set aside, some of its essential features were retained. Under the Northwest Ordinance of 1787, which became the basic law of the United States relative to territories, government was adapted to stages of population growth. The Northwest was to be divided into three to five districts, which in the earliest stage were to be ruled by a governor, a secretary, and three justices appointed by Congress. These officials were to act under the constitution and laws of any state they chose. When a district had 5,000 free male inhabitants, it was entitled to an elective legislature empowered to pass laws, which were subject, however, to the absolute veto of the governor. When population reached 60,000, the territory was free to draw up a constitution and apply for admission to the Union as a state. The Ordinance guaranteed personal rights and religious freedom. It provided for free public education and, within the Northwest Territory, the prohibition of slavery.

The Northwest Ordinance was a radical departure from the colonial policies of Old World nations. By providing for the eventual incorporation of new areas on terms of equality it eliminated the usual causes of hostility between colonies and mother country. This principle, it should be pointed out, was firmly established in the American tradition; from the first footholds on the east coast the colonies had grown by absorbing new settlements, although not always on the basis of political equality. In this respect, the Ordinance went beyond the practice of many states of the Union. But the Ordinance retreated considerably from the idea of self-governing frontier communities envisaged in Jefferson's Ordinance of 1784. Until statehood was actually achieved, the settlers were to be governed by federal officers less susceptible to popular control than the British governors once sent out to the American colonies. In this respect the Ordinance of 1787 represented a conservative trend, which was expressed at the same time by the movement for the Constitution.

The West in International Relations

Settlement of the northwest was obstructed by hostile Indians who frequently crossed the Ohio and carried their raids into Kentucky. Between 1783 and 1790 an estimated 1,500 Kentuckians were killed and 2,000 horses stolen. How many settlers north of the Ohio perished in unknown. Congress negotiated treaties under which the Indians ceded land, but the treaties were ignored by tribes which were not a party to them. In any case, treaties seldom forestalled violence on the frontier.

It was the universal belief of westerners that the Indians were incited by the British who, in violation of the peace treaty of 1783, retained possession of a string of forts and trading posts on American soil. The British justification for not evacuating the forts was the failure of the United States to fulfill treaty obligations with respect to prewar debts owed to British citizens. Inasmuch as the Privy Council made the decision not to withdraw from the forts the day before the peace treaty went into effect, it is evident that other considerations were involved. Among them was the fact that control of the lucrative fur trade of the region depended on holding the posts. Also, many Englishmen thought that the union of American states might disintegrate; retention of the posts would enable Britain to recover the territory without having to reconquer it. There was also fear of American expansion into the Canadian west and a desire to employ Indians as a barrier. All these motives were understood by Americans, to whom they furnished proof, if any were needed, of British hostility.

Americans did not understand the larger problem that faced Britain as a result of its cession of the northwest to the United

States. During the Revolution Britain had bound the Indians to its side as allies with the promise that it would never surrender their land. Evacuation of the posts would now disclose the broken pledge, undermine Britain's influence over the tribes, and expose its thin line of settlements in western Canada to Indian depredation. Britain therefore held on, assumed the role of patron and protector of the tribes, encouraged them to resist ceding land to the United States and, in the normal process of conducting the fur trade, supplied them with weapons.

An analogous situation existed on the southwestern frontier, where the United States confronted the remnants of Spanish power. Granted its last taste of imperial glory by the war of the American Revolution, Spain had recovered the Floridas, which, added to its existing possessions, gave it a vast empire stretching from the Gulf of Mexico to Canada and from the Mississippi River to the Pacific Ocean. Fortunately for America's future expansion, the empire contained only islands of white population. Backward in commerce and industry, Spain could not enforce an economic monopoly over the region, nor could it defend it against internal revolution or foreign encroachment.

Spain attempted to slow the westward advance of the United States in 1784 by closing the mouth of the Mississippi River to American commerce, an action in accord with its traditional exclusionist policy. The vital interests of the United States were less threatened by the immediate restriction, however, than by its potential effects. As settlers went into the Mississippi Valley, mountain ranges cut them off from easy communication with the east, and the only feasible outlet for their exports was the Mississippi River. In the first stages of the frontier, when little more was produced than a bare subsistence, the restriction was only a minor nuisance, but as the country developed it became intolerable. Spain's purpose was political as well as economic. By holding out navigation of the river as bait, Spain hoped to persuade westerners to secede from the Union and form a separate state under Spanish auspices. The strategy had some success. Washington, returning from a trip to the west in 1785, said of the inhabitants that "the touch of a feather would turn them away."

Congress instructed its Secretary for Foreign Affairs, John Jay, to negotiate a treaty with the Spanish minister to the United States, Diego de Gardoqui. The Mississippi question was not the only issue, for Congress also sought a commercial agreement which would lift Spain's restrictions on American trade with its colonies. A sharp division existed in Congress on these issues. The New England states were not concerned with the development of the west, which they feared would some day outweigh them in the Union. They were, however, intent upon getting a commercial treaty. The southern states, on the other hand, were vitally interested in the welfare of settlements in the southwest, which were still within their boundaries or their land claims. Gardoqui shrewdly played upon these differences. Under instructions from his government, he offered a commercial treaty in return for the renunciation of American rights to navigate the Mississippi for a period of 20 years. Jay signed an agreement on this basis in 1785, but the indignation that rose in the south and west prevented its acceptance by Congress.

In other respects Spain followed a policy similar to that of Britain in the northwest. Under the terms of the Anglo-American treaty of 1783, the southern boundary of the United States had been placed at 31° latitude. Spain claimed the land as far north as 32°28′, refused to abandon forts in the disputed area, and intrigued with the powerful Indian tribes in the southwest —the Creeks, Cherokees, and Choctaws—inciting them against the United States. Prominent western leaders, notably James Wilkinson, were bribed to support Spain's interest. Partly as a result of Spanish efforts to court favor among American settlers, the restrictions on navigating the Mississippi were eased. In 1787 Wilkinson was allowed to use the port of New Orleans on payment of 6 percent duty. The next year a royal edict authorized Spanish officials to extend the privilege to any Americans or their agents who might thereby be attached to Spain's cause; any other American was allowed to use the port subject to payment of a 15 percent duty. Under these terms a limited volume of American commerce moved down the river to the sea, and western discontent was held below the boiling point.

Loyalists and Planter Debts

The peace treaty contained a pledge that Congress would earnestly request the states to reimburse loyalists for confiscated property. It also stated that no lawful impediments should be placed in the way of the recovery of private debts owed to British citizens. Congress's requests that the states fulfill treaty obligations in these matters had little effect. There was no support anywhere for compensating loyalists. The sums were too large. State governments were already overburdened with debts owed to patriots. Moreover, the war had left a residue of bitterness against loyalists, not only those who remained in the country but those who returned. Riots sometimes greeted returning refugees, and in most states loyalists of all descriptions were subjected to some degree of persecution.

The treatment that loyalists received depended largely on the balance of political forces in state politics, in which loyalists were usually associated with conservative elements. They were often the friends and sometimes the relatives of conservative leaders, with whom they were likely to share opinions as to the vices of popular governments. Conservatives, on their part, tended to regard loyalists as a desirable social element, as sensible persons who supported good causes. Since loyalists were sometimes rich, they were appreciated for the wealth they contributed to the country. Conservative leaders therefore urged that the destructive hatreds of war should cease and argued that, in any case, reprisals were forbidden by the peace treaty.

This last point was the issue in a notable legal case, *Rutgers* v. *Waddington,* in which Alexander Hamilton was defense attorney for a loyalist prosecuted under New York's Trespass Act. The act permitted loyalists to be sued for taking over the property of patriots who had fled the British occupation. Hamilton argued that the act violated the peace treaty, which was superior to state law, and that the law was therefore invalid. Although the decision allowed damages to the plaintiff on a technicality, the New York supreme court upheld Hamilton's position.

Generally, wherever conservative influence prevailed in state politics, the war legislation against loyalists was soon dropped and they were quietly accepted. In New York and Pennsylvania, where the popular party was strong and exploited antiloyalist feelings for partisan purposes, the struggle was protracted. Not until near the end of the Confederation period were laws against loyalists repealed throughout the country.

In the south the loyalist issue involved the question of prewar debts. Many southern loyalists, as we have seen, were British merchants, who had resided only briefly in America before the Revolution. Many fled at the outbreak of war, to return after its end. Although there was much popular resentment against their return, the objection was less to their persons than to the efforts they immediately made to collect prewar debts. The south had been ravaged in the later stages of the war, and a multitude of slaves had been taken away by the British. Until basic production could be restored, American merchants and planters faced bankruptcy if debt collections were strictly enforced. Antiloyalist riots broke out in Charleston and Norfolk. State legislatures quickly passed laws preventing the collection of prewar debts. Later, when economic recovery had taken place, a difference of opinion arose on the debt issue. Since the laws obstructed recovery of all debts, creditors favored their repeal. Moreover, planters on the whole did not want to disown entirely their obligations to British merchants, upon whom they depended, as in colonial times, for continuing credit. Some planters were made uneasy, or their sense of rectitude was offended, by legislative violation of contract. Others, like James Madison and George Mason, felt that the country ought to observe the peace treaty. By 1787 all the southern states had gone through the motions of repealing their obstructive laws. In South Carolina and Virginia, however, debtor planters and debtor farmers were influential enough to maintain practical barriers against the collection of debts.

The Failure of Constitutional Revision

Until 1787 the main objective of those who wanted to strengthen the central government was to secure federal taxation. All during the Confederation, the modified version of the impost amendment adopted by Congress in 1783 was before the states for ratification. Meanwhile, Congress lacked funds to pay interest on a domestic debt which increased from $11 million to $28 million as private claims against Congress were settled after the war. Since Congress could not pay, the creditors applied to their own states, and at their insistence Pennsylvania, New York, and Maryland formally assumed federal debts owed to their citizens. They invited the creditors to bring in federal securities and exchange them for state securities, for which the states became responsible. By 1786 about one third of the federal debt had been converted into state debts in this way, and most of the states were absorbing additional federal securities by receiving them in the sale of land. In default of a federal power of taxation, the states were taking over the Revolutionary debt.

This relieved Congress of a burden, but in other respects Congress's financial condition was precarious. It never received quite enough money from the states to support operating expenses. Its annual deficit steadily increased up to 1789. A more urgent problem was the foreign debt, which amounted to about $11 million. Congress entirely stopped payment of interest due on wartime loans from France. Since Dutch bankers were still willing to lend money to the United States during the 1780s, Congress mustered all its resources to meet the interest on Dutch loans and keep its credit alive in Holland. Still, the future was very uncertain, for Congress would face the necessity, beginning in 1793, of paying not only interest but also installments of the principal of the French and Dutch loans. Congress had potential future wealth which would one day arise from the sale of western lands, but its immediate situation was not promising.

More serious was the complete failure of the impost amendment. Years of public discussion had spread conviction of the need for the impost. Even most states' righters agreed that Congress should be given a limited power to collect taxes. By 1786, in fact, all the states except New York had approved the impost. The legislature of that state then ratified it, but insisted that the state's paper money be accepted in payment of duties. Congress would not sanction this proviso, since it was not in line with the terms upon which the other states had ratified. New York refused to alter its stand. It was then discovered that, for completely different reasons, Pennsylvania's ratification was also unacceptable. A delegation from Congress appealed to the legislature, but it would not modify its position.

The current impasse in the movement to strengthen Congress was more critical than at any previous time. The states were rapidly absorbing the Revolutionary debt, and, as they did so, the main justification for federal taxation disappeared. Not much longer would the debt be a potential bond of union, nor would a creditor interest exist to support the central government. Parceled among the states, the debt would be a source of disunion, as each state justifiably committed its revenues to paying its own citizens. Left with few functions that required the expenditure of money, Congress could be expected to wither away. The method by which the Nationalists of 1781–83 had attempted to strengthen Congress had reached a dead end. The apparent futility of trying to amend the Articles of Confederation invited a resort to extraordinary procedures.

A crisis existed in 1786, although not the one envisaged by the old "critical period" thesis. The country was in no immediate danger from either attack or internal convulsion, but the future constitutional order was in jeopardy as a result of the failure to secure amendments to the Articles of Confederation which the majority of the country's leaders deemed necessary. The unanimous approval required for amendments proved to be a barrier not only to centralized tyranny but also to constructive reform.

The Revival of Social Radicalism

The sense of emergency inspired by these events was greatly reinforced by what conservatives regarded as an upsurge of social radicalism. The postwar depression inspired a wide demand for paper money, and seven states established land banks, in several instances coupling them with payments to federal creditors. The currency issued by New York, Pennsylvania, South Carolina, and Georgia held its value. New Jersey's currency depreciated gradually, while that of North Carolina and Rhode Island sank rapidly. In general, various states handled their currency with about the same degree of success as in colonial times. No particular conflict occurred except in Rhode Island, where the legislature engaged in the same kind of excess that had once brought down the weight of parliamentary restriction. The little state issued £100,000 on loan, an amount which, relative to population, was more than twice New York's emission. The money was declared legal tender in private transactions. Persons who refused to accept it at face value were subjected to heavy fines and deprived of citizenship. The merchants of Providence and Newport resisted, and many fled the state to avoid accepting the money. The state supreme court declared the "forcing acts" unconstitutional, but the legislature disregarded its ruling and discussed a bill to exact from every citizen an oath to support the currency. The bill did not pass, and at length the efforts of the mercantile community secured the repeal of the forcing acts. In the end, victory lay with the merchants.

All over the country, however, Rhode Island became symbolic of the iniquity of popular government. Before the Revolution, when elite rule had been more firmly seated and the elected assemblies were restrained by appointed councils and governors, propertied men in most colonies were not afraid of paper money. They now regarded it as instrument which the majority would surely use to despoil the rich. Their feeling of insecurity was increased by the fact that even in states which did not issue currency the paper money forces were barely held at bay. Moreover, in nearly every state the governments had been forced to pass laws of one kind or another to suspend collection of taxes and shield debtors from the demands of creditors. When the states were too slow in adopting such measures of depression relief, the collection of taxes and private debts was not infrequently resisted by force.

The final proof that the new republic was falling under that tyranny of mob rule predicted by all the philosophers was Shays's Rebellion. This outbreak climaxed years of growing resentment against the harsh policies of the state government of Massachusetts which served the interests of the wealthy without regard for the poor. Under a conservative government after 1780, the state consolidated its war debts in such a way that they were twice as large as they needed to have been. The state debt amounted to $5.5 million, and was held by the wealthy, who had made large profits from the method of consolidation. Amidst economic depression and scarcity of money during the postwar depression, the legislature levied heavy taxes to pay the debt. From 1780 to the fall of 1786 the total yield of taxes was about $6.5 million. About 40 percent of the state's revenue came from poll taxes, which bore most heavily upon the poor. Refusing to afford relief by issuing paper money or suspending payment of the state debt, the legislature not only continued to push tax collections but passed laws to enforce collection of private debts. Strict rules were prescribed for the forced sale of debtors' property and, if foreclosure did not raise a sufficient amount to discharge his obligations, the debtor could be put in jail. As early as 1782 some of the back counties of Massachusetts were in ferment, and by 1786 unrest had spread to all parts of the state. Numerous town meetings and county conventions sent protests to the legislature. Finally, in August 1786, groups of "insurgents" armed themselves and closed the courts in three counties.

Eastern conservatives interpreted this outbreak as a rebellion against a just government. Although probably half of the people of Massachusetts actively sympathized with the "rebels," the legislature outlawed Daniel Shays, a former Revolutionary officer, whom it somewhat arbitrarily singled out as the leader of the outbreak, and authorized the governor to suppress the insurgents. Funds were raised by private subscription among easterners to enlist a force of 4,000 men, which marched into the disaffected area under command of General Benjamin Lincoln. Without encountering much resistance, Lincoln's men dispersed the poorly armed and badly organized Shaysites, and the so-called rebellion came to an end.

When Thomas Jefferson, residing in France as American minister, heard of Shays's Rebellion, he wrote that he hoped it would not be suppressed with too great severity. "A little rebellion now and then is a good thing." Jefferson was reacting to the incident in terms of a tradition that justified popular resistance to government as a last resort. However, this tradition, appropriate to a monarchical system, had few defenders in the United States after the Revolution, when it was presumed that free and representative institutions afforded legal and constitutional means to obtain justice. But it gives a correct perspective to Shays's Rebellion, which was a protest demonstration rather than an attempt to seize power.

The armed outbreak was magnified by conservative propaganda, in which it was represented as attempted revolution. Nationalists argued that it demonstrated the imperative need for stronger central government. It was therefore convenient to their purposes, and some Massachusetts conservatives were "afraid the Insurgents [would] be conquered too soon." Secretary of War Henry Knox wrote in 1786: "The present moment is very favorable to the forming further and necessary arrangements for increasing the dignity and energy of the government." From Massachusetts, where he was Congress's observer on the scene, Knox spread rumors that the insurgents aimed at pillaging the wealthy and redistributing property. Other conservatives spread word that the rebels were linked with the British in Canada and would invite their military aid. Such tales were passed on by members of Congress to their state governments as official information. Conservatives everywhere were fearful of mob rule, and many now believed the country to be on the verge of social upheaval. Madison saw Shaysism emerging in Virginia. Edward Carrington advised the Virginia governor to notify the legislature that Shays's Rebellion might bring on civil war. In Philadelphia, a correspondent to a newspaper wrote: "A Federal Shays may be more successful than the Shays of Massachusetts. We are on the very brink of a precipice."

Origins of the Movement for the Constitution

The failure of constitutional revision, bitter internal conflicts in some states, depression-inspired demands for paper money and debtor relief, and finally the outbreak of Shays's Rebellion generated a national conservative movement dedicated to checking political democracy and protecting property rights. Whereas the Nationalists of 1781–83 had been strong only in the middle states and were closely tied to the person of Robert Morris, the Federalists of 1787 united northern merchants, southern planters, and middle-state conservatives in a common purpose. The political objectives of the movement were linked with the realization of important economic interests in federal regulation of trade, the payment of the Revolutionary debt, and the occupation of the trans-Appalachian west. The alliance had its extremist fringe, particularly among New Englanders, some of whom were so outraged by Shays's Rebellion that they wanted to go the whole way and establish a monarchy. Southern Federalists, on the other hand, were often nearly as apprehensive of strong central government as they were of popular rule. James Madison, writing about this time, probably expressed the sentiment that united the greatest number of Federalists. "Wherever the real power in a Government lies," he said, "there is the danger of oppression. In our Governments the real power lies in the majority of the Community, and the invasion of private rights is *chiefly* to be apprehended, not from acts of Government contrary to the sense of its constituents, but from acts in which the Government is the mere instrument of the major number of the constituents."

The Revolutionists of 1776 had defined liberty as the protection of individual rights against governmental tyranny. The Federalists of 1787 were determined to preserve liberty, as they understood it, against the tyranny of the majority.

CHAPTER X

The Formation of the
National Government,
1786–1790

Forces behind the Constitution

The failure to amend the Articles of Confederation invited resort to the extraordinary procedure of holding a national convention. The first step was taken in 1786, when Virginia proposed that all the states send delegates to a meeting at Annapolis, Maryland, to discuss trade regulation. It is apparent that the leading Nationalists welcomed the Annapolis Convention, not for its avowed purpose, but as groundwork for holding a second convention to recommend general changes in the structure of the Union. In drafting the resolution adopted at Annapolis, Alexander Hamilton declared that trade regulation could not be considered apart from other problems. He proposed a convention to be held at Philadelphia the next year to undertake a revision of the Articles of Confederation. The resolutions were submitted to Congress and the states, and after several states had decided to send delegates, Congress gave official recognition to the forthcoming convention. All the states except Rhode Island appointed delegates.

The meeting at Philadelphia in May 1787 was undoubtedly the most eminent gathering in American history. It represented the social, economic, intellectual, and official elite of the country. Its presiding officer was the deified Washington, whose presence gave it invaluable prestige. A few outstanding men were not elected as delegates or refused to attend, notably Patrick Henry, Richard Henry Lee, and Samuel Adams, whose views were not in harmony with the prevailing mood. Jefferson was away as minister to France. Benjamin Franklin attended, but had little influence; his libertarian ideas were regarded as visionary and sentimental. Of the 55 men who attended, many arrived late or departed early, and three delegates who stayed to the end— George Mason, Edmund Randolph, and Elbridge Gerry—refused to sign the finished document. Most of the delegates took little part in the proceedings beyond casting their votes. The active work of the Convention fell to about a dozen men.

One of the first decisions was to proceed in absolute secrecy, so that members could express their views freely without being intimidated or distracted by outside pressure. This decision no doubt contributed to the high level of debate and to the ability of the Convention to reach a compromise on vital issues. The differences among the members fell within a fairly narrow range. In basic social philosophy, most of them, certainly all who stayed to the end, had much in common. They were divided mainly by the separate interests of the states they represented.

The events of the Revolution and the postwar economic depression had dispelled among gentlemen whatever Lockean myths they might once have cherished as to a harmony of interest in society. They regarded the classical instruction in the evils of democracy and the necessity of defending property rights against majority rule as self-evident. The manifestations of democratic tyranny most often cited at the Convention were economic in character: paper money, tender laws, and laws obstructing the collection of debts. But the delegates also spoke of the unruliness of the people, their rejection of responsible leadership, and their tendency to follow demagogues who catered to their prejudices. History, as these gentlemen knew it, had never recorded an instance in which a government controlled by the people themselves had lasted very long. Most of them were convinced that the American experiment in republicanism had failed, or at least that it had reached a crisis. "What I most fear," John Jay had written in 1786, "is that the better kind of people, by which I mean the people who are orderly and industrious, who are content with their situations, and not uneasy in their circumstances, will be led by the insecurity of property, the loss of confidence in their rulers, and the want of public faith and rectitude, to consider the charms of Liberty as imaginery and delusive." Judge Edmund Pendleton was more forthright in addressing a grand jury in South Carolina. "The period is not far off," he predicted, "when the laws of the state must be voluntarily obeyed or executed by force; no society ever long endured the miseries of anarchy, disorder and licentiousness; the most vile despotism will be embraced in preference to it." Alexander Hamilton, who in his youth had once extenuated the evils of popular rule, was now so certain of them that he thought a good government could not exist if elective in all its branches. Although there was no complete remedy for this in a republican system, he thought that the president and senate should at least be elected for life.

Most members of the Convention were not such extremists. They wanted to restrain what they considered the licentiousness of the people, but most of them still harbored the traditional dread of centralized tyranny and shrank from instituting a regime so powerful and exclusive that it would itself endanger liberty and property. Their basic problem lay in the fact that America did not have a system of class privileges recognized by law and grounded in ancient right. In Britain, the recognized position of monarchy and aristocracy formed a natural base for balanced government. Since America lacked this social foundation, the essential task of the Convention was, by constitutional devices, to create a balance of classes under the forms of an elective government.

Constitutional revision was also linked with the realization of economic interests. Since its inception under financier Robert Morris, the movement for stronger government had been coupled with general economic reforms. It proposed to do away with state paper money, tender laws, and legislative abrogation of contracts, and, on the other hand, to establish a sound currency, pay the federal debt, increase the capital resources of the country, and restore public credit. This far-reaching program helped to enlist the commercial classes in support of a new constitution.

Much was said at the time, and has been written since, about the role of security holders, a group that would directly benefit from the establishment of a government that could pay its debts. Certainly they were a force behind the movement for the Constitution. From 1781 onward they advocated stronger government in their public statements, and the large holders among them had such a stake in the debt that one would have to suspend the ordinary canons of judging human behavior to believe that their political views were not affected by economic interest. By the time the Convention was held, the mass of securities, which had been issued originally to large numbers of people, was being rapidly transferred to men of substantial property and to speculators. By 1790 perhaps 80 percent of the domestic debt of $28,000,000, increased by the accumulation of unpaid interest to more than $40,000,000, was held in large and sometimes enormous concentrations. Of $12,300,000 in securities whose ownership has been determined, 280 persons held $7,880,000, nearly two thirds; a mere 100 individuals owned over $5,000,000. Although such large holders were usually brokers or acting in partnership with others and therefore did not own in their own right the entire sums listed in their names, the degree of concentration indicates that the small minority of the population which held most of the debt had a sufficient economic interest to be guided by it. Where information is available, it also denotes a sectional and class distribution of ownership. Sixty-one percent of all securities listed in Massachusetts were owned by residents of the single town of Boston. Eighty percent of all securities in the state belonged to persons described as merchants, brokers, esquires, and professional men. In neighboring Rhode Island, persons of the same description held 85 percent of the securities.

The creditor interest was of such magnitude as to leave little doubt that it was exerted on behalf of the Constitution. Its importance, however, can easily be exaggerated. Although the creditors included men of wealth and power in the community, they were but a small fraction of the population. In 1790 there were probably no more than 15,000 or 20,000 federal creditors, big or little, in the entire country. Moreover, their financial interest was fused with other and more general interests. The larger holders were likely to be merchants or propertied men, whose support of the Constitution was assured for the economic and political reforms it promised, irrespective of their security holdings. In defining the role of creditors in the formation of the national government, a recent historian has observed that, although they were its partisans, the movement for the Constitution was too broadly based in the country's general development to be attributed to a single pecuniary interest. The creditors "assisted the process, reaped its benefits, but did not create it."

Behind such material factors as we have described were patriotic sentiments and a rational interest in the solution of national problems. Virtually all Americans, whatever their political creed, subscribed to the idea of national unity rather than disunity. It was evident that the United States existed in a world of competitive states whose outposts ringed its borders. Fear was frequently expressed after 1783 that the nation would break up into confederacies and thus, as history taught, open the way to foreign intrigue and intervention. In many minds, therefore, the value of national strength offset the danger of centralized tyranny. Such considerations were reinforced by a growing sense of nationalism which the Revolution had fostered. How much it shaped attitudes toward the Constitution is impossible to say, but the general disparagement of the Confederation government for its weakness, and the pride which Americans took in their new government once it was formed, suggest that nationalism was a considerable force.

The Framing of the Constitution

It has been said that if a revolution in government like that wrought by the Constitutional Convention had taken place in

Europe, historians would describe it as a coup d'etat. The meeting at once formed itself into an extralegal body. In sanctioning the Convention, Congress had authorized it to propose amendments to the Articles of Confederation. The Virginia delegation, however, opened formal proceedings on May 29 by introducing a plan which departed completely from the existing frame of government. Under the Articles of Confederation, the Union was truly federal; Congress represented the states and operated on the states. The Virginia plan provided for a national government, which represented the people, operated directly upon the people, and was independent of the states. The Virginia plan envisaged a national legislature, to consist of a lower house elected by the people and a senate elected by the lower house from candidates nominated by state legislatures. Together, the house and senate would elect the president. Congress was to be given a commanding position over the states. It was to have a veto over their legislative acts, the power to legislate in any fields in which they were "incompetent," and the right to compel them to obey its laws by force. This was accepted by the Convention as the basis of discussion.

The introduction of the Virginia plan at once raised the central issue upon whose solution depended the success or failure of the Convention. Members as a whole were not at first opposed to giving sweeping grants of authority to Congress. The real point at issue was whether the large states were to dominate the government once it was formed. Under the Virginia plan, representation in both houses of Congress was based on population. This was to the advantage of the larger states, particularly Massachusetts, Pennsylvania, and Virginia, which together contained nearly half the country's population. They had long chafed under the equal representation accorded them by the Articles of Confederation, under which they had the same vote as Rhode Island. They were in a position to get their way: the large-state bloc had an effective majority in the Convention, since North Carolina, South Carolina, and Georgia sided with it in the expectation of one day becoming large themselves. As the discussion of the Virginia plan continued, the small-state delegates became increasingly alarmed by the lack of structural guarantees of the rights and interests of the small states and by the determination of the large states to make no concession on this point.

The small-state delegates embraced states' rights doctrine. Extreme Nationalists, like Alexander Hamilton and James Wilson, wanted to reduce the states to mere administrative agencies of the central government, deprive them of independent functions, and thus destroy the people's ancient attachment and loyalty to their own states. The large-state delegates in general supported this position for, in trying to put across the idea of representation according to population, they had to deny the importance of state distinctions or the value of local government. The small-state delegates perceived the ulterior motive, and in arguing the need to preserve the states, they got the support of extreme anti-Nationalists like Robert Yates and John Lansing of New York and Luther Martin of Maryland, who were ideologically committed to the principles of the Articles of Confederation. Eventually, they were also joined by such men as John Dickinson, George Mason, and Edmund Randolph—the latter two from Virginia—who objected to extreme centralization in the belief that the oppressive tendencies of central government ought to be balanced by the strength of local authority, and that the states should therefore be preserved as important entities. They also understood that the states had a hold on the allegiance of their citizens, and that this was a practical fact which would have to be taken into account in framing any plan of government.

The small-state delegates organized their forces, and on June 15 William Paterson of New Jersey presented their counterproposal. The New Jersey plan which they offered was not far behind the Virginia plan in conferring powers upon Congress, but it retained the federal organization of the Articles of Confederation. It provided for a single-house national legislature, in which each state would be equally represented, presided over by a plural executive which Congress was to elect from among its own members. The powers of the central government were strictly defined, but were to include taxation, the regulation of trade, and the conduct of war and foreign affairs. Acts of Congress and treaties of the United States were to be the supreme law of the land, interpreted by a federal judiciary which was also to have appellate jurisdiction over state courts. As a last resort, Congress was to have the right to execute its laws by force against state governments as well as individuals.

If the New Jersey plan had been introduced at the outset of the Convention and become the basis for discussion, it might well have altered the shape which the Union was to assume. At this stage, however, it represented the stand of the outvoted minority, and it was defeated seven states to three. Intent upon pushing their advantage, the large-state delegates went on with the Virginia plan, but there were sharp exchanges on the floor, and the small-state delegates threatened to walk out. It was at this point that Benjamin Franklin, in recognition of the critical nature of the debate, proposed opening each session with prayer, a procedure which the other members dismissed as irrelevant. The large states had a majority on June 29, when the Convention decided by a vote of six states to four that representation in the lower house should be by population. A few large-state delegates realized, however, that driving their program through would be ruinous, for it would break up the Convention and destroy any chance that the new constitution would be adopted. When the Convention next took up the question of whether representation should be equal or according to population in the upper house, the vote was tied, five states to five. Certain large-state delegates then decided to accept the so-called Connecticut Compromise, which provided for representation by population in the lower house and equal representation of states in the upper house. The vote was still close, five states to four with one divided, but the Convention was saved.

There were other major issues involving conflicts of state or sectional interests, but they produced no such hard alignments. Congress soon agreed that in determining representation and assessing direct taxes, three fifths of the slaves should be counted. This decision ended a complicated debate. It was the general belief that representation should take account of taxes which people paid, as well as their numbers; hence both wealth and population should be taken into consideration. The problem was to contrive some workable formula. The procedure had to rest on a counting of heads, modified by some principle that would register wealth. Southerners contended that the wealth of the thickly inhabited northern states would be sufficiently indicated by a mere census, but that a census would not show the wealth of the sparsely populated south. They therefore demanded that their representation be increased by counting slaves as well as white inhabitants. Northerners argued against this, saying that, if southern property in slaves was to be counted, why not northern property in horses. However, an established precedent existed on this issue. The Confederation Congress had proposed to amend the Articles by making population, rather than land values, the rule in determining each state's share of requisitions. The amendment provided for counting three fifths of the slaves as population. It had been ratified by 11 states. When the question came before the Convention, it was at once clear that a majority of delegates accepted the idea of counting slaves and that there was no effective support for any but the three-fifths ratio. It was early approved by a vote of nine states to three and added to both the Virginia and the New Jersey plans. The issue of slave representation, so charged with bitterness in the decades before the Civil War, was easily compromised in 1787.

Underlying the dispute over slave representation was the question of the potential balance of power between agricultural and commercial interests in the new government. New Englanders were afraid that slave representation would increase the political weight of the western states which would one day be admitted to the Union and that in combination with the south they would control the government in the agricultural interest. An effort was made to place permanent limitations upon representation to be given new states. That failed, but when the Confederation Congress in New York passed the Northwest Ordinance, which prohibited slavery in the Northwest Territory, the New Englanders were reassured. The issue lost some of its force, and dispute over slave representation virtually ceased.

Slavery gave rise to state and sectional divisions in still another way, although in this case, too, the issue did not have the importance sometimes imputed to it. Antislavery sentiment was a political force in the north, and although none of the delegates thought the central government should have the right to interfere with slavery where it existed, it was presumed that Congress's powers should extend to abolishing the foreign slave trade. Many southern delegates, particularly those of Virginia, which already had a surfeit of slaves, were as ardent as any northerners in demanding a stop to importations. A clear majority therefore existed in favor of early abolition of the slave trade. However, the Convention was again confronted by a vital interest that could be overridden only at the cost of forcing some of the states out of the new union. The delegates of North Carolina, South Carolina, and Georgia flatly declared that if the Constitution provided for an immediate abolition of the slave trade their constituents would never accept it. Many northern delegates were disposed to compromise for the sake of unity; nevertheless, the Convention tentatively adopted a provision to abolish the slave trade after the elapse of ten years.

The decision was soon altered in the course of debate over another sectional issue, federal regulation of trade. That Congress should have this power was scarcely in dispute. However, the commercial states of the north were certain to reap the benefits, and the major prize held out to them was the carrying trade of the south. Many southern delegates were perfectly willing to let the Yankees take their trade away from the British if they had enough ships to carry it, but they were aware that federal regulation could be pressed to the point of giving northerners a complete monopoly. Hence, they backed a proposal which required that navigation acts had to be approved by a two-thirds majority of both houses of Congress. The southern states would thus have an absolute veto over such legislation. A deadlock impended, for the southern delegates were determined on this point. Once more, however, the need for unity transcended particular interests. This time the south had to yield, for the desire to obtain effective trade regulation was a primary object in the northern states, and they would not consent to a constitution which did not provide it. The South Carolina delegates perceived the necessity for compromise and at the same time an opportunity to bargain. They voted in favor of federal regulation of trade by simple majority, and this measure passed. In return, northern delegates voted for a clause which restrained Congress from prohibiting the importation of slaves until 1808. This meant, in effect, a continuance of the slave trade for 20 instead of 10 years after the formation of the new government.

The Constitution as a Political Act

The adjustment of state interests cleared the ground for the erection of the central power. The significance of the Constitution as it emerged from the Convention has been obscured by the changes which have since occurred in the theory and practice of American government. As a historical fact the Constitution is best understood in terms of the conditions and the ideas prevailing at the time. Only in this context does the scale of the political revolution accomplished in 1787 become fully apparent. Measured against the Articles of Confederation and the Revolutionary state constitutions, and considered in the light of the traditional distrust of governmental power, the Constitution created a central authority of startling magnitude. In all but the vital element of republicanism, it invited comparison with the British system.

The continuity of early American history with its British past is apparent in the general structure of the federal government, which, like the state governments, is modeled on political forms with which Americans were familiar. The Constitution is a republicanized version of Britain's limited monarchy; the checks and balances built into it, which we shall discuss below, were an adaptation of the relations supposed to subsist between the branches of government in Britain. The Convention, moreover, was not afraid of power; it put nothing into the Constitution which would limit the ability of the government to deal with future problems or cope with emergencies. In view of the vital relationship then drawn between sovereignty and the power of taxation, it is significant that Congress was given unlimited authority to levy taxes (except on exports). This, observed George Mason, "does, of itself entirely change the confederation of the states into one consolidated government." Congress was given sweeping authority to perform the usual functions of a sovereign power: to declare war, maintain an army and navy, borrow money, and regulate trade. Besides its specified powers, Congress had undefined powers implicit in the so-called expansive clauses of the Constitution: the right to provide for the "general welfare," and "to make all laws which shall be necessary and proper for carrying into execution" its designated powers. As far as the Founding Fathers could contrive, a liberal construction of the Constitution was built into its fabric. The fact is sometimes overlooked that the original Constitution lacked the clause, present in the Articles of Confederation and later added by the Tenth Amendment, which reserved to the states all powers not specifically granted to the central government. Similarly, beyond the prohibition of ex post facto laws, bills of attainder, and suspension of habeas corpus in peacetime, the Constitution did not include a bill of rights to protect individuals against the abuse of power by the central government. The delegates considered it unnecessary, notwithstanding the fact that most of the states had seen fit to prefix bills of rights to their Revolutionary constitutions.

In all that related to federal functions, the superiority of the central government over the states was guaranteed. The Constitution, the acts of Congress, and treaties with foreign nations were declared the supreme law of the land, and obedience was enjoined upon state courts, regardless of state laws or constitutions. The states were laid under express prohibitions: they could not enter into engagements with foreign powers, maintain military forces in time of peace, levy duties upon imports or exports without the consent of Congress, coin money or issue paper currency, or pass laws abrogating contracts.

Federal law was to be enforced by a judiciary, headed by a Supreme Court with original jurisdiction in certain cases and appellate jurisdiction over federal courts and over state courts in cases involving federal laws. Most significantly, the Constitution provided for a system of lower courts. Thus, federal justice and the enforcement of federal law were brought down to the level of the individual citizen residing in the states.

In its adjustment of federal-state relations, the Constitution was a masterly attempt to resolve the historic conflict between central and local authority. This conflict had been implicit in the pre-Revolutionary disputes with Britain. The colonies had acquired practical sovereignty in local affairs, but, holding to a unitary conception of the state, Britain had refused to recognize a sphere of action in which local government was supreme. Britain's adherence to the idea of indivisible sovereignty was the downfall of its empire. The antithesis between local and central authority did not end with the Revolution. Under the Articles of Confederation, local government gained the upper hand, although the conflict between the authority of Congress and that of the states gave rise to most of the public issues of the period. By 1787 the delegates to the Convention were determined to reinvigorate central authority. Extreme Nationalists wanted to reduce the states to nothing, but that was impossible. The existence of strongly entrenched state governments had to be taken into account. At the other end of the political spectrum represented at the Convention, the advocates of the New Jersey plan wanted to preserve the importance of the states; these under their plan were to be the constituent members of the union, and the federal government was to operate upon them rather than upon the people. This arrangement posed a formidable problem. If the federal government operated only on the states, how could Congress enforce its will upon disobedient states? The only answer was a resort to force, but force employed by one government against another is not the execution of law but an act of war. The union would be continually embroiled in strife.

The solution arrived at by the Convention was to divide sovereignty between central and local government according to function. In general matters appropriate to action by the central authority, such as war, trade, and diplomacy, the national government was to be sovereign and fully equipped to operate by means of its own law and its own police directly upon individual citizens. Legally, the central government would never be in the position of coercing a state. The states, on the other hand, were to be supreme in matters appropriate to local authority, acting upon individuals through their own agencies. The occasions for a direct clash between central and local authority were thereby minimized. This "federal" solution was the outgrowth of American political experience in colonial and Revolutionary times.

The Founding Fathers tipped the balance of power heavily in favor of the central government. This imbalance was later redressed, in part by the adoption of the Tenth Amendment and in part, as the extreme Nationalists at the Convention feared, by the power that naturally clung to the preexisting states. The federal features of the Union—that is, the place and functions accorded to the states in the nation's political life—were for a long time the most effective restraint upon the growth of the central authority.

The Constitution as a Social Document

Examined in its historical context, the Constitution reveals the intent of the Framers to erect barriers against what they considered to be the excessively democratic spirit of American society. This purpose was implicit in the general plan of the new government, which was to have a "balanced" structure; it was explicit in the powers given to the various branches of government and in the mode of electing public officers.

The classical idea of balanced government, as understood by conservatives, had always presupposed the existence of distinct social classes; the underlying purpose was to protect and stabilize class interests by giving them separate representation. By the time of the American Revolution, as has been noted, some of the class content had been strained out of the concept, American writers often regarded a separate executive, judiciary, and legislature, the latter composed of two houses, as in themselves a good thing because they helped to prevent hasty and intemperate action and also because they placed barriers in the way of governmental tyranny. Nonetheless, the basic identification of "checks and balances" with the protection of class interests was never lost, either in the writings of Montesquieu, the chief theorist on the subject, or in political practice. Most of the state constitutions had provided for a senate, in which property qualifications for voting and holding office were higher than for the "popular" lower house; similarly the governor in several states had to have a large fortune, or he was elected by superior property owners. Such arrangements were designed to protect wealth and give the elite a special place in government. The chief complaint of conservatives, repeated frequently at the Convention, was that these devices had not worked. Nearly all the Revolutionary state constitutions gave the legislature superiority over the executive and judiciary; and the legislature, despite the existence of senates and property qualifications, was too susceptible to popular influence.

The Constitution was designed to erect a balanced government at the national level. The executive was made strong and independent. Whereas state governors were usually merely the heads of a council, without a veto over legislation or powers of appointment, the President of the United States was, by comparison, a kingly figure. He stood alone, unhampered by an executive council. He had sweeping powers to initiate and control policy, subject only to ultimate restraint by the legislature. He commanded the military forces, conducted foreign relations, appointed his department heads and numerous public officials, proposed legislation to Congress, exercised a veto over Congressional acts which could be overridden only by a two-thirds vote of both houses, and had power to rule by decree in times of national emergency. His election was independent of Congress, and he was protected against removal for purely political reasons. The main restraints upon his power were the necessity of securing Senate approval of major appointments, the obligation (which soon lapsed) to consult the Senate in negotiating treaties, and the requirement that treaties had to be approved by a two-thirds majority of the Senate. He could be indicted for criminal acts by the House and tried before the Senate, presided over by the Chief Justice, and, if found guilty by a two-thirds vote, removed from office.

The election of this great officer was not only independent of Congress, it was also removed from popular influence as far as was possible under a republican system. Electors chosen in any way which the state legislatures determined were to meet in their respective states and cast two votes. The person receiving the most votes was to be President, and the next highest Vice-President. In case of a tie or the absence of a majority for one person, the choice would be made by the House of Representatives, voting by states. This procedure was calculated to sift the popular will and keep the choice of the President in the hands of the elite.

The Senate was given powers superior to those of the House. Besides general powers to initiate and concur in legislative acts, it had special functions in reviewing executive appointments and participating in the conduct of foreign relations. It could amend money bills initiated by the House, a privilege which in fact gave it nearly equal power with the House in matters relative to taxation and the expenditure of money. The election of this branch of the legislature was shielded against direct popular vote. Senators were to be elected by the state legislatures, and their six-year terms were to be staggered in such a way as to prevent the retirement of more than one third of the members at any one time. The length of their terms was in marked contrast with the practice of many states, which had annual elections. Although the mode of electing Senators was appropriate to the fact that they represented the states, it was another barrier against popular influence.

The members of the Convention seriously considered setting up property qualifications for federal elections, but at length gave up the idea because any reasonable property qualifications were unlikely to accomplish the purpose. It was brought out in debate that too many farmers, from whom attacks upon property had come, were themselves landowners who could meet the customary requirements for voting. Besides, many of the states had reduced qualifications almost to the point of extinction; to erect higher qualifications for federal elections would deny the vote to large numbers of people accustomed to having it and virtually ensure rejection of the Constitution. Accordingly, it was decided to accept the suffrage requirements existing in the states and to rely upon indirect elections and checks and balances to curb popular influence.

The one part of the government directly elected by the people was the House of Representatives, which had exclusive right to originate tax bills and joint powers with the Senate in enacting legislation. The judiciary was appointed by the President with the consent of the Senate. Congress had power to organize the court system and determine the number of justices. In concert with the President, it therefore had ultimate control over the judiciary, which, as provided for by the Constitution, was not co-equal with the other branches of government.

Finally, conservative economic goals were written into the Constitution with the proviso that states could not issue paper money, make anything but gold or silver legal tender, or pass laws abrogating contracts. So deep was Federalist revulsion against these practices that for a time the Convention debated whether to extend the same prohibitions to the federal government itself. The idea was reluctantly given up on the grounds that bitter necessity might some day force the government to these expedients and that nothing should be done to tie its hands.

Ratification

Under the Articles of Confederation, which were still in effect in 1787, amendments had to be submitted by Congress to the state legislatures and unanimously ratified before they became effective. With past failures to amend the Articles in mind, the members of the Convention despaired of securing unanimous

ratification; moreover, they thought that members of state legislatures would be peculiarly resistant to the Constitution because
the elevation of the national authority would reduce their own
importance. Accordingly, the Convention provided for ratification, not by state legislatures, but by specially elected conventions. When approved by nine of the thirteen states, the Constitution was to become effective in the states that ratified it.

The Convention submitted the finished draft of the Constitution to the Confederation Congress, which after some debate
transmitted it to the states without recommendation. In due
course every state but Rhode Island called a convention to consider it. In the great debate that took place, the lines were drawn
between Federalists, as the supporters of the Constitution called
themselves, and the Antifederalists who opposed it. What the
majority of the people thought is impossible to say with any
precision, for there was no popular vote on the Constitution,
and what one can infer from the election of delegates to state
conventions is dubious. Property qualifications prevented some
people from voting, but many more were so little concerned that
they failed to vote even though entitled to. Many delegates
elected to the conventions were not instructed by their constituents; presumably they were to use their own judgment. It has
been said that if the Constitution had been submitted to a pleb-
iscite it would have failed. Certainly, there were initial majorities against it in the conventions held in New Hampshire,
Massachusetts, and New York. Opinion was evenly divided in
Virginia. North Carolina rejected the Constitution, and opinion
was so adverse in Rhode Island that the state did not hold a convention. John Marshall wrote:

> So balanced were the parties in some of [the states], that even
> after the subject had been discussed for a considerable time, the
> fate of the constitution could scarcely be conjectured; and so
> small in many instances, was the majority in its favor, so as to
> afford strong ground for the opinion that had the influence of
> character been removed, the intrinsic merits of the instrument
> would not have secured its adoption. Indeed it is scarcely to be

doubted that in some of the adopting states a majority of the people were in opposition.

Historians have endlessly debated the alignment of forces, asserting or denying the relative importance of economic interest, sectional and class divisions, ideological commitment, and concern for the national welfare. Alexander Hamilton, though perhaps overly cynical in assessing human motives, particularly those of his opponents, covered most of the ground in a statement made shortly after the Convention adjourned. Estimating the chances of the Constitution's adoption, he said it would have in its favor

> the good will of the commercial interests throughout the states which will give all its efforts to the establishment of a government capable of regulating, protecting and extending the commerce of the Union . . . the good will of most men of property in the several states who wish a government of the Union able to protect them against domestic violence and the depredations which the democratic spirit is apt to make on property—and who are besides anxious for the respectability of the nation— the hopes of the creditors of the United States that a general government possessing the means of doing it will pay the debt of the Union. A strong belief in the people at large of the insufficiency of the present confederation to preserve the existence of the Union and of the necessity of the Union to their safety and prosperity

Against the Constitution he put the influence of state officials whose importance would decline under the new regime, and that of ambitious men who would try to cultivate political advantage by opposing it. Other factors he considered adverse to ratification were

> . . . the disinclination of the people to taxes and of course to a stronger government—the opposition of all men much in debt who will not wish to see a government established one object of which is to restrain the means of cheating Creditors—the democratical jealousy of the people which may be alarmed at the ap-

pearance of institutions that may seem calculated to place the power of the community in a few hands and to raise a few individuals to stations of great preeminence.

As Hamilton's remarks imply, the motives of Antifederalists, like those of the Federalists, were compounded of economic interest and ideological attachment. Hamilton might have enlarged, however, on the fact that many people regarded strong central government—bureaucracy, rigorous taxation, and funded public debts, all of which he counted among the benefits of the proposed system—as the earmarks of governmental tyranny and aristocratic domination. Writing from the Massachusetts convention, Rufus King observed: "An apprehension that the liberties of the people are in danger, and a distrust of men of property or Education have a more powerful Effect upon the minds of our Opponents than any specific Objections against the constitution." In another letter he wrote that the opposition arose chiefly "from an opinion . . . that some injury is plotted against them—that the system is the production of the rich and ambitious . . . that the consequence will be the establishment of two orders in the society, one comprehending the opulent and great, the other the poor and illiterate. The extraordinary Union in favor of the Constitution in this State of the wealthy and sensible part of it is in confirmation of these opinions and every exertion hitherto made to eradicate it, has been in vain."

Although the point is disputed by some historians, it appears that except where particular local interests existed as in the desire of some parts of the west and the south to gain military support against the Indians, divisions over the Constitution tended to follow a sectional line: the east, the towns, and the commercial farming areas in general supported it; the subsistence farming regions opposed it. Something like organized political parties existed in New York and Pennsylvania, and in these states the division was along the already existing lines of local politics. In New York the party headed by Governor George Clinton, which represented small and middle-class farmers and subscribed to an anti-aristocratic tradition, opposed the Constitution. Federalist support for it centered in New York City and its environs and in the town of Albany. In Pennsylvania the Antifederalists drew chiefly from adherents of the Constitutionalist party, grounded in the western part of the state, which for more than a decade had fought the Quakers and merchants of Philadelphia and the eastern counties. In Massachusetts the heart of the opposition was the old Shaysite counties and the frontier districts of Maine. From South Carolina, Aedanus Burke wrote that four fifths of the people "from their souls detest it." Some allowance must be made for Burke's partisanship, since he was an ardent Antifederalist, but his analysis corresponds with the sectional division in the state. Included among supporters of the Constitution, he said, were "all the rich leading men, along the sea coast, and the rice settlements with few exceptions, Lawyers, Physicians and Divines, the Merchants' mechanics, the Populace and mob of Charleston. . . ." In the backcountry all was "disgust, sorrow and vindictive reproaches against the system, and all those who voted for it."

The Antifederalists were at a disadvantage in the contest. Few of them wholly endorsed the Articles of Confederation, which admittedly needed reform. The Federalists presented the Constitution as a concrete plan, agreed to by delegates of the various states. Their argument was that if it was rejected, the country would never be able to agree upon any other before the Union collapsed. The Antifederalists themselves had no concerted plan of their own to offer the people, and they disagreed among themselves. In none of the state conventions were they sufficiently well organized to make a frontal assault upon the basic principle of the Constitution, which lay in its creation of a national government in place of the federal structure of the Confederation. Instead, they dissipated their force in criticism of details, raising the spectre of suppositious evils: the President could become a dictator, the Senate a stronghold of aristocracy, the national government the conqueror of the states. While these possibilities could not be entirely denied, the Federalists were able to counter with arguments equally suppositious: that the balanced nature of the government would prevent such evils, that the government represented the people and was therefore incapable of tyranny, and that in any case objectionable features could be changed by amendment.

The "extraordinary Union . . . of the Wealthy and sensible part" of the community was the heaviest weight in the scale. The nation still deferred to its upper classes, and the opinions of its leaders were the active element in forming public opinion. The Constitution had the overwhelming endorsement of the country's outstanding men, in both the agricultural and the commercial states. Their superiority in education and ability, the dignity and force that they had acquired from habitual preeminence, went far to silence and overawe their lesser adversaries in debate. The newspapers, published mainly in cities, were predominantly Federalist, as was the clergy. The Antifederalist cause suffered further from the fact that its own leaders were drawn from the economic, professional, and office-holding elite that in the main supported the Constitution. They may have been afraid that the central power would crush the state governments and destroy the liberties of the people, but they were as apprehensive of democracy and the violation of property rights as most Federalists. They therefore had mixed views about the Constitution. In several crucial states, it was the defection of such Antifederalist leaders that swung the balance.

In state conventions where the Federalists had a solid majority, they secured unqualified adoption of the Constitution. In six states, however, including Massachusetts, New York, and Virginia, they won approval only by the promise of amendments. Some 150 different amendments were proposed in all. Analysis of their content indicates two basic purposes: to protect states' rights against federal power, and to safeguard individual rights. Some of the amendments in the first category would have seriously limited Congress's operations. It was proposed, for example, that a two-thirds vote be required to pass navigation acts, borrow money, raise troops, and declare war; that federal taxes be restricted to import duties and excise taxes, additional sums to be raised by requisitions on the states; that the jurisdiction of federal courts be limited; and that all powers not specifically delegated to the federal government be reserved to the states. In proposing amendments in the second category, designed to safeguard individual rights, the states repeated guarantees handed down in English constitutional tradition and already incorporated in many state constitutions: freedom of speech and religion, liberty of the press, trial by jury in civil cases, exemptions from unwarranted seizures and from cruel and unusual punishments. The leading Nationalists, including Alexander Hamilton, James Wilson, and James Madison, fought hard against making amendments the condition of ratification, but it was the only way that the Constitution won acceptance in Massachusetts, New York, and Virginia.

In 1789, after some prodding, the first Congress under the new government reviewed the amendments set forth by state conventions. Avoiding those which would impair its functions, Congress drafted a carefully chosen list and submitted it to the states for ratification. Thus the first ten amendments, the Bill of Rights, were added to the Constitution. Except for the Tenth Amendment, they related to the protection of individual rights, and nearly all Americans agreed with them. The Tenth, which reserved to the states all powers not expressly delegated to the federal government, was the only survival of a distinctly Antifederalist position.

Although nine states adopted the Constitution by June 1788, the struggle ended only when Virginia ratified in July. Virginia's adherence tipped the scales in New York, where Antifederalists had a strong majority in the convention and were corresponding with opposition leaders in other parts of the country with a view to holding a second convention to revise the work of the first. After Virginia's ratification, the new Union became a viable reality, and New York could not survive in isolation. In any case, the Federalists in New York City and environs were ready to secede from the state and join the Union. By a narrow margin, and on the condition of amendments, the New York convention endorsed the Constitution. An Antifederalist convention, sponsored by Pennsylvania Antifederalists, eventually met at Harrisburg, but the opportunity to defeat the Constitution had passed, and the Harrisburg Convention did no more than draw up a list of amendments. North Carolina, which rejected the Constitution in 1788, approved it the next year. Rhode Island stayed outside the Union even though Congress threatened to cut off her trade with the United States. The people of the state voted against the Constitution in 1789. Economic losses resulting from federal duties on Rhode Island's commerce proved too great, however, and a convention ratified the Constitution in May 1790. The union of the states was thus completed.

James Wilson's comment to the Pennsylvania ratifying convention was appropriate:

> Governments, in general, have been the result of force, of fraud, and of accident. After a period of six thousand years has elapsed since the creation, the United States exhibited to the world the first instance as far as we can learn, of a nation, unattacked by external force, unconvulsed by domestick insurrections, assembling voluntarily, deliberating fully, and deciding calmly, concerning that system of government, under which they would wish that they and their posterity should live.

The Inauguration of the Government

The Constitution was only the framework of a government. Aware that everything depended upon the men who would put it in operation, the Federalists exerted themselves to win the first elections. Washington was unanimously chosen President, and supporters of the Constitution gained majorities in both houses of Congress. The new government was Federalist in all its branches. Cabinet positions went to men of outstanding reputation and character: Alexander Hamilton in the Treasury, Thomas Jefferson in the Department of State, and Henry Knox in the Department of War. John Jay was named Chief Justice. Of the 39 men who signed the Constitution 26 got some kind of federal position, either as an elected delegate or as an appointed official.

The organization of the government took place amidst considerable pomp and ceremony. On his way from Mount Vernon to New York, Washington was greeted by official receptions in Georgetown and Philadelphia. At Trenton he passed through a triumphal arch bearing the inscription "The Defender of the Mothers will be the Protector of the Daughters," and his path was strewn with flowers by matrons and girls dressed in white, who recited an ode prepared for the occasion. Leaving Trenton, Washington proceeded to New York, whose inhabitants staged a mammoth celebration. Many Antifederalists were seen to exhibit unmistakable signs of pride in the new government.

In view of the struggle over ratification a certain amount of opposition had been expected, but as the members of Congress took their seats and passed the first acts of legislation, nothing of the sort materialized. The government's authority was respected, its regulations were obeyed, and the duties it levied upon commerce were from the start productive. It was a tribute to the political genius of the people and to the quality of their leaders that after the Constitution had been adopted the nation tried in good will to make it work.

The Funding Program

The crucial test came as Congress took up the controversial matter of providing for the Revolutionary debt. Funding the debt was the economic counterpart of the adoption of the Constitution. The two had always been linked in the movement for constitutional revision. Congress now had ample powers but, unless it exercised the right to collect and disburse revenues, its authority would remain unused and merely abstract. Hence the implementation of federal powers under the Constitution required paying the debt. The chief criticism of the Confederation government, moreover, had been its fiscal weakness, its inability to honor its pledges. The backers of the new government awaited Congress's action on the debt as a decisive test of the character of the regime.

Funding was a test in still another way. Agreement on the new plan of government had been reached by an adjustment of conflicting state interests achieved through compromise. Similarly, the means now chosen to deal with the debt, which was unequally distributed through the nation, had to take account of a diversity of interest if harmony was to prevail and the states were to be reconciled to the existence of the Union.

The key figure in the situation was Alexander Hamilton, Secretary of the Treasury, whose contributions to national policy were to place him among the country's great statesmen. He had behind him a brilliant career which in some ways was a commentary upon the rewards that American society held out to ability but in other ways demonstrated the power of aristocratic patronage to elevate those whom it embraced. Born in the British West Indies, he came to the United States as a young man, arriving just before the Revolution. He espoused the patriot cause, wrote pamphlets, and joined the army as an artillery captain, envisaging at that time a military career. His absolute courage, character, and conspicuous abilities drew the attention of men in high station. He was appointed aide to General Washington. For nearly five years he was at the center of events, taking part in high-level planning, dealing with members of Congress, and corresponding with the country's leading men. In his one opportunity to win military glory, he played a heroic role in the final assault at Yorktown. Meanwhile, he had married into the wealthy Schuyler family of New York, thus joining the elite.

As the war drew to a close, his interest turned to politics. A leading Nationalist, he served in Congress and in the New York legislature, where he was a champion of the conservative forces. He was too extreme in his political views to take much part in the practical accommodations of the Constitutional Convention, but he led the fight for ratification in New York, writing the bulk of the *Federalist Papers,* which some consider the greatest work of political philosophy ever written in America. Hamilton was bold and ambitious, gifted with extraordinary intellect, and his personal drive invariably thrust him into prominence. His appointment to the Treasury in 1789 met with the emphatic approval of Federalist leaders, who knew him by reputation.

The program which Hamilton recommended to Congress in his *Report on Public Credit,* issued in January 1790, had two major features. The first related to the federal domestic debt, which, with accumulated interest, amounted to more than $40,000,000. He proposed a government "loan," in which old securities were to be called in and exchanged at their face value for new federal "stock." The terms of the exchange were designed to force a reduction of interest upon the creditors from six percent due on their old securities to an immediate interest of a little more than four percent on federal stock. This was to be accomplished by issuing different types of stock in exchange for old securities. As finally determined by Congress, each creditor who brought in $100 in old securities was to receive stock of $100 par value, two thirds of which was to be stock bearing six percent interest and one third to be "deferred" stock which would begin to draw six percent interest after ten years. For all unpaid interest due on old securities, the creditor would get stock bearing an immediate interest of three percent. Hamilton justified the reduction of interest on the ground that the new government was a better risk than the old one, and hence the creditors could be legitimately asked to take a reduction. His real motive, however, was to ease the immediate burden of interest payments due from the government, so that it would be financially able to bear the additional load of providing for state debts.

The other major feature of Hamilton's *Report* was a recommendation that the federal government assume the war debts of the states, estimated at $25,000,000, but which later proved to be a little over $18,000,000. In urging the assumption he said the debts of the states were the price of victory in the Revolution no less than the federal debt and had an equal claim on the gratitude of the country. He also stressed political considerations: if state debts were not funded along with federal debts, a division of interest would exist between state and federal creditors. One group would oppose the other, and this would disrupt any system of funding. Payment of all debts by the federal government was therefore essential to a workable system. Of equal importance was the need to relieve certain states which still had large debts from the Revolution. Since Congress had taken over import duties and would probably levy excise taxes as well, the states were being deprived of major tax revenues. The heavily indebted states would face bankruptcy and their creditors would be stranded. Hamilton therefore recommended that Congress take over all debts incurred by the states in conducting the war. The terms, as eventually set by Congress, provided for the exchange of state securities for new federal stock on terms similar to but slightly less favorable than those given to federal creditors.

No period was set for the payment of the principal of the newly organized debt. The creditors were promised only that the interest would be paid. To redeem the principal a sinking fund was provided for, to be placed in the hands of a commission headed by the Secretary of the Treasury, who would enter the securities market at his discretion to purchase and retire federal stock.

In its full dimensions Hamilton's funding program amounted to a politico-economic revolution. At one stroke he repudiated paper money and the agrarian methods of public finance employed by the states, replacing them with specie payment. The funding of the federal debt and the assumption of state debts promised to revitalize $60,000,000 in securities, create capital for business enterprise, and lay the foundations for a stable currency. The political implications were no less important. With the assumption of state debts, virtually all the public debts in the country would pass to the federal government, which would then collect and disburse nearly all public revenues, thereby depriving the states of functions. The political centralization achieved by the Constitution would be fortified by attaching the self-interest of an enlarged body of creditors to the federal government.

In the months before Hamilton delivered his report to Congress, speculation in securities mounted to a frenzy. Security prices had reacted to the successive steps taken in forming the new government, rising from 15 cents to 21 cents on the dollar as the Constitution was ratified, to 30 cents in the summer of 1789, then suddenly to 33 cents in November and to 50 cents in December. The rapid increase was in part the result of large purchases by European capitalists, particularly the Dutch, who had begun to speculate in the American debt after the Constitution was ratified. Foreign purchases were made largely through orders placed with merchants of New York City, the seat of Congress and the center of a national securities market. By 1789 European capitalists owned millions, and it was apparent that the domestic debt was rapidly being transferred abroad. The demand for securities had become so intense and prices had gone up so high that investors were beginning to turn to state securities, which could still be bought for as low as 10 cents on the dollar. Inspired by rumors that Congress would assume state debts and, in the case of certain New York speculators, by Hamilton's premature indication that he intended to propose such a measure, big investors began moving into state securities. The most inviting were those of the southern states, which were still very cheap. Hamilton's actual delivery of his *Report* precipitated a mad rush southward as speculators hurried to make their purchases before the inhabitants heard the news.

Hamilton's recommendations with respect to funding the federal debt were quite satisfactory to the overwhelming majority of the members of Congress, who, as good Federalists, desired to establish the regime on a sound financial basis. The reduction of interest to four percent was a compromise, it was true, and some of the creditors loudly denounced it as a breach of faith, and yet the program constituted a sufficient observance of contract to satisfy their legitimate claims and to lay the foundation for the restoration of public credit. Political considerations, too, were heavily in its favor. All over the country the government's supporters were waiting for a display of financial integrity that would clearly repudiate the despised practices of the past. Any marked evasion of responsibility, any repudiation, was certain to provoke a reaction that would have disorganized the Union.

What opposition existed in Congress gathered behind a motion made by James Madison in the House of Representatives. Long an ardent Federalist, Madison surprised nearly everybody by taking an anti-administration line. He proposed to distinguish between original holders who had received securities from the government, and secondary holders who had purchased them in the market at a discount. Under his plan original holders who brought in securities for exchange would receive six percent federal stock for the full amount. Secondary holders, who had purchased securities originally issued to others, would, however, receive stock only to the amount of the highest price at which securities had sold in the market, that is, 50 cents on the dollar, and the balance would be issued in the form of federal stock to the original holders of the securities.

Madison argued that the nation was under no obligation to enrich speculators who had bought at a discount. The real debt was to the soldiers, farmers, and other patriots whose sacrifices had carried the country through the war. Now that the government could pay, the speculators should be given their due, but the sacred claims of the original holders should be honored. To this, Hamilton's supporters in the House replied that the new regime must start with a rigid observance of contract, that the government had no business inquiring into private transactions, that its only obligation was to make payment to the legal owner and that, if it did not do so, public confidence would be so undermined that the new federal stock would not be worth much, even to the original holders. Madison's adherents countered with the assertion that a nation was securely founded only in justice and in the loyalty of its people, that the patriotism of speculators was always for sale and would be a slender reed upon which to rely in time of need. A few members of Congress seized the opportunity to damn speculators, accusing them of having been Tories, for the most part, who had gotten rich during the war while such patriots as the original holders were making sacrifices. Most members of Congress, however, were more influenced by what they considered the necessities of public policy than by compassion for original creditors. The House of Representatives rejected Madison's proposal by a vote of 39 to 13, nine of the 13 supporting votes being cast by Madison's fellow Virginians.

The publicity given Madison's motion set off an intense debate outside Congress. Old resentments against loyalists and war profiteers were aired in the newspapers, speculators were vilified, and Hamilton's scheme was likened to European despotisms. "It is wished to sacrifice the *many* to a few . . . to make noblemen and nabobs of a few New York gentlemen, at the expense of all the farmers in the United States." However, the real ground of popular opposition to Hamilton's measures was not a desire to compensate original holders, but a wish to avoid paying speculators and by this means to reduce the amount of the debt. People saw no reason to redeem at par securities which had depreciated and changed hands at an eighth or a tenth of face value. They wanted to redeem the debt as far as possible at its depreciated market value and thereby get rid of it quickly. Most of the Revolutionary debts of Congress and the states had been disposed of in this way. Popular opinion would in all likelihood have supported the notion of paying the speculators, who held at least 80 percent of the debt, only the market value of their securities and ignoring the original creditors who had sold out. An alternative method of reducing the debt would have been to pay only three percent interest and redeem the principal by receiving securities in the sale of western lands. Such schemes would have eased the debt burden; they were destructive, however, of the larger aims of the Federalists, who were probably correct in saying that any repudiation would have a disastrous effect upon the government's credit, both at home and abroad. Certainly, a repudiation would have impaired the free negotiability of securities, limited their usefulness as the basis of a stable currency, and reduced the capital gains expected from funding. Above all, any resort to the former practices of the states and the Confederation Congress would have invited bitter opposition by a powerful segment of American society which had backed the new government in order to get rid of them.

Assumption of State Debts

Funding the federal debt was integral to the formation of the new government and supported by most of the country's leaders. Hamilton's proposal to assume state debts was less clearly necessary, and it ran afoul of conflicts of state interest which split the nation's leadership. Only Massachusetts, South Carolina, and, to a lesser extent, Connecticut had a vital interest in assumption. They were heavily indebted. Many of the states, on the other hand, had already discharged the bulk of their Revolutionary debts. Virginia, North Carolina, and Georgia, for example, had pulled in state securities by accepting them for taxes and in the sale of land. On the basis of population, their share of the total amount of debts to be assumed by Congress would be greater than their existing debts. Furthermore, if assumed by Congress, the debts would likely be paid in hard money rather than by the easier method of selling state land. Hence, these and other states opposed assumption, arguing that if Massachusetts and South Carolina had incurred large debts by their contributions to the Revolution, as they claimed, they would be compensated in the settlement of Revolutionary accounts between the states and the Union which was then taking place. In the meantime, the opponents of assumption favored letting each state pay its own debts.

The economic interests of the states were the pivotal issue in the debate over assumption, but its opponents also raised a constitutional point. The Virginia legislature formally declared that assumption was unconstitutional; it was not specifically included among the powers of Congress and would unduly increase the powers of the federal government at the expense of the states. Added to the constitutional issue was a moral, or, more truly, a sectional issue. The speculation of northerners in southern state debts set off by Hamilton's report had aroused great indignation among southerners, who saw all the anticipated gains from federal funding going to Yankees. They raised an outcry against what they said was a corrupt union between money dealers and the government.

Madison, who by this time had emerged as the chief anti-administration leader in Congress, led the fight against assumption. He was solidly backed by southern members of the House of Representatives, except for those of South Carolina, whose large debt gave them no choice. The leading supporters of assumption were the delegates of Massachusetts, Connecticut, and South

Carolina. Members from other states, whose interests were not vitally affected by the measure, voted according to their personal views. As the debate progressed, the opposition gained a small but firm majority, and finally defeated assumption by a vote of 31 to 29. The provision for assuming state debts was deleted from the funding bill, which was then sent up to the Senate.

The stage was now set for one of the better known political deals in American history. As the Senate prepared to act on the House measure, a bargaining situation was created by the introduction of a bill to determine the permanent residence of Congress. Ever since the removal of Congress from Philadelphia in 1783, its residence had been periodically debated. Each section of the country wanted to have the national capital, or at least wanted it located as close as possible. After 1783 the capital was at New York City, but the question of residence was reopened by the formation of the new government. The Confederation Congress discussed the location of the capital in 1788, and the new Congress took up the matter at its first session in 1789. Among the most interested parties were the Virginians, who had long desired a location on the Potomac, both for the political advantage it promised and for the economic stimulation expected from federal expenditures in the neighborhood. However, Virginia and her southern supporters did not have enough votes in Congress to get the capital; indeed no single section had. If Congress was to be moved from New York, the removal had to be accomplished by some kind of intersectional trade.

The introduction of the residence bill into the Senate set off flurries of negotiation as Congress saw the possibility of combining it with assumption. Many members of both houses were committed by the interest of their constituents to vote either for or against assumption. Some of the middle-state delegates, however, notably those of Pennsylvania, felt free to vote either way. They were thus in a position to deal, and what they wanted was at least the temporary residence of Congress for Pennsylvania. To James Madison's dismay, it appeared for a time that the Pennsylvanians would come to agreement with northern state delegates and trade votes for assumption in return for northern votes for locating the capital in Pennsylvania. The arrangement fell through, however, apparently because New York delegates refused to cooperate. They would not vote for any proposal to move the capital from their city, and without their support a coalition between northern states and Pennsylvania lacked sufficient votes to give the residence to Pennsylvania. Hamilton, who believed that assumption was absolutely essential to his program, finally realized that a trade would have to be made with the south and that southern votes could be had in only one way. At his instigation, Jefferson and Madison arranged to have two Virginia representatives, whose constituencies lay along the Potomac River, change their votes on assumption. The results of this negotiation quickly materialized. The residence bill passed: Pennsylvania got the capital for a period of ten years, and thereafter it was to be at some site on the Potomac River. The Senate approved assumption, sending it back to the House. This time, with the shift of two southern votes, it was approved. "And so," as Jefferson who later regretted his part in the affair, observed, "the Assumption was passed, and twenty million of stock divided among favored states, and thrown in as pablum to the stock-jobbing herd."

This was not his opinion at the time. Both Jefferson and Madison were nearly convinced that assumption was essential to the welfare of the Union; in any case, they were glad to have the permanent capital for Virginia. Indeed, if the Hamiltonian program is viewed against the background of the movement for the Constitution, its statesmanship is impressive. Confident of the support of most of the nation's leaders, Hamilton boldly implemented the Nationalist program of political centralization and economic reform. Beyond this, his problem was to reconcile conflicts of state interest. The assumption of state debts was a means to this end. It conciliated states which otherwise would have been disaffected, and it was auxiliary to his other general purposes. When assumption ran aground on divergent state interests, Hamilton threw the national capital to his adversaries, but in doing so he sacrificed nothing. The concession did not impair his program, which he managed to push through Congress without loss of any vital element.

Within the next year or two the market value of federal securities rose toward par, creating above $38,000,000 in profit for the owners. Robert Morris as well as Alexander Hamilton could take satisfaction in the consummation of the Nationalist program: a strong central government, the augmentation of business capital, and the construction of a system of credit and currency designed to foster the growth of business enterprise. Up to this time the country had lived with state paper money, land banks, commodity taxes—a system of "currency finance," which was adapted to an agrarian economy, to small-scale local government, and to American anti-statist conceptions of public liberty. By funding the debt in the British manner and blocking state functions in issuing currency and providing private credit, Hamilton instituted a big government system geared to implementing the power of the national government and promoting the development of financial and industrial capitalism. The new system did not at once envelop the whole economy; agrarian-oriented public finance still played a role. Nevertheless, the country had acquired a central core of advanced economic institutions that were to serve its needs as an emerging industrial nation.

The structure was completed by the incorporation in 1791 of the first Bank of the United States. Three fourths of its capital consisted of public securities subscribed by people who bought shares in it. The notes which it issued circulated as a national medium of exchange, replacing state paper money, prohibited now by the Constitution. Other banks, financial corporations, and internal improvement companies were organized, and a stock market grew up. The availability of private and public securities attracted long-term investment by foreign capitalists. As all these things materialized, familiar to Americans in the history of Great Britain, a critic of the government, John Taylor, wrote: "Is it not time to enquire, whether the constitution was designed to beget a government, or only a *British* system of finance." Unfortunately, the Hamiltonian program was also irremediably sectional in its effects. The agricultural south held little of the newly organized federal debt. Thus, the economic gains resulting from the establishment of the new government—from funding, assumption, and, later, the national bank—went to the north. The result was a disruption of the coalition of wealth, talents, and property which had produced the Constitution. The opposition of Madison and Jefferson to Hamiltonian measures was the first announcement of a rift in the aristocracy which gave rise to national political parties.

Epilogue

Creating a national government was a complex act which involved a numerous public constituency and a broad spectrum of material interests; not surprisingly, its significance can be defined on a number of levels. It restored an equilibrium between central and local government which had grown up in colonial times but succumbed to the anti-statist principles of the Revolution. Considered in terms of its effect upon social class relations, the formation of the national government checked, at least for the moment, the democratic impulses unleashed by the Revolution. In terms of economic effects, the new government and the adoption of the funding program represented preparation for the transition of the pre-industrial United States to a more advanced stage of economic development. More immediately, as some of these consequences unfolded, it became evident that in terms of the political ideologies familiar to Americans, a "court party" had materialized and gained control of the national government to the detriment of the "country party," with whose views most Americans were normally in sympathy.

The nation, nevertheless, had excellent prospects. Political disputes took place within a solidly established practice of elective government anchored in British history and colonial experience. The United States was more secure than most new nations. It was by far the largest and most powerful in the Western Hemisphere and was protected by the Atlantic Ocean from assaults from Europe. Its population had grown from about 2,500,000 at the beginning of the Revolution to nearly 4,000,000, including 700,000 slaves, an increase of 60 percent. The original area of the 13 states had been nearly doubled by acquisition of territory in the peace treaty, and settlers were swarming west at a prodigious rate. Having recovered from the worst of the post-war depression, the country was on the threshold of nearly two decades of enormous prosperity arising from pursuit of neutral trade while Europe waged war.

By a rational act, which has few precedents in history, the United States had without violence or intimidation altered its form of government to give the nation greater strength and unity. The event was propitious in its timing, for the country would soon live through an age of international revolution which with its spreading wars and divisive appeals to the loyalties of mankind might have disrupted a nation less well prepared.

Suggested Readings

SOURCES

Bailyn, Bernard, ed. *Pamphlets of the American Revolution, 1750–1776.* Cambridge, Mass., 1965.

Burnett, Edmund C., ed. *Letters of the Members of the Continental Congress.* 8 vols. Washington, D.C., 1921–1936.

Cooke, Jacob E., ed. *The Federalist Papers.* Middletown, Conn., 1961.

Elliot, Jonathan, ed. *The Debates in the Several State Conventions on the Adoption of the Federal Constitution.* 2d ed., 5 vols. Philadelphia, 1876.

Farrand, Max, ed. *The Records of the Federal Convention of 1787.* Rev. ed. New Haven, Conn., 1937.

Ford, Paul Leicester, ed. *Pamphlets on the Constitution of the United States.* Brooklyn, N.Y., 1888, Reprint New York, 1968.

Jensen, Merrill, ed. *English Historical Documents: American Colonial Documents, 1607–1776.* Vol. 9. New York, 1955.

———. *Tracts of the American Revolution 1763–1776.* Indianapolis, 1967.

Papers of prominent Americans sponsored by the National Historical Publications Commission, now in various stages of publication, including:

John Adams (L. H. Butterfield, ed.); *Benjamin Franklin* (Leonard W. Labaree, William B. Wilcox, eds.); *Alexander Hamilton* (Harold C. Syrett, Jacob E. Cooke, eds.); *Thomas Jefferson* (Julian P. Boyd, ed.); *Henry Laurens* (Philip M. Hamer, George C. Rogers, Jr., eds.); *James Madison* (William T. Hutchinson, Robert A. Rutland, eds.); *George Mason* (Robert A. Rutland, ed); *Robert Morris* (E. James Ferguson, John Catanzariti, eds.).

BRITISH BACKGROUND

Cantor, Norman S. *The English: A History of Politics and Society to 1760.* New York, 1967.

Carswell, John. *From Revolution to Revolution: England 1688–1776.* New York, 1973.

Dickson, Peter G. M. *The Financial Revolution in England: A Study in the Development of Public Credit, 1688–1765.* New York, 1967.

Kramnick, Isaac. *Bolingbroke and His Circle: The Politics of Nostalgia in the Age of Walpole.* Cambridge, Mass., 1968.

Mingay, G. E. *English Landed Society in the Eighteenth Century.* London, 1963.

Peckham, Howard H. *The Colonial Wars, 1689–1762.* Chicago, 1964.

Smellie, K. B. *Great Britain since 1688.* Ann Arbor, Mich., 1962.

Wilson, Charles. *England's Apprenticeship, 1603–1763.* New York, 1965.

POLITICAL AND SOCIAL STRUCTURE

Bonomi, Patricia U. *A Factious People: Politics and Society in Colonial New York.* New York, 1971.

Bridenbaugh, Carl. *Cities in Revolt: Urban Life in America, 1743–1776.* New York, 1955.

Brown, B. Katherine, and Eldon, Robert. *Virginia, 1705–1786: Democracy or Aristocracy?* East Lansing, Mich., 1964.

Buel, Richard, Jr. "Democracy and the American Revolution: A Frame of Reference." *William and Mary Quarterly* 3d ser. 21(1964):165–90.

Bushman, Richard L. *From Puritan to Yankee: Character and the Social Order in Connecticut, 1690–1765.* Cambridge, Mass., 1967.

Campbell, Mildred. "English Emigration on the Eve of the American Revolution." *American Historical Review* 61(1955):1–20.

Grant, Charles S. *Democracy in the Connecticut Frontier Town of Kent.* New York, 1961.

Greven, Philip G., Jr. *Four Generations: Population, Land, and Family in Colonial Andover, Massachusetts.* Ithaca, N.Y., 1970.

Hartz, Louis M. *The Liberal Tradition in America.* New York, 1971.

Henretta, James A. "Economic Development and Social Structure in Colonial Boston." *William and Mary Quarterly* 3d ser. 22(1965):75–92.

Hoffman, Ronald. *A Spirit of Dissension: Economics, Politics, and the Revolution in Maryland.* Baltimore, 1974.

Hofstadter, Richard. *America at 1750: A Social Portrait.* New York, 1971.

Jones, Alice Hansen. *American Colonial Wealth.* New York, 1977.

Kulikoff, Allan. "The Progress of Inequality in Revolutionary Boston." *William and Mary Quarterly* 3d ser. 28(1971):375–412.

Labaree, Leonard W. *Conservatism in Early American History.* New York, 1957.

Land, Aubrey C. "Economic Base and Social Structure: The Northern Chesapeake in the Eighteenth Century." *Journal of Economic History* 25(1965):639–54.

Lemon, James T. *The Best Poor Man's Country: A Geographical Study of Early Southeastern Pennsylvania.* Baltimore, 1972.

Lockridge, Kenneth. "Land, Population and the Evolution of New England Society, 1630–1790." *Past and Present: Studies in the History of Civilization* 39(1968): 62–80.

Main, Jackson T. *The Social Structure of Revolutionary America*. Princeton, 1965.

Morgan, Edward S. *American Slavery—American Freedom: The Ordeal of Colonial Virginia*. New York, 1975.

Nash, Gary B., ed. *Class and Society in Early America*. Englewood Cliffs, N.J., 1970.

———. "Social Change and the Growth of Prerevolutionary Urban Radicalism" in *The American Revolution: Explorations in the History of American Radicalism*. Edited by Alfred F. Young. DeKalb, Ill., 1976.

———. "Poverty and Poor Relief in Prerevolutionary Philadelphia." *William and Mary Quarterly* 33(1976):3–30.

Olton, Charles S. *Artisans for Independence: Philadelphia Mechanics and the American Revolution*. Syracuse, N.Y., 1975.

Pole, J. R. "Historians and the Problems of Early American Democracy." *American Historical Review* 67(1962):626–46.

Powell, Sumner Chilton. *Puritan Village, The Formation of a New England Town*. Middletown, Conn., 1963.

Sydnor, Charles S. *Gentlemen Freeholders: Political Practices in Washington's Virginia*. Chapel Hill, N.C., 1953.

Young, Alfred F. *The Democratic Republicans of New York: The Origins, 1763–1797*. Chapel Hill, N.C., 1967.

Zemsky, Robert. *Merchants, Farmers, and River Gods: An Essay on Eighteenth-Century American Politics*. Boston, 1971.

Zuckerman, Michael. *Peaceable Kingdoms: New England Towns in the Eighteenth Century*. New York, 1970.

POLITICAL AND PHILOSOPHICAL IDEAS

Bailyn, Bernard. *The Origins of American Politics*. New York, 1968.

Becker, Carl. *The Heavenly City of Eighteenth-Century Philosophers*. New Haven, Conn., 1932.

Colbourn, Trevor. *The Lamp of Experience: Whig History and the Intellectual Origin of the American Revolution*. Chapel Hill, N.C., 1965.

Gay, Peter. *The Enlightenment: An Interpretation; The Science of Freedom*. Vol. 2. New York, 1969.

Greene, Jack P., Bushman, Richard L., and Kammen, Michael. *Society, Freedom and Conscience: The American Revolution in Virginia, Massachusetts and New York*. Edited by Richard M. Jellison. New York, 1976.

Heimert, Alan. *Religion and the American Mind from the Great Awakening to the Revolution*. Cambridge, Mass., 1966.

Hindle, Brooke. *The Pursuit of Science in Revolutionary America, 1735–1789*. Chapel Hill, N.C., 1956.

Jensen, Merrill. "The American People and the American Revolution." *Journal of American History* 57(1970):5–35.

Kammen, Michael. *People of Paradox: An Inquiry Concerning the Origins of American Civilization*. New York, 1972.

Leventhal, Herbert. *In the Shadow of the Enlightenment: Occultism and Renaissance Science in Eighteenth-Century America*. New York, 1976.

McLoughlin, William G. "The Role of Religion in the Revolution: Liberty of Conscience and Cultural Cohesion in the New Nation" in *Essays on the American Revolution*. Edited by Stephen G. Kurtz and James H. Huston. Chapel Hill, N.C., 1973.

May, Henry F. *The Enlightenment in America*. New York, 1976.

Meyer, Donald H. *The Democratic Enlightenment*. New York, 1976.

Morgan, Edward S. "The Puritan Ethic and the American Revolution." *William and Mary Quarterly* 24(1967):3–43.

Leder, Lawrence H. *Liberty and Authority: Early American Political Ideology, 1689–1763*. Chicago, 1968.

Wood, Gordon S. *The Creation of the American Republic, 1776–1787*. Chapel Hill, N.C., 1969.

ECONOMIC FACTORS

Bidwell, Percy W., and Falconer, John I. *History of Agriculture in the Northern United States, 1620–1860*. Washington, D.C., 1925.

Bruchey, Stuart. *The Roots of American Economic Growth, 1607–1861: An Essay in Social Causation*. London and New York, 1965.

Carman, Harry J., ed. *American Husbandry*. New York, 1939.

Egnal, Marc, and Ernst, Joseph A. "An Economic Interpretation of the American Revolution." *William and Mary Quarterly* 3d ser. 29(1972):3–32.

Ernst, Joseph A. *Money and Politics in America, 1755–1775: A Study in the Currency Act of 1764 and the Political Economy of the Revolution*. Chapel Hill, N.C., 1973.

Ferguson, E. James. "Currency Finance: An Interpretation of Colonial Monetary Practices." *William and Mary Quarterly* 3d ser. 10(1953):153–80.

Gray, Lewis C. *History of Agriculture in the Southern United States to 1860*. Washington, D.C., 1933.

Nettels, Curtis P. *The Emergence of a National Economy, 1775–1815*. New York, 1962.

Pares, Richard. *Yankees and Creoles: The Trade between North America and the West Indies before the American Revolution*. London, 1956.

Price, Jacob M. *France and the Chesapeake: A History of the French Tobacco Monopoly, 1674–1791, and of Its Relationship to the British and American Tobacco Trades*. Ann Arbor, Mich., 1973.

Shepherd, James F., and Walton, Gary M. *Shipping, Maritime Trade, and the Economic Development of Colonial America*. Chicago, 1972.

Williams, William Appleman. "The Age of Mercantilism: An Interpretation of the American Political Economy, 1763 to 1828." *William and Mary Quarterly* 3d ser. 15(1958):419–37.

URBAN LIFE, SOCIAL PROBLEMS, AND THE STATUS OF WOMEN

Benson, Mary Sumner. *Women in Eighteenth-Century America*. New York, 1935.

Blake, Judith. "The Changing Status of Women in Developed Countries." *Scientific American* 231(1974):136–47.

Bridenbaugh, Carl. *The Colonial Craftsman*. New York, 1950.

Carr, Lois Green, and Walsh, Lorena S. "The Planter's Wife: The Experience of White Women in Seventeenth-Century Maryland." *William and Mary Quarterly* 3d ser. 34(1977):542–71.

Coleman, Peter J. *Debtors and Creditors in America: Insolvency, Imprisonment for Debt and Bankruptcy, 1607–1900*. Madison, Wis., 1974.

De Pauw, Linda Grant. *Four Traditions: Women of New York During the American Revolution*. Albany, N.Y., 1974.

Mohl, Raymond A. *Poverty in New York, 1783–1825*. New York, 1971.

Randall, Edwin T. "Imprisonment for Debt in America: Fact and Fiction." *Mississippi Valley Historical Review* 39(1952):89–102.

Shryock, Richard H. *Medicine and Society in America, 1660–1860*. New York, 1960.

Spruill, Julia Cherry. *Women's Life and Work in the Southern Colonies*. Reprint. New York, 1972.

Wilson, Jean Hoff. "The Illusion of Change: Women in the American Revolution" in *The American Revolution: Explorations in the History of American Radicalism*. Edited by Alfred F. Young. De Kalb, Ill., 1976.

BLACKS, INDIANS, SLAVERY, AND RACE RELATIONS

Anstay, Roger. *The Atlantic Slave Trade and British Abolition, 1760–1810*. Atlantic Highlands, N.J., 1975.

Berlin, Ira. *Slaves Without Masters: The Free Negro in the Antebellum South*. New York, 1974.

Cotterill, R. S. *The Southern Indians: The Story of the Civilized Tribes before Removal*. Norman, Okla., 1954.

Curtin, Philip D. "Epidemiology and the Slave Trade." *Political Science Quarterly* 83(1968):190–216.

Davis, David Brion. *The Problems of Slavery in the Age of Revolution, 1770–1823*. Ithaca, N.Y., 1975.

Degler, Carl N. *Neither Black nor White: Slavery and Race Relations in Brazil and the United States*. New York, 1971.

Donnan, Elizabeth, ed. *Documents Illustrative of the History of the Slave Trade to America*. Washington, D.C., 1930–1956.

Elkins, Stanley M. *Slavery: A Problem in American Institutional and Intellectual Life*. 2d. ed. Chicago, 1968.

Fogel, Robert William, and Engerman, Stanley L. *Time on the Cross: The Economics of American Negro Slavery*. Boston, 1974.

Freehling, William W. "The Founding Fathers and Slavery." *American Historical Review* 77(1972):81–93.

Genovese, Eugene D. *Roll, Jordan, Roll: The World the Slaves Made*. New York, 1975

Graymont, Barbara. *The Iroquois in the American Revolution*. Syracuse, N.Y., 1977.

Gutman, Herbert G. *The Black Family in Slavery and Freedom, 1750–1925*. New York, 1976.

Hagan, William T. *The American Indian*. Chicago, 1961.

Harris, Marvin. *Patterns of Race in the Americas*. New York, 1964.

Hudson, Charles. *The Southeastern Indians*. Knoxville, Tenn., 1976.

Jordan, Winthrop D. *The White Man's Burden: Historical Origins of Racism in the United States*. New York, 1974.

Josephy, Alvin M., Jr. *The Indian Heritage of American*. New York, 1968.

Klein, Herbert S. *Slavery in the Americas: A Comparative Study of Cuba and Virginia*. Chicago, 1967.

McLeod, Duncan J. *Slavery, Race, and the American Revolution*. Cambridge, Mass., and London, 1974.

McManus, Edgar J. *Black Bondage in the North*. Syracuse, N.Y., 1973.

Mullin, Gerald W. *Flight and Rebellion: Slave Resistance in Eighteenth-Century Virginia*. New York, 1972.

Nash, Gary B. *Red, White, and Black: The Peoples of Early America*. Englewood Cliffs, N.J., 1974.

Owen, Roger C., Deetz, J. F., and Fisher, Anthony D. *The North American Indians: A Source Book*. New York, 1967.

Peckham, Howard H. *Pontiac and the Indian Uprising*. Chicago, 1947.

Rice, C. Duncan. *The Rise and Fall of Black Slavery*. New York, 1975.

Robinson, Donald L. *Slavery in the Structure of American Politics, 1765–1820*. New York, 1971.

Silversmidt, Arthur. *The First Emancipation: The Abolition of Slavery in the North*. Chicago, 1967.

Walker, James W. St. G. *The Black Loyalists: The Search for a Promised Land in Nova Scotia and Sierra Leone, 1783–1870*. New York, 1976.

Washburn, Wilcomb E. *The Indian in America*. New York, 1975.

Wood, Peter H. Black Majority: *Negroes in Colonial South Carolina from 1670 through the Stono Rebellion*. New York, 1974.

SECTIONAL CONFLICTS

Brown, Richard M. *The South Carolina Regulators: The Story of the First Vigilante Movement*. Cambridge, Mass., 1963.

Countryman, Edward. " 'Out of Bounds of the Law': Northern Land Rioters in the Eighteenth Century" in *The American Revolution: Explorations in the History of American Radicalism*. Edited by Alfred F. Young. De Kalb, Ill., 1976.

De Mond, Robert O. *The Loyalists in North Carolina during the American Revolution*. Durham, N.C., 1940.

Hooker, Richard J., ed. *The Carolina Backcountry on the Eve of the Revolution: The Journal and Other Writings of Charles Woodmason, Anglican Itinerant*. Chapel Hill, N.C., 1953.

Kay, Marvin L. Michael. "The North Carolina Regulation, 1766–1776: A Class Conflict" in *The American Revolution: Explorations in the History of American Radicalism*. Edited by Alfred F. Young. De Kalb, Ill., 1976.

Lincoln, Charles H. *The Revolutionary Movement in Pennsylvania, 1760–1776.* Philadelphia, 1901.

Mark, Irving. *Agrarian Conflicts in Colonial New York, 1711–1755.* New York, 1940.

POPULISM, THE "DISAFFECTED," AND THE RESISTANCE TO BRITAIN

Aldridge, Alfred Owen. *Man of Reason: The Life of Thomas Paine.* Philadelphia and New York, 1959.

Bailyn, Bernard. *The Ordeal of Thomas Hutchinson.* Cambridge, Mass., 1974.

Becker, Robert A. "Revolution and Reform: An Interpretation of Southern Taxation, 1763 to 1783." *William and Mary Quarterly* 3d ser. 32(1975): 417–32.

Berthoff, Rowland. *An Unsettled People: Social Order and Disorder in American History.* New York, 1971.

Brown, Richard D. *Revolutionary Politics in Massachusetts: The Boston Committee of Correspondence and the Town, 1772–1774.* Cambridge, Mass., 1970.

Brown, Richard Maxwell. "Violence and the American Revolution" in *Essays on the American Revolution.* Edited by Stephen G. Kurtz and James H. Huston. Chapel Hill, N.C., 1973.

Brown, Robert Eldon. *Middle-Class Democracy and the Revolution in Massachusetts, 1691–1780.* Ithaca, New York, 1955.

Douglass, Elisha P. *Rebels and Democrats: The Struggle for Equal Political Rights and Majority Rule during the American Revolution.* Chapel Hill, N.C., 1955.

Foner, Philip S. *Labor in the American Revolution.* Westport, Conn., 1976.

Forbes, Esther. *Paul Revere and the World He Lived In.* Boston, 1942.

Hoerder, Dirk. "Boston Leaders and Boston Crowds, 1765–1776" in *The American Revolution: Explorations in the History of American Radicalism.* Edited by Alfred F. Young. De Kalb, Ill., 1976.

————. *Crowd Action in Revolutionary Massachusetts, 1765–1780.* New York, 1977.

Hoffman, Ronald. "The 'Disaffected' in the Revolutionary South in *The American Revolution: Explorations in the History of American Radicalism.* Edited by Alfred F. Young. De Kalb, Ill., 1976.

Labaree, Benjamin W. *The Boston Tea Party.* New York, 1964.

Lemisch, Jesse. "Jack Tar in the Streets: Merchant Seamen in the Politics of Revolutionary America." *William and Mary Quarterly* 3d ser. 25(1968):371–407.

McLoughlin, William G. "The American Revolution as a Religious Revival: The Millennium in One Country." *New England Quarterly* 40(1967):99–110.

Maier, Pauline. *From Resistance to Revolution: Colonial Radicals and the Development of American Opposition to Britain, 1765–1776.* New York, 1972.

Miller, John C. *Sam Adams, Pioneer in Propaganda.* Boston, 1936.

Rudé, George. *The Crowd in History: A Study of Popular Disturbances in France and England, 1730–1848.* New York, 1964.

Rudolph, Lloyd L. "The Eighteenth-Century Mob in Europe and America." *American Quarterly* 11(1959):447–69.

Ryerson, R. A. "Political Mobilization and the American Revolution: The Resistance Movement in Philadelphia, 1765–1776." *William and Mary Quarterly* 3d ser. 31(1974):565–88.

Skaggs, David Curtis. "Maryland's Impulse toward Social Revolution, 1750–1776." *Journal of American History* 54(1968):771–86.

Walsh, Richard. *Charleston's Sons of Liberty: A Study of the Artisans, 1763–1789.* Columbia, S.C., 1959.

Wood, Gordon S. "A Note on Mobs in the American Revolution." *William and Mary Quarterly* 3d ser. 23(1966):635–42.

Zobel, Hiller B. *The Boston Massacre.* New York, 1970.

ANGLO-AMERICAN CONTROVERSY

Andrews, Charles M. *The Colonial Background of the American Revolution.* New Haven, Conn., 1931.

Bailyn, Bernard. *The Ideological Origins of the American Revolution.* Cambridge, Mass., 1967.

Bridenbaugh, Carl. *Mitre and Sceptre: Transatlantic Faiths, Ideas, Personalities, and Politics, 1689–1775.* New York, 1962.

Christie, Ian R., and Labaree, Benjamin W. *Empire or Independence, 1760–1776: A British-American Dialogue on the Coming of the American Revolution.* New York, 1976.

Dickerson, Oliver M. *The Navigation Acts and the American Revolution.* Philadelphia, 1951.

Evans, Emory. "Planter Indebtedness and the Coming of the Revolution in Virginia." *William and Mary Quarterly* 3d ser. 19(1962):511–33.

Greene, Jack P. *The Quest for Power: The Lower Houses of the Assembly in the Southern Royal Colonies, 1689–1763.* Chapel Hill, N.C., 1963.

Guttridge, G. H. *English Whiggism and the American Revolution.* Berkeley and Los Angeles, 1942.

Harper, Lawrence A. "The Effects of the Navigation Acts on the Thirteen Colonies" in *The Era of the American Revolution.* Edited by Richard B. Morris. New York, 1939.

Jensen, Merrill. *The Founding of a Nation: A History of the American Revolution, 1763–1776.* New York, 1968.

Morgan, Edmund S., and Helen M. *The Stamp Act Crisis: Prologue to Revolution.* Chapel Hill, N.C., 1953.

Oliver, Peter. *Origin & Progress of the American Rebellion.* Edited by Douglass Adair and John A. Schutz. San Marino, Cal., 1961.

Shy, John. *Toward Lexington: The Role of the British Army in the Coming of the American Revolution.* Princeton, 1965.

Varg, Paul. "The Advent of Nationalism, 1758–1776." *American Quarterly* 16(1964):160–81.

REVOLUTION, MILITARY OPERATIONS

Billias, George, ed. *George Washington's Generals.* New York, 1964.

Freeman, Douglas Southall. *Washington.* [An abridgement by Richard Harwell of the seven-volume edition] New York, 1968.

Higginbotham, Don H. *The Way of American Independence: Military Attitudes, Policies, and Practices, 1763–1789.* New York, 1971.

Peckham, Howard H. *The War for Independence: A Military History.* Chicago, 1958.

Quarles, Benjamin. *The Negro in the American Revolution.* Chapel Hill, N.C., 1961.

Shy, John. *A People Numerous and Armed: Reflections on the Military Struggle for American Independence.* New York, 1976.

Smith, Page. *A New Age Now Begins: A People's History of the American Revolution.* New York, 1976.

Sprout, Harold H., and Margaret. *The Rise of American Naval Power, 1776–1918.* Princeton, 1939.

Van Doren, Carl. *Mutiny in January.* New York, 1943.

Van Every, Dale. *A Company of Heroes: The American Frontier, 1775–1783.* New York, 1962.

Weigley, Russell F. *The Partisan Wars: The South Carolina Campaign of 1780–1782.* Columbia, S.C., 1970.

A brilliant work on the American Army by Charles Royster is scheduled for publication by the University of North Carolina Press.

REVOLUTION: THE BRITISH AND THE LOYALISTS

Billias, George A., ed. *George Washington's Opponents.* New York, 1969.

Calhoon, Robert M. *The Loyalists in Revolutionary America, 1760–1781.* New York, 1973.

Mackesy, Piers. *The War for America, 1775–1783.* Cambridge, England, 1964.

Nelson, William H. *The American Tory.* Oxford, England, 1961.

Norton, Mary Beth. *The British-American: The Loyalist Exiles in England, 1774–1789.* Boston, 1972.

Robson, Eric. *The American Revolution in Its Political and Military Aspects, 1763–1783.* New York, 1955.

Shy, John. "The American Revolution: The Military Conflict Considered as a Revolutionary War" in *Essays on the American Revolution.* Edited by Stephen G. Kurtz and James H. Hutson. New York, 1973.

Smith, Paul H. *Loyalists and Redcoats: A Study in British Revolutionary Policy.* Chapel Hill, N.C., 1964.

Wallace, William S. *The United Empire Loyalists: A Chronicle of the Great Migration.* Toronto, 1914.

REVOLUTION: DOMESTIC AND FOREIGN POLICY

Alexander, John K. "The Fort Wilson Incident of 1779: A Case Study of the Revolutionary Crowd." *William and Mary Quarterly* 3d ser. 31(1974):589–612.

Bemis, Samuel F. *Diplomacy of the American Revolution.* New York, 1935.

Ferguson, E. James. "Business, Government, and Congressional Investigation in the Revolution." *William and Mary Quarterly* 3d ser. 16(1959):293–318.

———. *The Power of the Purse: A History of American Public Finance, 1776–1790.* Chapel Hill, N.C., 1961.

Henderson, H. James. *Party Politics in the Continental Congress.* New York, 1974.

Jensen, Merrill. *The Articles of Confederation: An Interpretation of the Socio-Constitutional History of the American Revolution, 1774–1781.* Madison, Wis., 1948.

Kohn, Richard H. "The Inside History of the Newburgh Conspiracy: America and the Coup d'Etat." *William and Mary Quarterly* 3d ser. 27(1970):187–220.

Morris, Richard B. *The Peacemakers: The Great Powers and American Independence.* New York, 1965.

Stinchcombe, William C. *The American Revolution and the French Alliance.* Syracuse, N.Y., 1969.

Van Alstyne, Richard. *Empire and Independence: The International History of the American Revolution.* New York, 1965.

Ver Steeg, Clarence. *Robert Morris, Revolutionary Financier: With an Analysis of His Earlier Career.* Philadelphia, 1954.

REVOLUTION: SOCIAL CHANGE

Bailyn, Bernard. "The Central Theme of the American Revolution: An Interpretation" in *Essays on the American Revolution.* Edited by Stephen G. Kurtz and James H. Hutson. Chapel Hill, N.C., 1973.

Greene, Jack P. "Changing Interpretations of Early American Politics" in *The Reinterpretation of Early American History.* Edited by Ray Billington. San Marino, Cal., 1967.

Henretta, James A. *The Evolution of American Society, 1700–1815: An Interdisciplinary Analysis.* Lexington, Mass., 1973.

Jameson, J. Franklin. *The American Revolution Considered as a Social Movement.* Princeton, 1926.

Jensen, Merrill. "The American People and the American Revolution." *Journal of American History* 57(1970):5–35.

———. *The American Revolution Within America.* New York, 1974.

Kenyon, Cecelia. "Republicanism and Radicalism in the American Revolution: An Old Fashioned Interpretation." *William and Mary Quarterly* 3d ser. 19 (1962):153–82.

Lockridge, Kenneth. "Social Change and the Meaning of the American Revolution." *Journal of Social History* 6(1973):403–39.

Main, Jackson T. *Political Parties before the Constitution.* Chapel Hill, N.C., 1973.

Morgan, Edmund S. "Conflict and Consensus in the American Revolution" in *Essays on the American Revolution.* Edited by Stephen G. Kurtz and James H. Hutson. Chapel Hill, N.C., 1973.

Palmer, Robert R. "The Revolution" in *The Comparative Approach to American History.* Edited by C. Van Woodward. New York, 1968.

Tolles, Frederick B. "The American Revolution Considered as a Social Movement: A Re-evaluation." *American Historical Review* 60(1954):1–12.

Ver Steeg, Clarence. "The American Revolution Considered as an Economic Movement." *Huntington Library Quarterly* 20(1957):361–72.

Williamson, Chilton. *American Suffrage from Property to Democracy, 1760–1860.* Princeton, 1960.

CONFEDERATION

Gates, Paul W., and Swenson, Robert W. *History of Public Land Law Development.* Washington, D.C., 1968.

Horsman, Reginald. *The Frontier in the Formative Years, 1783–1815.* New York, 1970.

Jensen, Merrill. *The New Nation: A History of the United States during the Confederation, 1781–1789.* New York, 1950.

Morris, Richard B. "Insurrection in Massachusetts" in *America in Crisis.* Edited by Daniel Aaron. New York, 1952.

CONSTITUTION AND THE FUNDING PROGRAM

Beard, Charles A. *An Economic Interpretation of the Constitution of the United States.* New York, 1913.

Brant, Irving. *The Fourth President: A Life of James Madison.* Indianapolis, 1970.

De Pauw, Linda Grant. *The Eleventh Pillar: New York State and the Federal Constitution.* Ithaca, N.Y., 1966.

Elkins, Stanley, and McKitrick, Eric. "The Founding Fathers: Young Men of the Revolution." *Political Science Quarterly* 76(1961):181–216.

Farrand, Max. *The Framing of the Constitution of the United States.* New Haven, Conn., 1913.

Ferguson, E. James. "The Nationalists of 1781–1783 and the Economic Interpretation of the Constitution." *Journal of American History* 56(1969):241–61.

Jensen, Merrill. *The Making of the American Constitution.* Princeton, 1964.

Kenyon, Cecelia. "Men of Little Faith: The Anti-Federalists on the Nature of Republican Government." *William and Mary Quarterly* 3d ser. 12(1955):3–43.

Lynd, Staughton. "The Compromise of 1787." *Political Science Quarterly* 71 (1966):225–50.

McDonald, Forrest. *We the People: The Economic Origins of the Constitution.* Chicago, 1958.

Main, Jackson T. *The Anti-Federalists: Critics of the Constitution, 1781–1788.* Chapel Hill, N.C., 1961.

Peterson, Merrill D. *Thomas Jefferson and the New Nation: A Biography.* New York, 1970.

Rutland, Robert A. *The Ordeal of the Constitution: The Antifederalists and the Ratification Struggle of 1787–1788.* Norman, Okla., 1966.

Schachner, Nathan. *Alexander Hamilton.* New York and London, 1946.

Index

This book has been set Linotype in 11 point and 10 point Baskerville, leaded 3 points. Chapter numbers are 30 point Goudy Open and Chapter titles are 18 point Goudy Bold italic. The size of the maximum type area is 27 x 45 picas.